Ocean Traders

MICHAEL W. MARSHALL

Ocean Traders

from the Portuguese discoveries to the present day

Facts On File
New York • Oxford • Sydney

OCEAN TRADERS

Copyright © 1990 by Michael Marshall

Facts on file, Inc.
460 Park Avenue South
New York NY 10016
USA

Printed in Great Britain

10 9 8 7 6 5 4 3 2 1

This book is printed on acid-free paper.

Library of Congress Cataloging-in-Publication Data
Marshall, Michael
  Ocean traders : a history of merchant shipping from the
Portuguese discoveries to the present day / Michael Marshall.
    p.   cm.
  Includes bibliographical references.
  ISBN 0-8160-2420-0
  1. Merchant ships–History.   2. Merchant marine–
History.   3. Shipping–History.   4. Navigation–
History.   I. Title.
  VM15.M368   1990
387.5'09–dc20   89-48361
                                                        CIP

Facts On File books are available at special discounts when
purchased in bulk quantities for businesses, associations,
institutions or sales promotions. Please contact the Special Sales
Department of our New York office at 212/683-2244 (dial 800/322-
8755 except in NY, AK or HI).

For my mother Vera

———————

For Julie and Sylvie

Contents

List of Maps

Acknowledgements

I am grateful to the following for useful discussions and for reading and commenting on draft manuscripts:

P. Atkinson, Alison Boyle (née Hinks), A. Hinks, A. Livington, A.P. McGowan, S. McGrail, E.D. Mackie, D.R. MacGregor, A. Osler, E. Pacitti, P. Padfield, A.W.H. Pearsall, J. Roome, A. Small.

Any errors are, of course, my own responsibility.

Special thanks are due to Mrs R. Baker, Ms C. Dubois, Ms J. Hinves and Ms J.O. Peachey for their critical comments during the preparation of the book. Also my brother, Peter, whose encouragement is always there. Thanks also to Dr David Jones of Batsford for seeing the book through the press.

The copyright source is given alongside each photograph and illustration, and I am indebted to the staff of all the maritime museums mentioned.

The maps and drawings are by Sutton.

Introduction

This book describes the evolution of merchant ships that trade across oceans: wooden, iron and steel merchantmen, powered by wind, coal, oil and split atom. The heyday of the sailing ship is arrived at through Viking longship, cog, carrack, galleon, clipper and Indiamen. The book shows how ocean traders were evolved to defend themselves, to carry cargo, to economise on crews, to drift through the Doldrums, to pound into head seas or run with the trade winds. It examines the fall of sail and the rise of steam-power, and the evolution of iron and steel hulled traders, from early passenger liners, steam tramps, and tankers, to today's gigantic ships that almost ignore Nature.

There is a romantic appeal in the merchant sailing ships of the eighteenth and nineteenth centuries, and much has been written about them. In a square-rigged merchantman, beauty and function appear to be perfectly balanced: man had finally harnessed the wind. But these ships were often man-killing and 'cranky', and life aboard for the crew was often short and brutish. Some skippers drove their crews without mercy, uncontrollable headsails tossed men over-board with an alarming frequency, and ships were often leaky, overloaded and undermanned. Seamen, living for months in sea-soaked forecastles, died of pneumonia or were crippled prematurely with arthritis. But, comparatively, labourers ashore often suffered more than the men afloat. Some merchant seamen took a special pride in their ships and trade, some captains even built up special relations with their crews, who followed them from ship to ship. But many hated their skippers, and many stayed at sea only because they knew no other way of life.

The evolution of ocean trade and the trader is, of course, intimately connected and both are part of the development of world history: maritime history being but one focus of world history. Adventurers, merchants, bankers, kings and queens, national expansionism and competitive empire-building played major roles in the development of trade and trader. A maritime nation, intent on obtaining trade and colonies, soon realized that power depended not only on the number, size and speed of its warships but also, and ultimately, on the size of its merchant fleet. Cargo ships supported armies, fed citizens and traded within and beyond the confines of every large empire. The citizens of Rome would have soon starved if the Empire's cargo ships had been unable to supply them with Egyptian grain. Control of ocean trade was essential if Great Britain was to keep and use her Empire.

The continuous desire of nations to develop empires brought about rapid advances in merchant shipping. For example, the Portuguese caravel played an important part in the early ocean explorations; the Spanish and English galleons were developed as both traders and warships for the defence of and exploitation of their colonies. The combination of propeller, efficient steam engine and large iron ship brought about the rapid fall of the sailing ocean trader, but ensured Britain's position as the major maritime power for over 150 years.

The dawn of ocean trade was in the early 1400s, and much has been made of the role of Portugal's Prince Henry the Navigator as the 'father of ocean trade'. He was, however, one of the originators of the slave trade and, like many famous people in history, happened to be, 'the right person, in the right place, at the right time'. Prior to the fifteenth century men had undoubtedly made ocean voyages: the Chinese as well as the Arabs had visited India and Africa; the Vikings had crossed the North Sea and North Atlantic and the Polynesians had ranged far in their canoes across the Pacific Ocean. The Vikings probably arrived in North America nearly 500 years before Columbus' voyages to the West Indies, and the Chinese probably sailed westwards around the

Cape of Good Hope before the Portuguese went around it in the opposite direction. Early Chinese ships were large, had sophisticated rigging, were multi-masted, and were crewed by hundreds. It was the Chinese, most likely, who brought the compass to Europe: an essential piece of equipment which allowed the Portuguese navigators to leave the coasts and sail off-shore.

Chapters in the book (approximately) divide the historical evolution of the ocean trader into periods, and each chapter starts with a brief overview of world and maritime history for its period. I deal only with ocean-going merchant ships; I have largely ignored the coastal trade and have only discussed warship design when it affected or was affected by ocean trader evolution. It is difficult to survey over 5000 years of maritime history and give all sources; but some are mentioned in the text and in the Select Bibliography. Books that were always close to hand were C. Ernest Fayle's *History of The World's Shipping Industry*, R. and R.C. Anderson's *The Sailing-Ship*, G.S. Laird Clowes' *Sailing Ships*, and

E. Smith's *A Short History of Naval and Marine Engineering.* I especially enjoyed S. McGrail's *Ancient Boats in North-West Europe*, R. Davis' *The Rise of The English Shipping Industry* and A. McGowan's two volumes, of a 10-volume publication, *The Ship*, edited by B. Greenhill. The three volumes of D.R. MacGregor's *Merchant Sailing Ships*, covering 1775–1875, contain a wealth of detail as do S.E. Morison's two volumes on *The European Discovery of America.* All Basil Lubbock's books on sailing ships were never far away, and Falconer's 1769 Marine Dictionary was invaluable.

This book was a delight to research. It was fascinating examining maritime and picture archives, talking to historians, shipwrights and welders, designers and yard managers, looking up articles, reading books, climbing inside wooden, iron and steel hulls and wriggling along double bottom tanks. There were also breathtaking visits to special collections in maritime museums and seaports in France, Britain and the USA. It is an enthralling and complex story. I hope I have done it justice.

CHAPTER ONE

The Long Dawn

The true birth of ocean trade was around AD 1400, the beginning of the 'Age of Discovery' (c1400–1600). But ocean trade had been evolving over thousands of years before Portugal's ships made their first tentative probes, westward into the Atlantic Ocean. The drive, usually the acquisition of wealth or competitive empire building, began over 5000 years ago in the ancient Near East and continued up to the twentieth century. England's Walter Raleigh (1554–1618) summarised the Elizabethan view:

Whosoever commands the sea commands trade; whosoever commands the trade of the world commands the riches of the world, and consequently the world itself.

Ocean trade was almost inevitable: from man's restless spirit, a ceaseless search for power and wealth, and a need to exchange goods. From hollowed log, raft and reed craft came *caravel, carrack* and *galleon*, and Europe's great Age of Discovery.

Empires and city states (2600 BC–AD 1400)

Ocean voyages were undoubtedly made before the Age of Discovery. According to the legend of St Brendan, Irish monks sailed the North Atlantic in leather boats. Arab merchants crossed the Arabian Sea to India, the Chinese sailed the Indian Ocean, and the Vikings made regular trips across the North Sea and took their longships as far as Greenland, Newfoundland and Labrador. One of the earliest records of sea trade was when Pharaoh Sneferu of Egypt (2613–2589 BC) sent 40 ships to Phoenicia to bring back cedar wood from the forests of Lebanon. The Egyptians were then a powerful trading nation, exchanging goods with the Phoenicians and Syrians. They were active in the Red Sea at least as far down as Somalia, and under Nikau II, c600 BC, they attempted to build a ship canal from the Nile estuary, via the Bitter lakes, to the Red Sea—forerunner of

the Suez Canal by over 2000 years. But it was not completed until the sixth century BC after the Persian conquest of Egypt by Darius of Persia (521–486 BC).

When ancient Egyptian civilization declined the Phoenicians (whose major cities Tyre, Sidon and Byblos were all ports) became the most powerful trading nation in the Mediterranean. They had natural harbours, situated along the present-day Syrian coastline, and they were strategically placed on the caravan routes from the wealthy inland empires such as Cathay, Persia and Babylonia. The Phoenicians acted as middle-men for trade to the western Mediterranean, north Africa and down the Red Sea. Herodotus wrote of a remarkable voyage by Phoenician seamen who, in 600 BC, circumnavigated Africa clockwise from the Red Sea, returning to the Mediterranean via the Straits of Gibraltar. During the sixth and seventh centuries BC the Phoenicians were at the height of their power; the shores of the Mediterranean contained numerous ports and trading settlements and their city, Tyre, had a large population.

Until the fifteenth century most northern and Mediterranean sea-trading voyages were undertaken in spring and summer. Cargo ships generally travelled close inshore, navigating by sight from headland to headland, and stopping-over each night at sheltered anchorages or safe harbours. Hesiod, writing around 740 BC, had good advice for merchants:

Praise a small vessel, but put your cargo in a large one ... For fifty days after the summer solstice, when the summer season of labour is past, sailing is seasonable for men: neither would you wreck your ship, nor would the sea drown the crew, unless of design Neptune, who shakes the earth, or Jupiter, king of the Gods, should choose to destroy them, for these decide the end of good folk and of bad. But at that season the winds blow steady, the sea is

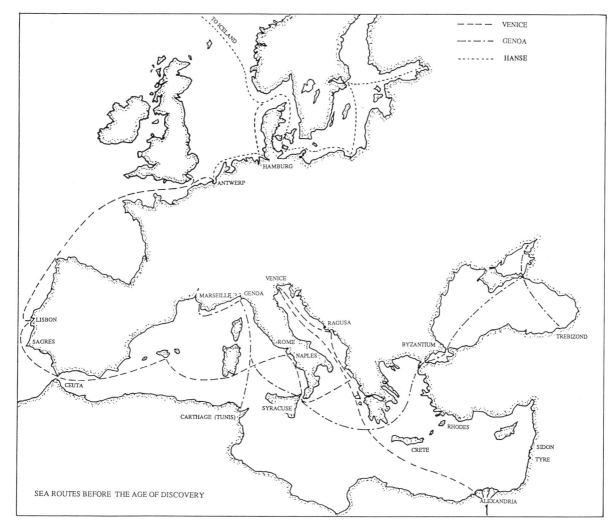

VENICE

GENOA

HANSE

TO ICELAND

HAMBURG

ANTWERP

VENICE

MARSEILLE   GENOA

RAGUSA

LISBON

SAGRES

ROME

BYZANTIUM

TREBIZOND

NAPLES

CEUTA

SYRACUSE

CARTHAGE (TUNIS)

RHODES

CRETE

SIDON

TYRE

SEA ROUTES BEFORE THE AGE OF DISCOVERY

ALEXANDRIA

Map 1   *Sea routes before the Age of Discovery. (after Moyse-Bartlett, 1937)*

safe; then you are safe to trust the winds and drag down your swift ship to the water's edge and put the cargo on board ... Another good time for sailing is in the spring ... (but) I praise not the spring voyage, for it must be performed in haste ... Death in the waves is fearful. (from F.G. Aflalo's, *The Call of the Sea*)

After the Egyptians other sea powers rose and fell—Minoan, Mycenaean, Greek—but for over a thousand years the Phoenicians were the dominant seafarers in the Mediterranean until, in 332 BC, when Alexander the Great sacked Tyre, slayed most of the inhabitants and started the Macedonian-Greek empire's raise to maritime supremacy.

From 220 to 160 BC the Roman Empire became so powerful that it brought peace and stability to the shores of the Mediterranean, even controlling sea trade in the Black Sea and Indian Ocean. Under Pax Romana the link between the Mediterranean and the Red Sea was re-opened, piracy was almost eradicated, lighthouses and beacons were brought into operation, the first seamen's pilot books (*Peripli*,

see p 65) were written and an efficient maritime legal system was developed. The city of Rome depended on trade for its survival, and it was cheaper to sail cargo from one end of the Roman Empire to the other than to transport it some 100 miles overland.

But the Roman Empire crumbled, and by the eighth century AD the Islamic Empire controlled much of North Africa, Asia Minor, parts of Greece and most of Spain. The Arabs were fine seamen and there is evidence of early trading voyages across the Indian Ocean to India and beyond. During the period of Islamic expansion in the seventh century scattered Mediterranean sea ports developed into city-states and built war fleets to protect themselves and their cargo ships: Venice, Genoa, Marseille, Barcelona were all to become important.

The Crusades (1096–1270) encouraged the growth of the city-states, as the Crusaders arrived in the Mediterranean and needed seamen, war- and cargo-ships. Venice, Amalfi, Trani, Pisa and Genoa all grew in importance. Genoa and Venice were particularly well placed, Genoa in the northwest corner of Italy, covering the Gulf of Lyons. Venice, at the head of the Adriatic sea, was eventually to gain the title 'Queen of the Adriatic' and to become so powerful that in the fourth crusade in 1202, it alone was able to supply 1200 ships and 20,000 soldiers. Venice and Genoa became so dominant that northern cargo ships rarely entered the Mediterranean, even though the Crusaders had stimulated the Europeans' desire for exotic Eastern goods. To supply this market, Venetian galleys (*galleasses*) went to Egypt and Syria to collect cargoes from China, India and the Spice Islands (The Molucca Islands), taking them first to North African ports and then on to northern Europe. Travelling in convoys, they slowly rowed and sailed their way across the Bay of Biscay, carrying silk, tapestries, precious stones and spices which they traded for wool, fur, timber and pickled herrings. Sea voyages were nearly always made along the coast from headland to headland, and between the months of April and December. The Venetian galleasses were, by 1400, some 130 ft long and 16 ft wide, and were powered by up to 25 oars on a side and rigged with small triangular sails. They could travel at five knots when rowed and carry up to 100 tons of cargo. The Venetians considered them so efficient that by decree valuable spice cargoes had to be carried by galleys and not sailing ships. In 1255 Venice, secure of itself as a maritime nation, published its own maritime laws.

Cargo ships were not only at work in the Mediterranean. In the North and Baltic Seas the Vikings were active from the late eighth to the eleventh centuries. They conquered lands, made settlements and built ships specifically for carrying cargoes. Non-Mediterranean maritime laws were developed around 1200 and were known as the *Rules of Oleron (La Ley Olyroun)*, after the small, then English-held, island of Oleron, and important twelfth-century trading post off the French port of La Rochelle. These laws were possibly instigated by Richard I, Coeur de Lion, on his return from the Third Crusade in 1192. The *Rules* provided conditions for seamen, ships and trade, and awarded fines to be paid in 'tuns', or wine barrels. At that time northern European ship sizes were given as the number of tuns they could carry, and in 1380 northern ships were hired by the 'tun-tight', based on the capacity taken up in the single-hold merchantman by 80 wine jars. The English measure of weight, the ton, was eventually obtained from the tun, which was standardised as a cask that could hold 252 gallons of wine (2240 lbs or 1016 kgs). Because of their shape, when packed into a hold casks occupied more space than the wine they carried. This gave rise to the term 'deadweight' tonnage, which was applied to the

volume occupied by the casks, as opposed to tuns 'burden', which was the weight of the wine. Deadweight tonnage was defined as one third greater than tuns 'burden' (see also p 97).

From the middle of the thirteenth century the Hanseatic League played a major role in developing trade in northwest Europe. The League was developed when the most powerful North German trading towns banded together, partly to curb piracy and to form a trans-national trading alliance which, at its height between the early fourteenth and late fifteenth centuries, included over 60 cities. The League had cargo ships, warehouses, exchanges and banks, and set up its own code of maritime practice. Peculiarly, by today's standards at least, its agents were sworn to celibacy. The League became the most important force in northern European waters for over 200 years, and had its own freighters, clinker built 'Hansa cogs'. The English, French and Dutch all had sea-going trading vessels, but most medieval English seamen, for example, either worked on coasters or were pirates.

Throughout the fourteenth century European thirst for Eastern luxuries—spices, silk, porcelain, precious stones—remained unabated, and merchants made large profits by supplying the European market. But in 1370 revolution in China closed her markets to foreign trade. The Ottoman Turks began to make the overland caravan routes to the East difficult, and Venice and Genoa had a strangle-hold on the Mediterranean trade. For western and northern Europeans there was only one way left to the riches of the orient: eastwards across the Indian Ocean. Portugal, a small country of around one million inhabitants in the early fifteenth century, was ideally situated as the European point of departure to sail the Atlantic Ocean, round Africa and cross the Indian Ocean to load the spices of the Orient. Portugal had the vessels—square-sailed *naus,* and *carvels.* Caravels were rigged with triangular sails which could drive them against the Atlantic northeast trade winds, prevailing winds down Portugal's western coast. Along Portugal's southern coast there were good harbours and sheltered anchorages: ideal points of departure.

The drive of one man, Prince Henry or the Infante Henrique, was inspirational in making Portugal, for a short period, a wealthy maritime power. In 1385 Prince Henry's father, King John I, had with the Portuguese army successfully beaten off a Castilian invasion. The three sons of King John—Prince Henry was the youngest—were eager to go to war to win their spurs, just as their father had done, and in 1415 Portugal attacked the rich Moslem port of Ceuta, for its wealth and to extend Christian influence. After a short sail through the Straits of Gibraltar some 200 Portuguese ships arrived off the port and the city fell after only a short battle. The Age of Discovery was about to begin, and with it the true ocean trader.

But long before the Age of Discovery the ocean trader had been evolving. For thousands of years Mediterranean warships had been sleek galleys made for ramming. They carried soldiers who boarded and fought sea-battles as if they were fighting on land. Galleys were V-shaped in cross-section and, built for speed. Although they carried small, square sails, they were mainly powered by slaves working dozens of long oars. In contrast to warships cargo ships were round ships, slow vessels, U-shaped in section powered mainly by large square sails, and rowed by their small crews only when necessary. A round ship's main function was to carry as much cargo as cheaply as possible. The basic hull-building material for a sea-going vessel was wood.

Shell and skeleton

The earliest known wooden-planked vessels were 'shell constructed'. Historical analysis of the evolution of shipbuilding suggests that man used two basic forms of hull construction, 'shell' and 'skeleton' (see Sean McGrail, *The Ship*, vol. I and *Ancient Boats in North West Europe*). Shell construction involves building the hull first, perhaps of animal skins, bark or wood, and then adding the internal strengthening structures (such as knees, frames or ribs, transverse floor timbers). In skeleton construction the frames are assembled first, to give the overall shape of the hull, and then the outer covering (animal skin, bark, wood) is attached to the framework.

In a planked, shell-constructed hull, the wooden planks can be either overlapped, or tightly butted together ('non-overlapping' or 'flush-laid' hull planking). The edges of the planks were joined using animal sinews, skins, ropes or even tree roots, or by wooden pegs ('treenails') or by iron nails. Viking longships had, for example, shell-constructed hulls with overlapping planks fastened together by nailing their overlapping edges, a technique known as 'clinker' or 'clench' building. Iron nails were driven through the two planks from the outside and the nail points led through a metal washer on the inboard face of the planking before being turned over or 'clenched'.

In skeleton-constructed wooden hulls, planks are flush-fitted and fastened by metal nails, or wooden treenails, to the previously erected frames. This technique is sometimes known as 'carvel' building, and the gaps between the planks are filled, or 'caulked', with tarred hair or some such material to make the hull watertight. Caulking also has the added advantage of increasing hull rigidity.

Early Egyptian tomb drawings, around 2600 BC, show sea-going ships with flush-laid hull planks. Pharaoh Sahure's tomb (about 2450 BC) has pictorial representations of eight ships returning from Syria after a military expedition. They were edge-planked

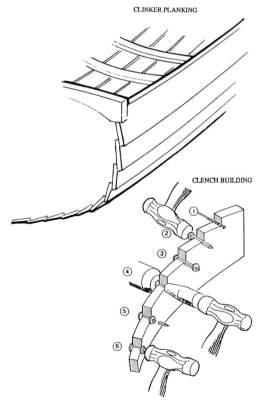

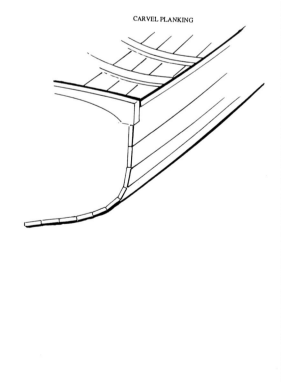

CLINKER PLANKING

CARVEL PLANKING

CLENCH BUILDING

1 *Clinker (shell construction) and carvel (skeleton construction) building. (1) drilling the hole (2) driving home the nail (3) roving the end (4) striking the roving punch (5) nipping the nail (6) clenching the end. (after Eric McKee in* Clenched Lap or Clinker)

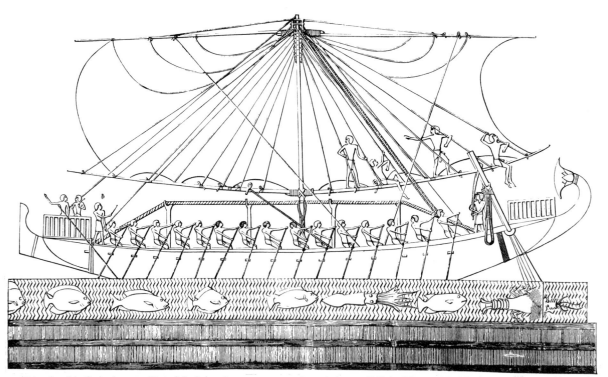

2 *Egyptian ship from the punt 'Expedition' showing truss ropes and steering oars. (Science Museum, London)*

3 *A model of a Roman merchant ship cAD 200 with two steering oars, artemon and swan-neck in the stern. (Science Museum, London)*

sailing craft, probably without a keel, with single masts, square sails and oars. Around 2000 BC, models of ships recovered from tombs show masts, square sails and large-bladed oars lashed to vertical posts in the aft end of the boat. These oars were powerful enough to row or 'haul' the stern round, to set the bow on a new course. On the ruined walls in the temple of Deir el-Bahri, Thebes, there are beautiful representations of 'double-ended' boats (stem and stern similar) with steering oars, deck beams, single masts and a complicated sail rig. They were 70 ft long and 18 ft wide. The drawings illustrate an Egyptian expedition to Punt (possibly present-day Somalia) c1480 BC. The expedition ships had heavy 'truss' ropes that passed from the bow to the stern. The truss could be shortened and tightened by inserting a spar amongst the ropes and turning, creating what is known to later seamen as a 'Spanish windlass'. The truss rope, used in Egyptian ships for at least a 1000 years before the Punt expedition, acted as a longitudinal stiffener and prevented these long, narrow boats from 'hogging': the sagging of the stem and the stern when the boat was supported in the middle by a wave. In earlier Egyptian ships, lateral strengthening ropes passed around the hull, but the Punt-expedition were reinforced with 16 deck beams that passed across the ship and out through the hull planking.

By the time of the Punt expedition wide square sails were hung from a transverse spar (yard), and the bottom fixed to a second yard (spreader). Ropes between the yards supported the spreader and helped shape and reduce strain on the sail material. The square sail could be swung into the wind by ropes (braces) that ran from the ends of the upper yard. Other ropes (halliards or halyards) were use to hoist the sail, and three rope 'stays' (two forward, one aft) acted as part of the supporting rig. Two stern-mounted steering oars, one on each side, were used, so that when the ship was heeled by the wind one oar would always be in a better position: the windward oar would rise in the water while the leeward oar would dig deeper into the water and steer the boat more effectively. Models of sailing ships recently taken from the tomb of Tutankhamen, dated around 1350 BC, are similar to those ships used in the Punt expedition, but one development was that the two steering oars are hung from a large transverse beam that overhangs the sides of the vessel near the stern.

In 400 BC Herodotus described the Egyptian vessels as 'frameless with hulls made from acacia blocks, pinned together as if building a wall'. Perhaps Egyptian acacia and sycamore trees would only give planks of short lengths and the timbers had to be joined together with intricate joints. Egyptian vessels, from around 2000 BC, show end-butted planks connected together with longitudinal running wedges.

The Phoenicians has a plentiful supply of cedar from the forests of Lebanon and they built ships from planks that ran the whole length of the vessel. Their ships, like those of the Egyptians, were pointed at both ends, but were broader, rounder-hulled and without truss ropes, suggesting that they were structurally sounder. Phoenician ships of c1400 BC depended more on sails than oars; they had single masts with single square sails on two yards. At the stem and stern the planks entered into solid timbers. They were steered by two oars mounted on either side of the stern. There is evidence that they carried grain, exported timber and pitch, and that there was regular trade with the Egyptians from as early as 2000 BC. C. Torr (Ancient Ships, 1894) suggested that fishing vessels built on the lines of Phoenician merchantmen—known as Hippi because their figure-heads were carved in the shapes of horses—doubled the Cape of Good Hope, sailing from Cadiz right around to the east coast of Africa.

The Greeks between 750 and 500 BC used sailing ships to establish their new colonies. Greek and Roman cargo ships were large and strong (80 ft long, 25 ft abeam and 10 ft draught), and could carry up to 200 tons of cargo. Like earlier vessels they were double-ended, single-masted, square-sailed and steered with two oars.

Imperial Rome became a great maritime power in the Mediterranean and Western sea, only exceeded by the global maritime power of the British Empire in the nineteenth century. Roman grain ships c200 AD carried some 150,000 tons of grain each year along well defined sea-lanes, anticipating the ocean trade wind routes of the Age of Discovery. A Roman cargo ship often carried a corbis, or basket, at the top of the main mast (the ships were known as corbitae), to indicate that it transported both cargo and passengers. Roman cargo vessels carried a large square mainsail and a short mast that pointed forward in the bow of the ship, a forerunner of the bowsprit. From here a small square foresail (a spritsail or artemon) was set, which would reduce the helmsman's steering effort by preventing yawing, especially important in rough weather. The spritsail might have allowed corbitae to sail closer to the wind, perhaps even with the wind a little forward of the beam, but it curiously disappeared with the fall of the Roman Empire and did not re-appear until centuries later. It was common practice to extend the stern timbers of a corbitae into a beautiful curved neck of a swan. According to C. Torr, in Ancient Ships, by about AD 50 triangular topsails were in common use on mainmasts, and about this time also, larger Roman merchantmen could have been rigged with a third or 'mizzen' mast. Thereafter there was

4 *Roman ship with triangular topsail. (from Torr, 1894)*

no further progress and additional masts and sails were regularly discarded. However, the three-masted ship was to make a dramatic re-appearance in the fifteenth century.

Hulls from the Classical period were shell-constructed with flush-laid planking. Roman hulls were made of pine, as were the keels. False-keels (see Fig. 123) were of oak. Hulls were caulked with tow (coarse flax) and other material and covered with wax or tar. Planks were fastened together by beautifully cut tenons contained within the thickness of the planking. On Roman merchantmen, iron nails were used to attach the deck beams and frames to the inside of the hull planks, but bronze bolts and nails, because of their better resistance to corrosion, were sometimes used below the waterline.

By the first century BC there is evidence that in the Mediterranean region shipbuilders were leaving shell construction to experiment with a simple form of skeleton building. By the seventh century AD southern shipbuilders were mixing shell and skeleton construction in one ship. During the Crusades (1095–1291) northern European vessels started to enter the Mediterranean, interaction between northern and southern ship-building occurred.

Perhaps the oldest type of northern European sea-going ship was the Scandinavian longship. Although the origin of the Viking ship is still debated, it is the classic example of the shell, clinker-built, hull construction often associated with northern shipbuilders. Between cAD 400 and 1200 the essential characteristics of the Viking longship changed little. The Nydam boat of c400 is 75 ft long, 11 ft wide and 4 ft deep at its widest point. Clinker-built, the boat has five overlapping planks on each side, through-rivetted with iron nails. Nineteen ribs, fitted after the hull was built, were made from naturally curved wood and attached to the planks by lashing them to projections, 'cleats', that were left on the hull planks. In the Nydam boat there is a keel-plank rather than a keel, and there is no evidence that it was sailed. Steering was carried out with a single steering oar set aft on the right-hand side (facing forward): 'steering board' is the origin of the term 'starboard' for this side of a ship. The steering oar was attached at two places to the hull, the upper attachment possibly by a leather loop around the oar shank and the lower attachment by a length of flexible tree root passed through the blade of the rudder and a projection from the lower part of the hull. At the top of the steering oar a tiller was led off at right angles to the oar shaft, to pass transversely across the boat. The oar was moved, and the boat steered, by the helmsman either pulling or pushing the tiller.

The ninth-century Gokstad ship was uncovered in Norway in 1880. It is 78 ft long, 66 ft on the keel, 16.8 ft wide and 6.8 ft deep. Clinker-built in oak, it is a beautifully preserved example of a double-ended, shell-built ship. There are 16 planks on each side. The lower parts of the frames are lashed to the eight lowest planks by a complicated cleat arrangement, while the upper parts are nailed with iron nails to the upper strakes. Strengthening beams tie the two sides of the ship together, and were fitted after the hull planking had been completed. The beams touch the hull at the tenth plank up from the keel and are attached to the frames. There was a large, T-shaped gallows which might have been used to rig a shelter. In the clinker style, each plank overlapped another and the points of iron rivets were deformed over square washers ('roves'). A single pine mast was stepped in a large wooden house, and oars on each side were led through oarports cut some 18 in. below the gunwale.

Raiding Viking longships were fast, sleek and manoeuvrable. However, the Norsemen did not only

5 *The ninth-century Gokstad ship, discovered almost complete in a burial mound near Sande Fjord, with a reconstructed steering oar on the starboard side and oar ports. (Science Museum, London)*

build warships. Cargo carrying ships of reduced length, wider beam and rounded hull were also built. The ship most used by the Vikings in their voyages to Greenland and Vinland, and to carry cargoes, was a round ship called a *knarr*. In 1962, six ships were excavated at Skuldelev in Rostildefjord, Denmark, one of which was a 54 ft long, 14 ft 9 in. beam *knarr*. Dated at around 1000 AD, this knarr was double-ended, clinker-built, and had a single mast and a rudder over its starboard side. The overlapping planks were fastened with nails and made watertight with animal-hair caulking soaked in pine tar. The planks were made of soft pine, but the frames were

of oak. The boat was partially decked-in at both ends and was big enough to transport both cattle and cargo amidships.

Seals, cogs and hulcs

For the twelfth and thirteenth centuries there are few primary sources on the structures of cargo ships, either from northern European or Mediterranean waters and much of the available information comes from contemporary drawings, often celebrating battles.

6 *Drawings of town seals. (drawn from photographs)*

One primary source of ship design in the twelfth and thirteenth centuries can be obtained from seaport seals. Official documents were sealed with hot wax and then stamped with a carved seal. The date of the document would not give the exact date of manufacture of the seal but would, at least, give an upper limit. Seals, although distorting many of the features of the boat, indicate that most northern ships were clinker-built, with square sails and single masts. In order to protect themselves from attack, ships developed fortifications: forecastles and aftercastles. The seals also trace the gradual replacement of the side rudder hung off the quarter by a centre-line, stern-hung rudder: an important evolution in ship design. For example, a stern-hung rudder is clearly seen on an Ipswich town seal dated at 1200, and an often-quoted source is a ship carved on the font (dated 1180) of Winchester cathedral, which seems to show a stern-hung rudder. A seal dated 1242 and a church wall, dated 1284, in Gotland, Sweden, also show stern-hung rudders. The cinque port seals (and gold coins struck in Edward III's reign in 1344) show forecastles and aftercastles, bowsprits and possibly small triangular, 'lateen' (see p 40 ff) sails.

The northern cargo ships of the twelfth, thirteenth and fourteenth centuries are known as *cogs*. Only recently have a number of medieval ships been excavated from coastal mud or raised from the sea bottom. A clinker-built, single-masted cog found at Kalmar, Sweden, and dated to be c1250, had a stern-hung rudder.

In 1962 a well-preserved cargo ship, known as the Bremen cog, from c1380, was found in the River Weser. The ship was 77ft long, 24 ft 6 in. wide and 16ft deep, and could carry some 130 tons of cargo. The Bremen ship shows how cog sterns were straightened to take the newly evolved stern-hung rudders. Thus, unlike Norse longships, cogs were no longer double-ended. The Bremen cog could be considered to be of a 'composite construction, the sides clinker built (shell constructed) but with the flush-laid bottom ('floor') planking attached to the transverse running floor timbers, a feature typical of skeleton construction (see p 15).

Cogs had fore- and aftercastles and from their single masts they set a square sail. Ropes, or 'bowlines', were led from the leading edge of the sail to a 'bowsprit'. Bowlines tensioned the leading edge of the sail, and the bowsprit improved the direction of the pull. Together they enabled a cog to be sailed closer to the wind.

With their clinker-built sides, stern rudders and deep, U-section holds (sometimes with a keel plank, sometimes flush bottomed), cogs were the working freighters of the merchants of the Hanseatic League. Early ninth century cogs were probably built without decks, but by the twelfth century cogs were likely to have been fully covered-in, a real advantage over the partially decked knarrs. And in a fully-decked 'Hansa cog', seawater would no longer collect in the bilge to spoil cargo and upset trim. The cog's castles were primarily for defence, but were later adapted to other

WINCHESTER CATHEDRAL FONT   (1180)

7 *Drawing of the ship carved on Winchester Cathedral font, possibly showing a stern-hung rudder. (drawn from photograph)*

uses. The aftercastle, or 'summercastle', became a cabin and a protective housing for the helmsman, while the forecastle contained stores and provided accommodation. The fully developed cog, with bowsprit, large sail, broad-beamed, deep hull, covered holds, stern rudder and tiller steering, was a major advance in cargo ship design.

By the end of the fourteenth century the northern cog appeared to be replaced by a single-masted, clinker-built ship: the *hulc*. References to hulcs occur as far back as the tenth century and continue until the fifteenth century, but their heyday was short-lived; at the most a hundred years. Their main characteristics appear to be the stern-hung rudder attached to the hull, which has some clinker-built planking, a marked fore and aft curve and is perhaps more round-bottomed than the cog. The vessel carved on the font of Winchester Cathedral is thought to be a hulc, and the ship depicted on the New Shoreham seal is said in the inscription to be a hulc (S. McGrail, *Ancient Ships*).

By the end of the fourteenth century, therefore, there were two broad developments in shipbuilding. They were not necessarily mutually exclusive, but one was in northern Europe and the other in the Mediterranean region. Northern cargo ships were mostly shell-constructed, with clinker-built side-planking, with flush-plank bottoms and single masts supporting large square sails. They had horizontal keels to take the ground at low water, and a blade rudder was hung off a straight stern post. They were steered by a large tiller attached to the rudder head. In general northern ships were heavy, wide-beamed, deep-draughted and slow-moving, and for defence there were fore- and aftercastles (see R. Morton Nance, *The Ship of the Renaissance*).

Mediterranean cargo ships were, like their northern counterparts, heavy and slow, but differed in having skeleton-constructed, carvel-built hulls and more than one mast. The common two-masted, square-sailed rig of the Roman ship of cAD 200 was replaced by the two-masted, lateen rigged ship, possibly the result of the Arab influence from the seventh century onwards. The small artemon mast of the Roman trader developed into a large mast (often the larger of the two) to give the two-masted, lateen-rigged southern trader. By 1200 lateen sails were a distinguishing feature of southern ships. By 1400 most southern ships were still two-masted but the main mast might have a square sail—perhaps a direct influence of the northern cog—and a triangular lateen sail on the aft or mizzen mast.

Northern and southern ships also differed in the method of supporting the mast where it passed through the deck. In the Mediterranean region the mast was contained in a deck socket, made up pieces of timber lashed vertically around the mast and carried well above deck level. In northern Europe, the mast was secured with wedges driven down between the deck and mast until they were flush with the deck.

Another difference might have been that southern ships rarely took to the ground in the almost tideless Mediterranean. Thus southern keels were curved and, when the stern-hung rudder was introduced, rudders were shaped like half-moons to fit concave stern posts.

Southern rigging was also different: the shrouds (ropes that supported the mast on either side of the ship) were attached below any 'top' that was made fast to the mast. A 'top' was a platform at the head of the mast used for fighting or as a look-out. In southern ships' shrouds were tensioned using blocks and tackles and going aloft to the top or yard of the sail was by means of a ladder run up the back of the mast. In the north, shrouds were tightened by 'deadeyes' and lanyards (see p 45 and Fig. 34), and seamen went aloft on 'ratlines'—ropes stretched between the shrouds to make a ladder. Northern methods of rigging were to become common to both northern and southern ships by the end of the fifteenth century.

It is arguable that square-sailed northern cogs, introduced into the Mediterranean during the fourteenth century, returned north in the following century as three-masted 'hybrid ships', with the best features of northern and southern ships. What is certain is that during the fifteenth century cargo ship design underwent dramatic changes. The three-masted, skeleton-constructed, ocean-going *carrack* appeared in the 1400s with such remarkable speed that today there is little documentary evidence describing its evolution. In only 50 years the single-masted cog had been virtually replaced by the three-masted carrack. With large square sails on the fore- and mainmasts and lateen sails on the mizzen, these ships turned out to be ideal for the trade winds of long ocean passages. Carracks became the first true ocean traders.

8 **Opposite top** *a southern ship with steering oars, a tilt frame in the stern, wales and a deck socket, from a mosaic in St. Mark's cathedral, Venice.* **Bottom** *clinker-built cog from an illumination to a 15th-century Spanish manuscript, showing a stern castle and stern-hung rudder. (Both illustrations re-drawn from Morton-Nance, 1955)*

SOUTHERN SHIP (AFTER NANCE)

THE COG (AFTER NANCE)

CHAPTER TWO

The Ocean Trader Comes Of Age

The Age of Discovery (1400—1600)

Trans-oceanic trade began in the fifteenth century when Portuguese merchant adventurers, driven by a desire for wealth, curiosity, and a missionary zeal, pushed first west and then south into the Atlantic Ocean. European nations began to compete to build trans-oceanic empires, a process that continued for over 500 years.

In the Age of Discovery, the adventurers usually backed by rich merchants, bankers or kings and queens, opened up the Atlantic and Indian oceans to trade. Commanders were brave and reckless, and would often go to any lengths to obtain their goals. By the 1500s square-sailed, slow-moving cargo ships, heavily laden with all manner of exotic cargoes—precious gems, gold and later silver, fragrant oils and exotic spices—voyaged along the trade-wind routes from the East and West Indies, to feed European markets that were to remain insatiable for hundreds of years.

If one man can be said to have caused the break away from the coastal, summer-sailing, fourteenth-century cargo ship to the ocean trader, it was Prince Henry of Portugal (1394–1460). He was the third son of King John I and Philippa of Lancaster, the daughter of John of Gaunt of England. (Her brother, John Beaufort, was to become the first holder of the title 'Lord Admiral of England'.) Although Prince Henry played an important role in opening up ocean trade routes, he owed a debt to those who had sailed and traded before. Ship design, ship propulsion and navigation techniques had been developing over thousands of years. The discoveries of Columbus, Magellan and da Gama had their origins in the sea voyages made by early Egyptians, Chinese and Arab traders, Hanseatic merchants and Mediterranean fishermen. Although the fifteenth and sixteenth centuries were the 'Age of Discovery' as far as

Europeans were concerned, most newly 'discovered' lands had indigenous populations with rich local customs and cultures: usually quickly destroyed by the arrival of European merchant adventurers.

In 1414 Prince Henry was in North Africa, at the siege of Ceuta, Morocco. There he eagerly talked to merchants about the countries crossed by the inland caravan routes. He learnt much, and returned to Portugal with a passion to discover the wealth and lands that lay beyond Europe's shores. Although Europe, North Africa and parts of India and China had been mapped, most uneducated sailors thought the earth flat, and that they would be drowned by sailing over a gigantic waterfall at the edge of the sea or boiled alive in the waters of the African coasts. Prince Henry's leadership, drive and ambition, his captains and their ships, were to help the ordinary seamen overcome their fears.

But the early ocean voyages were not just due to Prince Henry: European intellectual climate was ready for the Age of Discovery. Around 1400 much excitement had been generated by the re-discovery of Ptolemy's *Geographia*, a compendium of geographical knowledge about the middle of the second century AD. Marco Polo had journeyed overland to China in the thirteenth century and, while imprisoned by the Genoese in 1298, wrote an early geographical encyclopaedia of China and the East. There was the legend of the Christian king, Prester John, thought at this time to be a ruler in eastern Africa; rumours circulated of untold wealth in the East; and much was being made of Chinese scientific knowledge.

The acquisition of wealth was probably the major drive of the merchant adventurers in the Age of Discovery. Prince Henry declared it as one of his main aims in sending out discovery ships. His other aims were to extend geographical knowledge for Portugal's advantage and, with the missionary zeal

2000BC/ 16thCENTURY

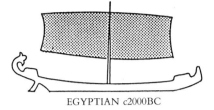

EGYPTIAN c2000BC

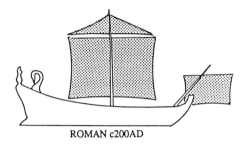

ROMAN c200AD

VIKING c10th CENTURY

HANSA COG c1350

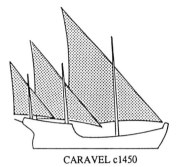

CARAVEL c1450

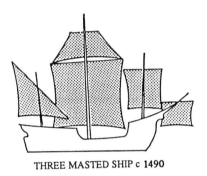

THREE MASTED SHIP c 1490

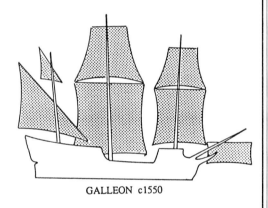

GALLEON c1550

9 *Sail Plans. (after Kihlberg, 1986)*

typical of the period, prevent the overrunning of Africa by the Moslems by linking his forces with those of Prestor John. In 1419 Prince Henry became governor of the Algarve and moved from Lisbon to southern Portugal, near Lagos, to the village of Villa do Infante, very close to Cape St. Vincent, the southwest tip of Portugal.

At Cape St. Vincent barren cliffs rise steeply out of the ocean, their surfaces dried to a powder by the sun. Deep sea-caves echo rhythmically, unceasingly, to the boom and crash of the Atlantic swell. Stiff, wind-filled, canvas sails suddenly flap and lose shape, blocks start to rattle and taut ropes become slack as the Cape is rounded: the North-East trade winds die,

10 *Prince Henry the Navigator. Detail from a 15th-century painting by Nuño Goncalves. (Museu Nacional de Arte Antiga, Lisbon)*

smothered by the lee of the high cliffs. During an onshore gale the Atlantic throws spray high into the air, showering the rocks until they stream with water. Later, dried sea-salt glistens on the cliff faces, gleaming white in the hot Algarve sun. Little grows here, but it was on these high, barren cliff tops, at Sagres, that Prince Henry set up a School of Navigation that was to become world famous. He surrounded himself with the best cartographers, astrologers and mathematicians and sent out expeditions, west into the Atlantic, and south down the west coast of Africa, his commanders armed with the finest maps and instruments of the day. One of his most important acts was to instruct captains to record all that they saw and experienced, so as to build a collection of sailing pilots or *rotarios* ('rutters', as they became known in English).

Prince Henry's early explorations in the Atlantic Ocean were later to become important for the development of the Portuguese empire. Goncalo Cabral, for example, discovered in 1427 the eastern-most rocky outpost of the Azores—the Ants. During Prince Henry's lifetime more islands in the archipelago were discovered and colonized, and they played an important role as a staging post for Portuguese cargo and warships returning home to Lisbon.

One of Prince Henry's main African objectives was to round Cape Bojador (Boujdour: Bulging cape) a small cape just south of the Canaries. In 1434 Gil Eanes rounded it in a small, square-sailed ship, a *barca*, and saw the African coast running away southwards: the sea was not boiling and the sun did not turn the seamen black. Fears of reefs, shallows, rapid currents and contrary winds that had built up over decades were shown to be groundless. Cape Bojador was just another minor African headland.

Prince Henry's continued voyages to Africa met with criticism because of their expense, but in 1443 Lancarote, one of the Prince's retainers, brought back 235 black Africans. It was the beginning of the lucrative European slave trade that was to transport or kill some 20 million Africans. By the time of Prince Henry's death in 1460, he had organized over 30 oceanic and African coastal expeditions; he had increased geographical knowledge of the Canaries; he had either discovered or started the colonization of the Madeiras (Porto Santo, 1419), the Azores (The Ants, 1427) and the Cape Verde Islands (1456); he had set up regular trade routes with Senegambia; and, finally, his ships had travelled to within 500 miles north of the equator. Portugal was well on the road to becoming one of the richest and most powerful nations in Europe.

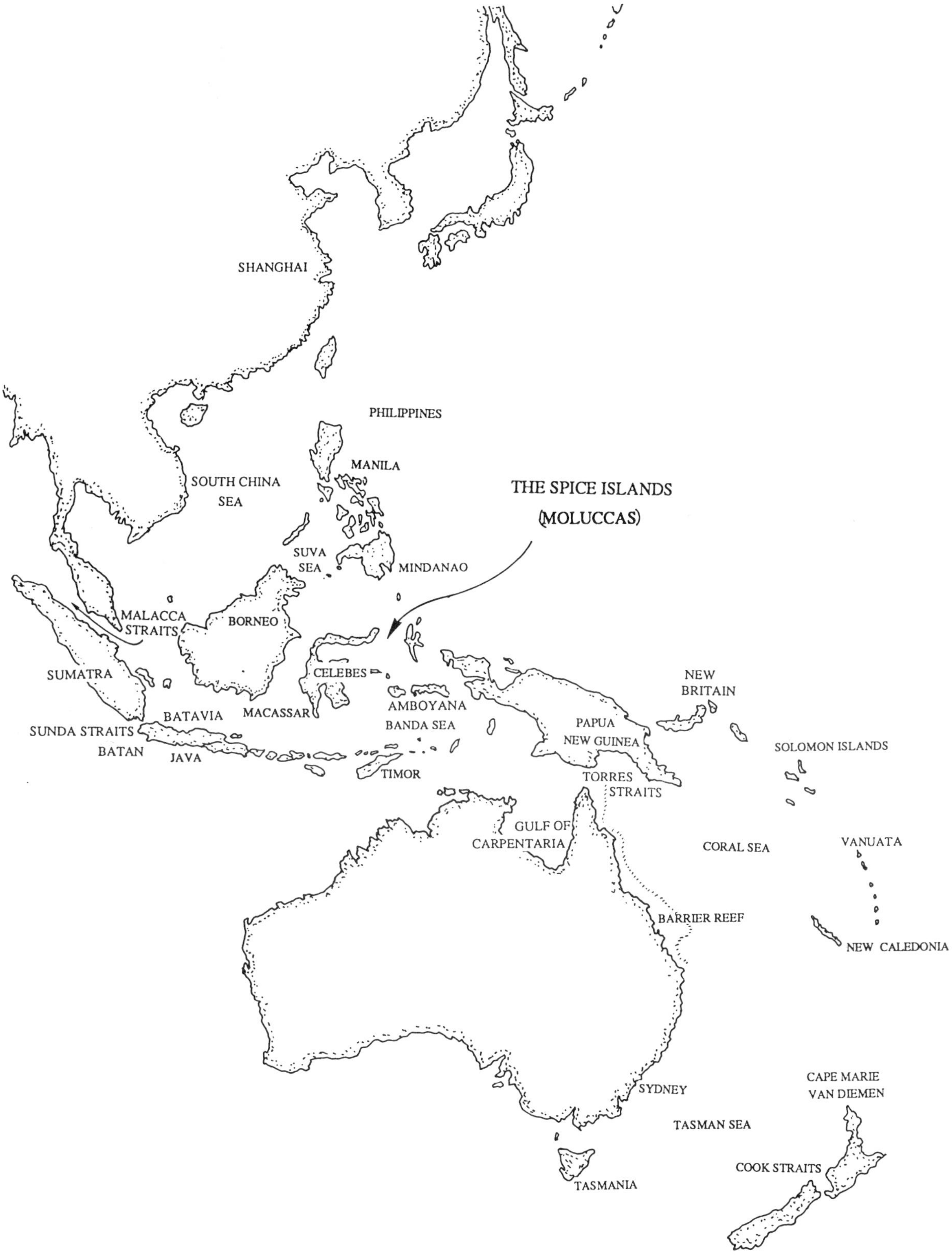

SHANGHAI

PHILIPPINES

MANILA

SOUTH CHINA
SEA

THE SPICE ISLANDS
(MOLUCCAS)

SUVA
SEA

MINDANAO

MALACCA
STRAITS

BORNEO

SUMATRA

CELEBES

NEW
BRITAIN

BATAVIA

MACASSAR

AMBOYANA
BANDA SEA

PAPUA
NEW GUINEA

SOLOMON ISLANDS

SUNDA STRAITS

BATAN

JAVA

TIMOR

TORRES
STRAITS

GULF OF
CARPENTARIA

CORAL SEA

VANUATA

BARRIER REEF

NEW CALEDONIA

CAPE MARIE
VAN DIEMEN

SYDNEY

TASMAN SEA

COOK STRAITS

TASMANIA

Map 2   *The Spice Islands.*

27

In 1481 John II (1455–1495) came to the throne and continued to encourage Portuguese empire-building and expansionism. In 1486 he gave Bartholomeu Dias a fleet of three ships with orders to press southwards, down Africa's west coast. For 13 days Dias ran before a terrible storm in the South Atlantic. Finally the storm passed; lost he turned east, hoping to find land, but none appeared. He turned north and soon made a landfall, on Africa's east coast: unknowingly he had broken through into the Indian Ocean. He named the southernmost tip of Africa the Cape of Storms; John II renamed it the Cape of Good Hope. Dias landed in present-day Algoa Bay and set up *padraos*: stone pillars as tall as two men, crowned with a cross, and used by the Portuguese as proof of their discoveries and a claim to their sovereignty over the land.

John II ordered a small fleet to be built in order to reach India and put Dias in charge of its construction. He broke from the traditional Portuguese discovery ship, the *caravel*, to build larger, heavier, square-sailed vessels: *naus*. John II died before the fleet was completed and his successor, Manuel I (1469–1521), chose Vasco da Gama as Commander-in-Chief.

The tiny fleet was ready to set sail on 7 July 1497. The ship's officers had spent the night in prayer in the chapel of Our Lady of Belem, a chapel that had been built by Prince Henry. Thousands had come to send them off on perhaps the longest sea voyage yet undertaken by man. The moment, one of Portugal's greatest, was described by the poet an adventurer Luis de Camoes (c1524–1580), in 'The Lusiads':

Now in the famous port of Lisbon town
(where golden Tagus mingles his sweet flood
With the ocean and his sands doth drown)
With noble longings, and transported mood,
The ships lye ready. There no sullen frown,
No frosty fear benumbs the youthful blood:
For both the seamen and the landmen there,
Will go with me about the world they sweare.
(from 'Camoes and his epic', W. Freitas)

In order to pick up favourable winds, da Gama bravely sailed southwestwards out of Lisbon, across uncharted Atlantic Ocean, to almost reach Brazil before turning south and east to round the Cape of Good Hope. It was a stroke of nautical insight, and the British Admiralty sailing directions still recommends this route for sailing round the Cape of Good Hope. In 1498 de Gama, with the aid of an Arab navigator, Ahmed ibn Majid, finally crossed the Indian Ocean and arrived off the Malabar coast, a few miles north of Calicut, West India. To mark the return of da Gama to Lisbon in 1500, Manuel I ordered the building of a great cathedral at Belem, near where da Gama had prayed before setting out.

In 1500 Pedro Cabral followed da Gama's tracks and arrived at Brazil, which he claimed for Portugal. Sailing southeast, towards the Cape of Good Hope, his fleet of 13 ships ran into a violent storm and only nine survived. Batholomeu Dias, the discoverer of the Cape, went down with his vessel. Only seven ships returned to Lisbon, but their cargoes were so valuable that the voyage made well over a hundred per cent profit. Cabral and the next two voyages of da Gama established the Portuguese-India run and by 1515 Portugal had pushed so far east that it had trade connections with China at Macau and Canton.

While the Portuguese were busily expanding their overseas possessions in the East, Spanish ships were voyaging west. Columbus, a Genoese seaman sailing under the Spanish flag, believed that by travelling west he could reach the Orient. In 1492, six years before da Gama's voyages to Calicut, Columbus was the first European to cross the Atlantic and discover many Caribbean Islands. But he was convinced, until his death, that he had found the route to the 'West Indies'. Unfortunately, Columbus' original log is lost, perhaps because of the 'policy of secrecy' which may have surrounded the early discovery voyages—although some historians now question if there ever was such a policy. A copy of the log was found in 1552 by a Spanish priest, Las Casas, who re-wrote it in the third person. Occasionally Las Casas used the first person, and it is now assumed that these were the original words of Columbus. Las Casas described the first European siting of a Caribbean island of San Salvador:

Wednesday, 10th of October (1492)

The course was W.S.W., and they went at the rate of 10 miles an hour, occasionally 12 miles, and sometimes 7. During the day and night they made 59 leagues counted as no more than 44. Here the people could endure no longer. They complained of the length of the voyage. But the Admiral cheered them up in the best way he could, giving them good hopes of the advantages they might gain from it. He added that, however much they might complain, he had to go to the Indies, and that he would go on until he found them, with the help of our Lord.

Thursday, 11th of October.

The course was W.S.W., and there was more sea than there had been during the whole of the voyage. They saw sandpipers, and a green reed near the ship. Those of the caravel *Pinta* saw a cane and a pole, and they took up another small pole which appeared to have been worked with iron: also another bit of cane, a land-plant, and a small board. The crew of the caravel *Niña* also saw signs of land, and a small branch covered with berries. Everyone breathed afresh and rejoiced at these signs. The run until sunset was 26 leagues.

After sunset the Admiral returned to his original west course, and they went along at the rate of 12 miles an

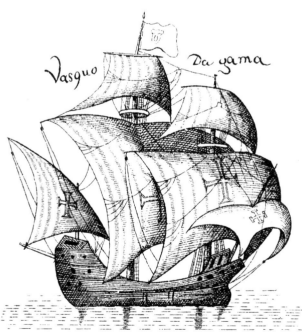

11 *The Da Gama fleet of 1497, showing three-masted* naus; *from a painting ordered by Jorge Gabral in 1550. (Science Museum, London)*

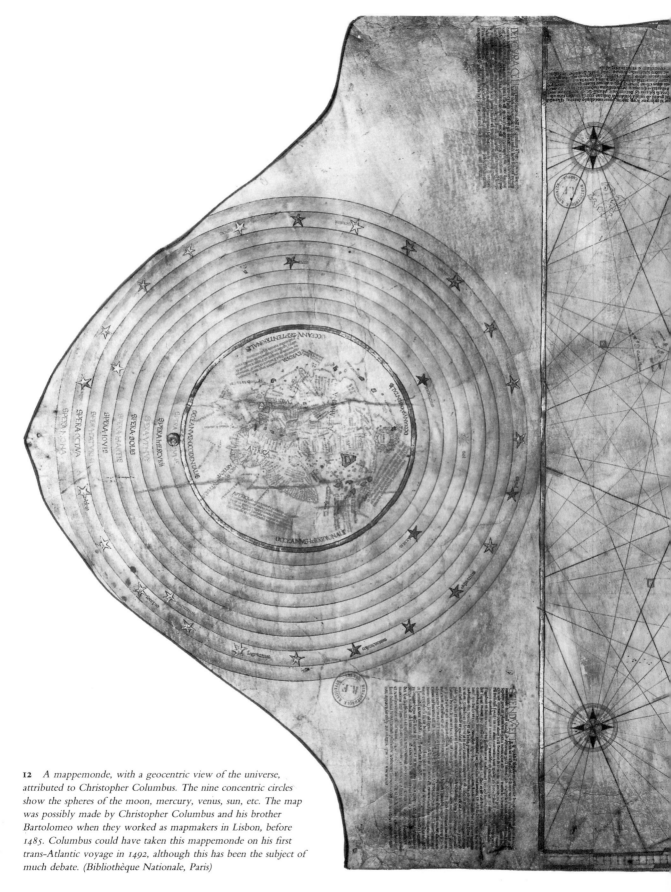

12 *A mappemonde, with a geocentric view of the universe, attributed to Christopher Columbus. The nine concentric circles show the spheres of the moon, mercury, venus, sun, etc. The map was possibly made by Christopher Columbus and his brother Bartolomeo when they worked as mapmakers in Lisbon, before 1485. Columbus could have taken this mappemonde on his first trans-Atlantic voyage in 1492, although this has been the subject of much debate. (Bibliothèque Nationale, Paris)*

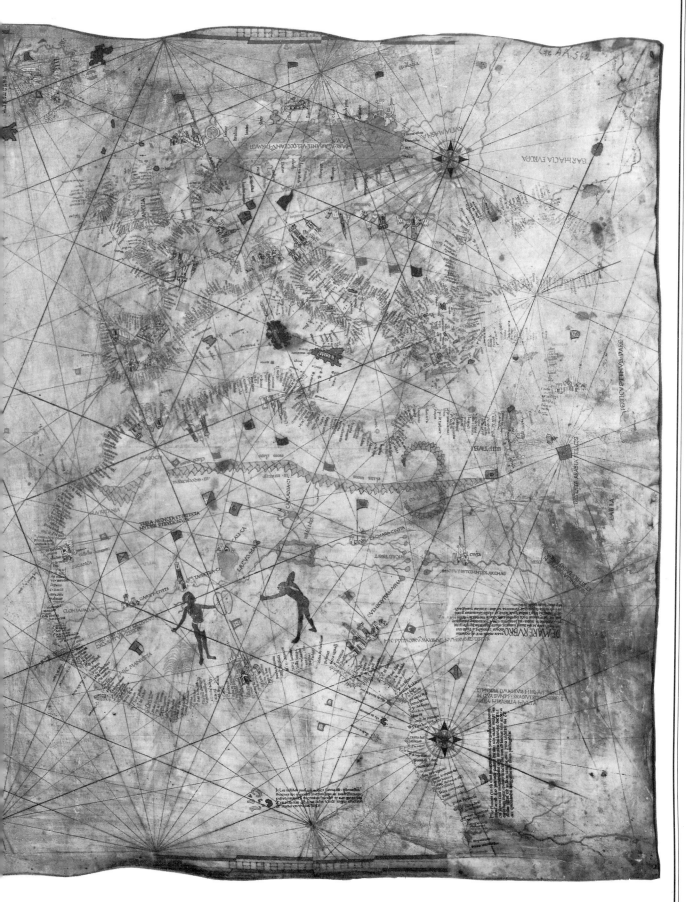

hour. Up to two hours after midnight they had gone 90 miles, equal to 22½ leagues. As the caravel *Pinta* was a better sailer, and went ahead of the Admiral, she found the land, and made the signals ordered by the Admiral. The land was first seen by a sailor named Rodrigo de Triana.

[20 leagues was one degree of latitude, which is 60 nautical miles. So one league is between three and four land miles. The above extract is from a translation of Las Casas, published by the Hakluyt Society. The speeds given by Las Casas for 10th October were very fast and unlikely to be correct.]

On October 12th, Columbus landed at Bahia Longa on the west coast of San Salvador and claimed the land for Spain. On December 24th he lost his ship, the *Santa María*, on a reef off Hispanola and had to transfer to the *Niña* for his return to Spain. Altogether, Columbus made four West Indian voyages, the second was to Cuba and Jamaica (1493–1496); in the third he visited South America and Trinidad (1497–1500) and on his last voyage he visited parts of Central America (1502–1504). He died in 1506 at the age of 55, in Valladolid, one of the great men of the Age of Discovery.

England took little part in the first century of the Age of Discovery. Henry VII (1457–1509, king 1485–1509) hired two Genoese seamen, John Cabot and his son Sebastian, to voyage northwest across the Atlantic. In 1497 they discovered Cape Breton Island thinking, like Columbus, that they too had found the way to the Orient. But the English crown did not follow-up the voyage, partly due to its fear of the maritime superpowers Spain and Portugal.

As a result of a Spanish-Portuguese treaty in 1493 (the treaty of Tordesillas), the Spanish pope Alexander VI issued two papal bulls. He gave Spain the rights to all lands discovered west of a line that connected the north and south poles and ran a 100 leagues west of the Azores and the Cape Verde islands. Spain could monopolise trade in this region and have the rights to grant trading licenses to other nations. Portugal was given the lands discovered east of the line. In 1494 the line was fixed 370 leagues west of the Cape Verde islands, so that Portugal could include its recent Brazilian discoveries. Not surprisingly, other European nations resented the line and refused to recognize it.

THE FOUR VOYAGES OF COLUMBUS

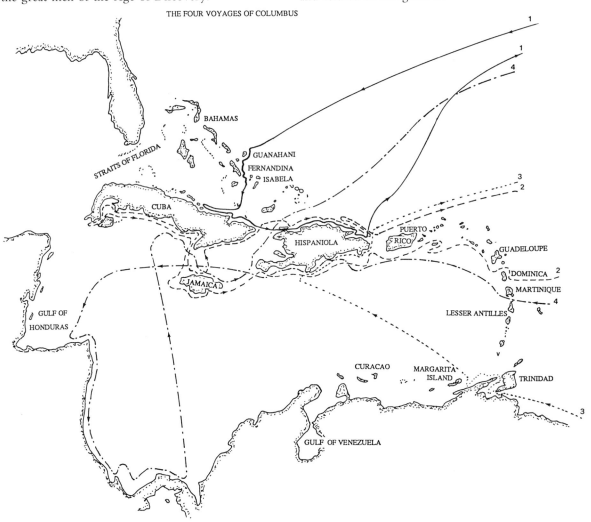

Map 3 *The four voyages of Columbus. (after D. Castlereagh)*

Throughout the fifteenth century development of ocean trade was generally linked to the expansionist policies pursued by Portugal and Spain. As a direct result of their discoveries, the balance of power, commercial and military, had begun to swing away from the Mediterranean city-states and towards the Iberian Peninsula. In the sixteenth century the great trading empires of Venice and Genoa would collapse and their oar-powered galley fleets disband. Ocean traders were to come of age.

The sixteenth century saw the continued rapid expansion of the ocean trading routes and cargo ships evolved to meet the needs of the trading nations. Spanish ships carried bullion back from new territories in Central and South America, while Portugal's chief interest was in the spices from India and the East. Spain, the greatest ocean trader in the sixteenth century, soon had a fast, seaworthy vessel: the galleon. The other maritime nations quickly built their own versions.

With the Spanish Pope's blessing, in the late fifteenth and early sixteenth centuries Spain continued to expand her empire in the west and Portugal expanded hers in the east. In the 1520s Spanish Conquistadores overran the Aztec empire in Mexico and by 1533 they had control of most of the Peruvian Inca empire. Portugal held its overseas territories under a strong, often ruthless, thumb.

Throughout the sixteenth century maritime explorations continued at a steady pace. In 1519 the Portuguese Ferdinand Magellan (c1480–1521) set out to travel west around the world under the flag of Spain. Charles V of Spain gave him five, three-masted ships: *Santo Antonio, Trinidad, Concepcion, Victoria* and *Santiago*, vessels that ranged from 120 to 75 tons. Only one of the ships, the *Victoria*, returned to Seville and Magellan, famous for his 'Straits' and for being the first European to sail the Pacific, was killed in the Philippines. Men from his fleet were the first to circumnavigate the world. His voyage was one of the greatest of all the voyages of Discovery.

Portugal, a small country with few inhabitants and scarce natural resources, ruled its possessions from fortified settlements, supplied when necessary from Lisbon, with armed convoys and reinforcements. Portugal's main gains in the East were made by a great soldier and sailor Alfonso de Albuquerque (1453–1515), who became the Governor of Portuguese India from 1509—1515. In 1511 he sent the first of many Portuguese expeditions to the Spice Islands or Moluccas. In a series of brilliant campaigns Albuquerque siezed a number of strategic locations: in 1510 he captured Goa in India; in 1511 Malacca in the Malay Peninsula; in 1514 Calicut was fortified; the island of Hormuz in the Arabian Gulf was his in 1515. His only failure was when he attempted to take

Aden in his bid to control the Red Sea and destroy Mecca.

In 1518 Manuel I of Portugal decided to commission his cartographer, Lopo Homem, to record Portugal's early discoveries by drawing a set of 'sea maps'. (They were probably to be sent as a gift for Francis I of France.) Lopo Homem was still relatively inexperienced and procured the help of Pedro Reinel and his son. Together they produced a series of beautifully illustrated early charts (Portolans, see p 65). Their Azores chart was complete with sketches of Portuguese ocean traders, with three masts and Order of Christ crosses painted on their sails. The Order was founded in 1317 and had been closely associated with Henry the Navigator. Their sea map of India and East Africa featured all the discoveries and conquests of Albuquerque, as well as those of the earlier explorers Cabral and da Gama. Perhaps the charts were meant to define Portuguese possessions for the King of France. By 1600 Portugal had more than 50 forts between Africa and India, but with its gains in the Spice Islands it had begun to over-extend itself.

France, resenting the world's division by the Pope into Spanish and Portuguese halves, and wanting her share of the new trades, went to war against Spain. Speedy French privateers from the Biscay ports were particularly effective against the homeward bound, heavily-laden Spanish galleons.

England in the second century of the age of Discovery did not play a pioneering role. Cabot's successful trans-Atlantic voyage in 1496 was followed by John Rastell's disastrous voyage to Newfoundland in 1517. Setting sail with two ships manned by English seamen he was marooned by the crews in Ireland. The seamen preferred to turn their ships south to search for a more profitable cargo from Bordeaux than risk a hazardous voyage across the north Atlantic. Dorothy Burwash, in *English Merchant Shipping, 1460–1540*, wrote:

Nor did English navigators and scholars take the lead in the development of scientific and celestial navigation. The comparative lack of original scientific treatises composed in England before the middle of the sixteenth century; the use of Portuguese and Genoese pilots on important expeditions; and John Rastell's discouraging experience when he attempted to employ English pilots on his western voyage, all indicate that English seamen and scholars were not yet equipped to take their place in the forefront of Renaissance exploration and investigation.

Henry VIII (1491–1547), as his father Henry VII (1457–1509) had done, encouraged the English in all maritime affairs. Both kings built warships which were important in giving protection to the country's merchant shipping. In 1514 Henry VIII founded the Corporation of Trinity House for the 'advancement of navigation and commerce' and to train pilots for

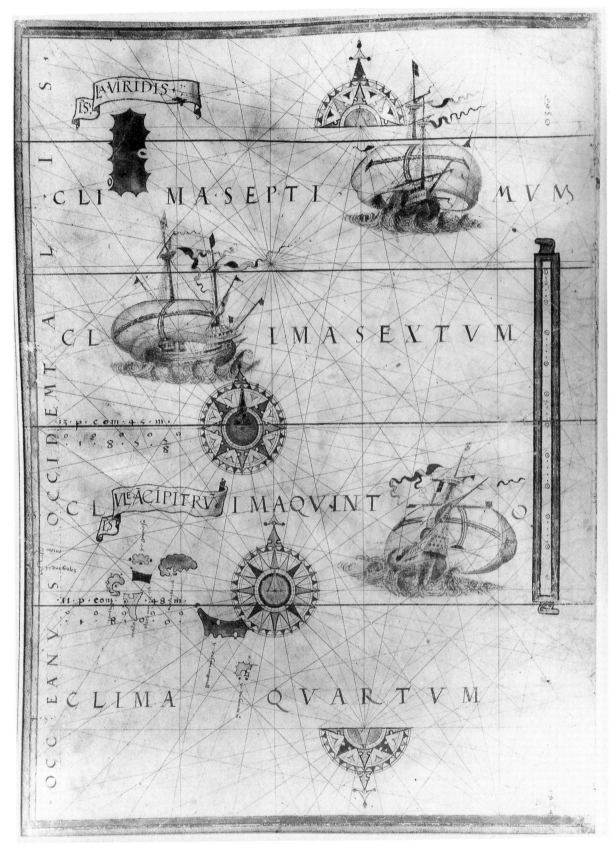

13 *The Azores Chart attributed to Lopo Homem and Pedro Reinel c1518–1519, showing three-masted naus with lateen-rigged mizzen masts, round tops, and topsails. Crosses of the Order of Christ are painted on the ships' sails. (Bibliothèque Nationale, Paris)*

English waters. An important outcome of both Henrys' interests in English shipping was that the state now took an active interest in both ship design and building. Merchant shipbuilders were also active: in the Elizabethan period, for example, Walter Raleigh built a ship of advanced design and sold it to the state.

The Henrys passed laws which stipulated that English freight had to be carried by English ships. These laws lasted, in one form or another (see p 78, the Navigation Acts), until the middle of the nineteenth century. Henry VIII's daughter, Mary I (1516–1558), married Philip II of Spain in 1554. Her aim was to restore Roman Catholicism to England and technically Britain and Spain were united under one crown until her death in 1558. She brought England into the Spanish-Franco wars, and she soon became as unpopular as her policies.

By 1580 Spain and Portugal were united under one crown. The sixteenth century was Spain's 'golden age', her colonies supplying her with enormous wealth, her merchant fleet the largest in Europe. But there was dissent within the empire. In 1579 the Spanish Netherlands (today's Holland and Belgium) declared themselves independent of Spain, partly as a result of Spain's suppression of Protestantism. These northern provinces continued their struggle for independence until 1648 when the 'United Provinces of the Netherlands' were finally recognized. By the seventeenth century the Dutch had created a great merchant shipping industry of their own.

English shipping under Elizabeth I (1558–1603) began to ascend for the first time. Ralph Davis wrote in *The Rise of the English Shipping Industry* that in 1588:

The English (in contrast to the Spanish), so far from being at that time heirs to generations of seagoers were newcomers to ocean trade and shipping … The basis on which England established itself in 1588 as the first naval power of Europe was created only during the previous two decades. The mid-sixteenth century may well mark the nadir of English merchant shipping.

There was an English sympathy for the Dutch Protestants' struggle for independence from Spain, and Elizabethan England produced a band of merchant adventurers who raided Spanish ships in Spain's Caribbean colonies. In 1532 English ships began to appear in the Mediterranean, trying to break the trade stranglehold of the Venetians. In 1533 Hugh Willoughby had tried to find the North-East passage to the Spice Islands. In 1553 Thomas Wyndham was trading on the Gold Coast of Africa and by 1554 French and English ships were fighting the Portuguese for the right to trade on the West African coast.

Many famous English navigators and seamen like John Hawkins (1532–1595), Martin Frobisher (c1535–1594), Humphrey Gilbert (c1539–1583), Francis Drake (1540–1596) and John Davis (c1550–1605) sailed on voyages of discovery with English government encouragement and approval. Many attacked and looted Spanish treasure ships, and Elizabeth I's unwillingness to condemn English piracy and privateering was another factor that resulted in war with Spain in 1587. The English galleon and the weather played key roles in the failure of the Spanish Armada in 1588. The war reached its height in the 1590s, only to continue into a war of attrition that was finally ended in 1604 after Elizabeth's death.

Partly due to the failure of the 1588 Spanish Armada (there were two others), Spain and Portugal began to lose their ocean trading monopolies. Portugal rapidly declined, but Spain continued as a major, if not the world power, until losing its dominant position to France in 1659 after the Thirty Years War.

Francis Drake was the first English sea-captain to circumnavigate the world and there were attempts by other Englishmen to find a North-West or North-East passage to the Spice Islands. Attempts on the North-East passage resulted in a lucrative trade agreement being made with Ivan (the Terrible) of Russia and the formation of the British-Muscovy Company. Richard Hakluyt proudly wrote about the exploits of the British explorers, and in 1589 published his famous *Principal Navigations, Voyages and Discoveries of the English Nation*. English merchants gradually became more powerful, competed with the Hanseatic League and soon began to control their own manufacturing processes. By 1598 the Hansa had been expelled from England and in 1599 one of the most powerful of all the British ocean trading companies came into existence: the Honourable English East India Company (HEIC).

14 **pp 36–7** *Attributed to Homem-Reinel c1518, this sea map was drawn after the voyages and discoveries of Da Gama, Cabral and Albuquerque: seven-masted Arab ships with steering oars, and half-moons on their sails; Portuguese naus with the crosses of the Order of Christ. The Maldive islands are shown exaggerated, clustered off the southwest tip of India. (Bibliothèque Nationale, Paris)*

15 **pp 38–9** *Homem-Reinel sea map of northern Europe, c1518. Scotland is shown as a separate island. (Bibliothèque Nationale, Paris)*

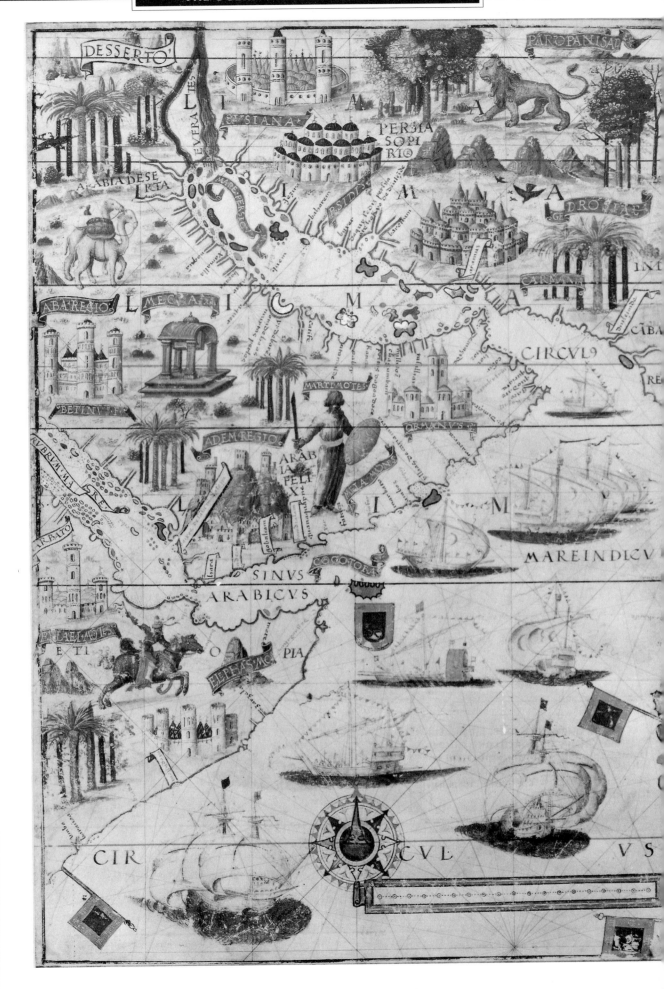

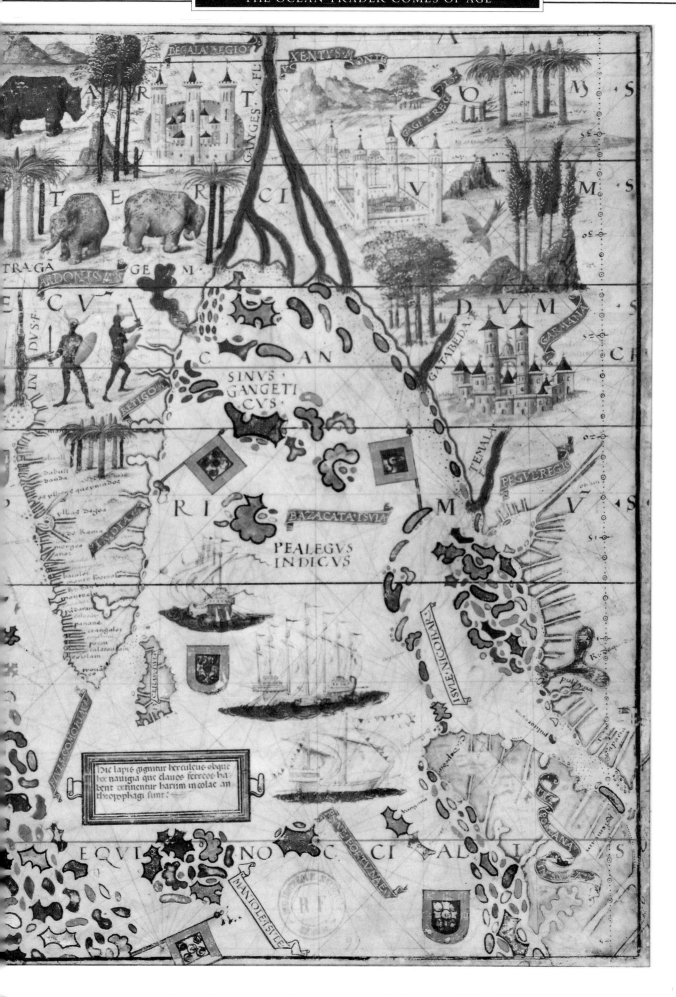

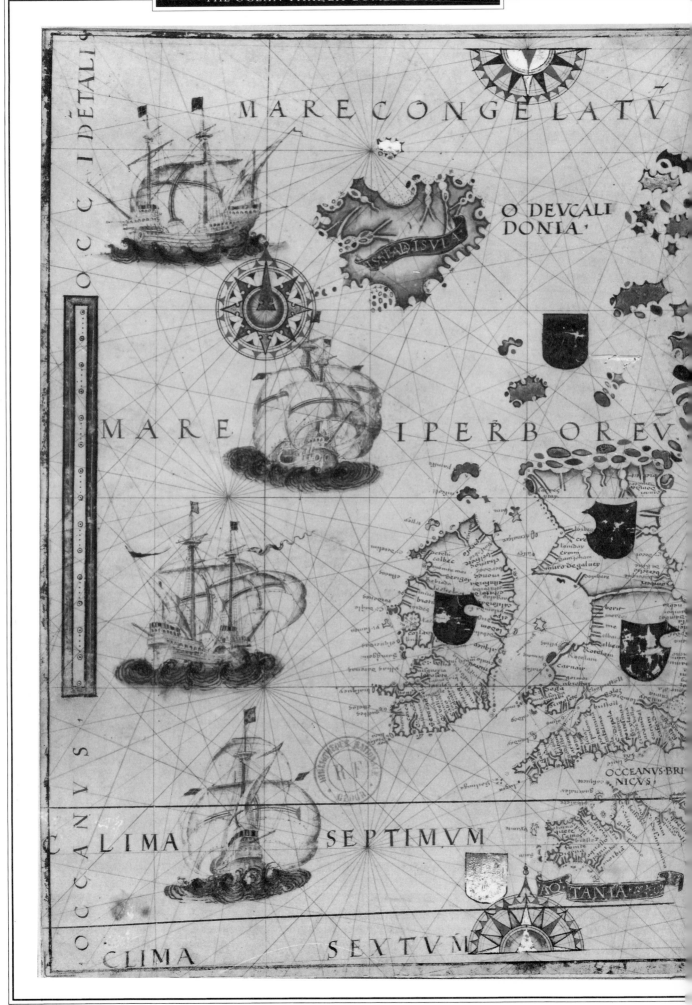

MARE CONGELATŪ

O DEVCALI
DONIA·

ISTLADISVLA

MARE IPEŘBOREV

OCCANVS IDĒTALIS

OCCANVS BRI
NICVS

CLIMA SEPTIMVM

CLIMA SEXTVM

Caravel

The origins of the three ocean-going ships—*caravel, carrack* and *galleon*—that played the most important roles in the Age of Discovery are obscure. The caravel could have come from a Portuguese fishing boat or from an Arab trader; the three-masted carrack appeared so fast that there is little historical evidence of its evolution; and the galleon was probably developed by the Spanish, or possibly the Italians. Historically the caravel preceded the carrack and galleon, but at one time all three types co-existed.

The caravel, with its triangular lateen sails, played its role in the early part of the first century of the Age of Discovery. Caravels were important because of the prevailing winds in the Atlantic Ocean. North and South Atlantic sailing ship routes have to follow the paths traced out by the winds that circulate around two high pressure systems that are situated north and south of the equator. These winds are the trade winds that travel clockwise around the northern system, and anti-clockwise around the southern system. As a result, the prevailing winds along Portugal's coast, and down towards the northwest African coast, are the northeast trade winds (winds are named for the direction from which they blow), or the 'Portuguese trade winds' as they are sometimes known.

A square-sailed ship sailing from Portugal towards Cape Bojador on the African coast has an easy outward voyage: it just spreads out its sails and runs, with the Portuguese trades blowing steadily over the quarter or stern. The problem is to return; ships with square sails will not sail efficiently, or even at all, with the wind forward of the beam. In the fifteenth century ships with square sails were doing well if they could sail with the wind 10° forward of the beam.

A homeward-bound Portuguese ship, for example, returning to Lisbon from the Orient, once over the equator and through the windless zone of the Doldrums, would still have to travel north and west out in to the North Atlantic, until out of the influence of the northeast trades. Ships would sail as far north as the latitude of the Azores, before turning east for Lisbon. These ocean traders would call in at the Azores, which soon became an important staging post for any homeward-bound Portuguese ships.

A caravel's lateen sail is an example of a sail rigged 'fore and aft' (that is parallel with a line connecting the ship's stem and stern). It is a triangular sail set on a spar that is hung at an angle of some 45° from around the top of the mast. John Morwood, in *Sailing Aerodynamics*, describes the lateen sail as 'probably as good a sail as has ever been devised to take a boat to windward and could only be improved by streamlining and shifting the yard to make it straight'.

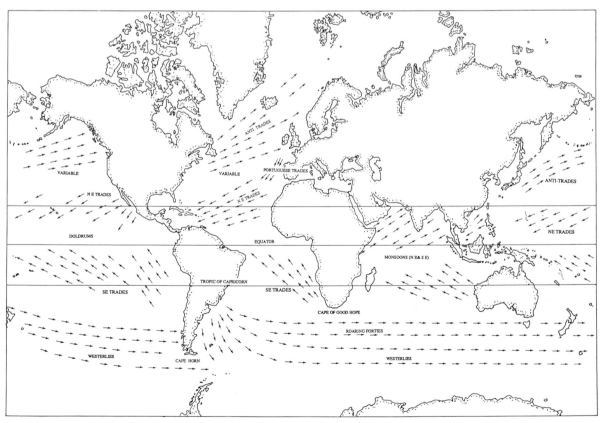

Map 4   *The Trade Winds. (after Knight, 1973)*

16 *A model of a four-masted Portuguese* caravel *(c1536). A* caravela redonda *with the foremast square-rigged, and the other three with lateen sails; a round top on the foremast and a spritsail yard below the bowsprit. (Science Museum, London)*

No ship can sail directly into the wind but fore and aft rigged ships (and even ships with square sails, provided they angle them into the wind) can move upwind by 'tacking', that is making a zig-zag course into the wind. A fore and aft rigged ship can sail much closer to the wind than a ship with square sails. To return home to Portugal from West Africa, caravels would often travel westward, far off-shore, and then beat their way northwards: a long daunting, but at least possible voyage in lateen-rigged ships.

During the early part of the explorations, caravels (caravela or carabela) were between 60 and 90 ft long with either two, three or possibly four single-sailed, lateen-rigged masts. The largest mast was usually placed in the middle of the hull and the spar of the

lateen sail could be as long as the vessel. Typically they had no forecastles, low stern castles and were sleek looking craft for their period. By the late fifteenth century some caravels carried small, square sails for running when the wind was aft of the beam. As Portuguese seamen became more experienced, they began replacing the long-yarded lateen-rig with square sails on the foremast, as the square sail was easier to handle in strong wind. These caravels were known as *caravela redonda* (round caravels) and might, in addition to the square rigged foremast, have three other lateen rigged masts. There were a number of different types of caravels used by the Portuguese: the *caravela de armada* (fleet caravel), usually caravela redondas; the *caravelao* (a small

41

caravel); and the *caravela mexeriqueira* (a patrol boat). The ocean-going caravels were square-sterned and decked-in for safety.

Caravels were small, cheap to build and shallow draughted. Like all sailing ships they sailed best with the wind over the quarter. Not drawing much water they were ideal for voyaging up African rivers (they penetrated some 200 miles inland) but this was a disadvantage when beating to windward: they tended to slip side-ways ('make leeway') since they lacked a deep keel to grip the water. A discovery caravel on a voyage of discovery would be around 100 tons with a crew of 50. Large crews were needed for shore parties, to fight when necessary, and to handle the large yards of the lateen rigs. To tack, the lateen yards had to be manhandled around the mast. Sometimes the vessels would 'wear' ('wearing' is when the stern is passed through the wind; 'tacking' is when the bow passes through the wind).

The origins of the lateen rig are obscure: it might have been developed by Mediterranean fishermen for use in a sea famous for its calms and sudden squalls. A lateen sail has an advantage in that the long yard carries a lot of canvas for light winds, yet easily bends to spill wind from the sail in a strong gust. Alternatively the lateen rig might have originated from Arab traders working the Indian Ocean or Arabian Gulf. Lateen rigs are still found on present-day working craft in these areas. Arab *dhows* and, for example, the *baggala*, a double-masted, lateen-rigged boat found in the Indian Ocean. Baggala lateen sails have a short, vertical section on their leading edges and are sometimes known as 'settee' sails.

Caravels were not used on the earliest Portuguese voyages. For example a square sailed *barca* was used to conquer Cape Bojador. But from 1441 caravels increasingly became the vessel of choice for voyages of discovery down the African coast. For example Bartolomeu Dias survived a severe Atlantic storm and rounded the Cape of Good Hope in a caravel when he unwittingly entered the Indian Ocean. Dias's decision to build the three-masted, *naus* with square sails for da Gama's 1498 crossing of the Indian Ocean was probably based on the inability of the caravel to carry the quantities of stores needed for a long ocean voyage.

Lateen-rigged caravels did not appear in northern Europe until the mid-fifteenth century. Even then there seems to be confusion as to whether ships were caravels, with lateen rigs, or simply had 'carvel-built' hulls.

From carrack to galleon

Carrack is a general term used to describe the new three-masted ocean traders that appeared around 1400. It is an English derivation of the term *kraeck* used by the Flemish artist, 'W.A.', after drawing a three masted ship, sometime in the middle to late fifteenth century, and labelling it a kraeck. The origins of the three-masted ship in both northern and Mediterranean waters remain obscure. The originators could have been the Genoese, the Venetians or even the Spanish and Portuguese.

In the early part of the fifteenth century England was still producing clinker-built square-sailed ships. In 1419 Henry V (1387–1422) built the *Grâce Dieu*. In the early tradition of northern European shipbuilding, *Grâce Dieu* was shell constructed (see p 15), but broke with tradition by having two, possibly three, masts to drive a hull that was probably over 100 ft. These clinker-built ships were approaching the limit of the size that can be obtained using shell construction techniques alone. Hull strength obtained by bonding together overlapping planks does not increase linearly with the weight of the timber used. Or, put more simply, large clinker-built hulls are less strong than smaller ones. Large ships need more sail power to drive them. *Grâce Dieu* had at least two masts, an enormous main or 'great' mast and an aft, 'mesan or mizzen' mast. G.S. Laird Clowes, in *Sailing Ships* discusses the origin of the term 'mizzen' (or 'mizen'):

Unfortunately, however, contemporary pictures of two-masted vessels of the fifteenth century are extraordinarily scarce, and it is consequently very difficult to decide whether the term 'mesan' should be understood in the English sense of mizen, the after-mast, or the French sense of 'misaine', the foremast. The word is derived from the Arabic 'mizan', a balance or adjustment, and consequently applies equally well to the foresail, by means of which early Mediterranean craft were balanced on a wind, and to the small mizen sail which served to lighten the labours of the steersman.

Ships grew in size throughout the fifteenth century and more masts were added. Two exceptionally large English ships were the four-masted, clinker-built *Regent* (1,000 tons) and the *Sovereign* (800 tons). Built by Henry VII in the 1480s, they were among the first four-masted ships in Europe, the two mizzen masts being rigged with lateen sails. Both fore and main masts carried topsails, but these ships were still built carrack-fashion, with large forecastles carried over the bow of the ship. In peace time cannon were used by merchantmen to defend themselves against attacks by pirates and privateers. In the late 1400s English hulcs and carracks mounted their cannon in the aft and forward castles and fighting was largely by grappling and boarding.

17   Henry Grâce à Dieu, *carvel-built in 1514 with four masts, and topsails and topgallants. (National Maritime Museum, Greenwich)*

Since the hulls were mainly clinker-built, cannon ports cut through the outer shell would have caused a significant loss of strength. The *Regent* and *Sovereign* were both clinker built and had cannon mounted in the fore and aft castles but without gun ports. In contrast, Henry VIII's *Henry Grâce à Dieu*, carvel-built in 1514, had gun ports cut below the upper decks. A huge 1500-ton, four-masted, carrack-type ship with a four-decked forecastle and a three-decked aftercastle, 'Great Harry' never fired a gun in battle. *Henry Grâce à Dieu* had an extended rig with topsails and topgallants on the fore- and mainmasts, as well as topsails and topgallants on the two lateen-rigged mizzen masts.

Primary sources of the early three-masted ships are few: the usual town seals, contemporary artists' drawings and paintings and an interesting Hispano-Moresque bowl that is in the Victoria and Albert Museum, London. There is a beautiful picture of the bowl in David Divine's *The Opening of the World*, and it is described by A. McGowan in Vol. 3 of *The Ship*. Dated 1425, the bowl shows a three-masted ship complete with a furled square spritsail set below

A SPANISH-MOORISH BOWL SHOWING A THREE MASTED SHIP(1425)

18   *A three-masted ship, c1425, drawn from the bowl in David Divine's* The Opening of the World.

43

the bowsprit, one of the earliest illustrations of such a sail. The spritsail is similar to the small, square artemon sail used by Roman cargo ships to balance their steering oars (see p 17).

W.A.'s kraeck is acknowledged to be one of the best early examples of a three-masted ship, but it is by no means perfect. There are two square sails on the fore and main masts and a lateen-rigged mizzen, but a spritsail below the bowsprit is absent. The ship, which looked as if it was at anchor, shows two anchor cables, one of which is passing out through a

'hawse hole'. R. Morton Nance in his article *The Ship of the Renaissance* considers that hawse holes, which developed during the fourteenth century, probably originated from a groove cut in the planks on either side of the bow. The grooves located the lanyards that attached the 'mainstay' to the stem of the ship. The mainstay was a rope that went over the head of the mast and along with the shrouds and backstays held the mast in position. Stays are part of the 'standing rigging' of a ship. As the century progressed larger grooves were cut in the bow which

19   *A model based on a northern carrack, like W.A.'s, with tilt frames above the forecastle and aftercastle. (Science Museum, London)*

were big enough to take an anchor cable. Eventually there were only hawse holes ('hawse pipes' today) which allowed the anchor cables to pass in and out of the ship.

The model shown here of a 'W.A.-type' carrack has many shrouds to hold up the main mast, a few of which are led aft as backstays. Morton Nance suggested that W.A.'s carrack was of northern origin as the shrouds were tensioned by means of 'deadeyes'—circular, hardwood blocks with a groove cut around the edge to take the eye of the shroud. Deadeyes had three holes, and their resemblance to the eye sockets and nose of a skull gave them their macabre name. Lanyards attached two deadeyes together and tension was increased by shortening the distance between them.

On W.A.'s carrack, there are well-developed fore- and aftcastles, when compared to the simple, defensive structures seen on the early cogs (Fig. 8). R. Morton Nance describes hull evolution from 1400–1600 and considers that castles were developed from a tilt-frame that supported some form of protective netting (figure 2). The frame supports soon held a second castle, with its own tilt frame. Tilt frames are seen in the fore- and aftcastles in the model of a 'W.A. type' carrack, and also in Morton Nance's figures 3a and 3. His figures 4 to 7 show the development of these castles into the enormous poops and forecastles of the later carracks, before they were replaced by the lower fore- and aftcastles of the galleon (figures 8 to 10).

20 *Hull evolution 1400–1600 (1) carrack: 'castles' only. (2) carrack: 'somercastle' brought forward, tilt-frame aft. (2a) carrack: variant tilt-frame of lean-to form. (3) carrack: poop, raised on stanchions, with thwartships tilt-frame over it, forecastle tilt-frame. (3a) carrack: variant tilt-frame of longships form. (4) carrack: stage added to forecastle also, tilt-frame over it. (5) carrack: poop joined to hull, arched openings, guns on gunwhale. (6) carrack: forecastle consolidated, poop built raking, guns in round open ports. (7) carrack: two counters aft, heavy forecastle, boomkin beneath it, guns in rectangular ports with lids. (8) first galleon: low-down beak, reduced forecastle. (9) intermediate form between carrack and galleon: low-down forecastle. (10) later galleon: beakhead, reduced upperworks, stern gallery. (after Morton Nance, 1955)*

Carracks were skeleton-constructed, with flush laid planking. On the model of a W.A. type, in the Science Museum, London, there is a suggestion of a 'gallery', or walk-way, in the stern. The bowsprit carries a peculiar structure which might have acted as a sort of grappling hook for boarding another vessel or perhaps was used as a third anchor. The hull has vertical 'skids' which act as fenders and strengthen the inward turn, or 'tumble-home', of the hull, as well as longitudinally running planks, 'wales', that act as fore and aft strengtheners and follow the run of the stern in towards the rudder.

There are 'lifts' to support the yards on W.A.-type carracks, to which the three sails are furled and there are round 'fighting tops' on each of the three masts. In contrast to the cog, where the sails were 'hauled' (hoisted or pulled) up to the yards when sail area was reduced, carrack's yards were probably lowered to the deck and then the sail furled by lashing it to the yard. During lowering, 'clew lines' hauled up the lower corners of the square sails and 'martnets', attached above the bowlines on the side or 'leech' of the square sail, pulled up the slack in the middle 'belly' of the sail. (In the seventeenth century martnets were to be replaced by 'leechlines' and 'buntlines' which helped pull in the middle belly of the sail.)

On the model there are no extra sails above the three large sails. On the fore- and mainmasts the sails are square, while on the mizzen mast the sail is triangular. The main mast was set in the middle of the ship, from which hung the mainsail, the main power unit. The position of the forward and mizzen masts, at the stem and stern respectively, held balancing sails which helped the helmsman steer the ship. It is not known when or exactly how sail area from a W.A.-type carrack was increased by adding sails about the three basic sails. Possibly, as in Roman ships (p 17), a topsail on the mainmast was the first. In his article, *The Ship of the Renaissance*, Morton Nance also described the evolution of the sail plan from 1430–1600. He describes a square-rigged ship which has a small main topsail and two extra 'fill-in' sails, on either side, which ran along the main yard. These extra sails were attached to the main top (figure 2). An obvious development of this was to attach the triangular sails to the sides of the topsail and the clews of the topsail to the yard of the mainsail (figure 3). The other figures suggest the evolutions of the sail plan from carrack to galleon.

A mid to late fifteenth-century Portuguese carrack, or nau (nau, is Portuguese for large sailing ship), might be 80 ft long with the beam a third of that. The ship had heavy wales, for extra fore and aft strength and also perhaps to help reduce downwind rolling. The foremast and mainmast had large square mainsails or 'courses' and the mainmast was led

through all the decks, to rest on the 'keelson' of the ship. The foremost and mainmast might carry, about their courses, fore and main topsails which would give extra drive in light airs. There would be a spritsail below the bowsprit, and the mizzenmast was lateen-rigged. Sails were made of flax (linen), as was the rigging. On a nau of these dimensions, with all the sails set, some 4,000 square feet of sail area could be presented to the wind. According to V. Jones in *Sail the Indian Sea*, the naus, built by Dias for Vasco da Gama and his brother Paullo da Gama, the *Sao Gabriel* and *Sao Raphael*, were similarly rigged. They would have been crewed by c60 men.

Ballast was stones and gravel, shovelled into a single hold and would be added to as the stores were consumed. Steering was by means of a long tiller; the helmsman was under the poop deck and probably steered partly by instructions shouted down from the upper deck and partly by compass, since he was unable to see either the sails or the ship's head, important indicators if a sailing ship is to be steered well and safely. In bad weather deck openings in the nau could be partially closed off, and the hull made as watertight as possible, but there was always a danger of following seas entering the opening where the tiller entered the ship. At least three, usually six and sometimes as many as eleven, anchors were carried, each with iron shanks, wooden stocks and a ring for attaching the rope cable. Spare anchors would be carried in the forward compartment of the hold. All ships when completing a voyage would anchor, and anchoring was the last resort for a ship with blown-out sails, forced towards the coast in an onshore gale.

The ship's hold might have been divided into three compartments: the forward compartment for spare sails as well as the anchors; the midships, cable and water barrels; and the aft for gunpowder, iron and stone cannonballs. Anchors would be raised with a capstan, the men pushing the bars as they walked around to haul the rope anchor-cables aboard. The lower deck, which was above the hold, might be divided into three compartments, two of which contained the provisions.

The hull was coated with a mixture of fish-oil and tallow which helped, to some extent, to prevent the build-up of weed. The oustide seams—gaps between the hull planks—were caulked with 'oakum' (small teased bundles of hemp).

In fair weather, 'bonnets' were attached to the lower halves of the square sails and to further increase surface area in light airs a 'drabbler' could be lashed to the bonnet. In strong winds bonnets and drabblers would be detached and the yards lowered to the deck and sails furled by lashing them with short lengths of rope to the yards. In a good, following breeze naus would travel at around eight knots.

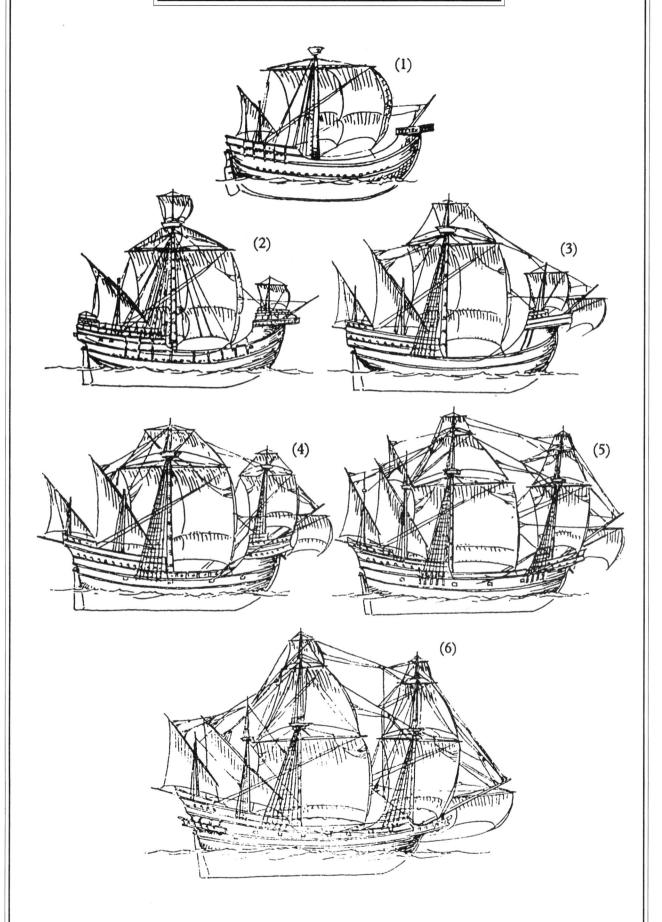

21 *Evolution of sail plan 1430–1600: (1) c1430; (2) c1450; (3) c1500; (4) c1530; (5) c1560; (6) c1600. (after Morton Nance, 1955)*

DESCRITTIONE DELLA GRAN CARACCA
Sopra la quale la facra Religione Cierosolimitana Venne a Malta.

22 *An engraving of a 16th-century, four-masted carrack by Van de Velde. It has two lateen-rigged mizzens, and topsails and topgallants on the foremast and mainmast. (Musée de la Marine, Paris)*

In 1499 da Gama brought his small fleet to Calicut in India, to open up one of the most important ocean trading routes to the East. Soon, enormous carracks would be sailing the ocean routes. A Portuguese carrack might be as large as 2000 tons and could carry hundreds of tons of cinnamon, cochineal, cloves, peppers, porcelain, and silk back to Lisbon.

Such a carrack would be some 160 ft long, 100 ft on the keel, with a 47 ft beam and a 31 ft draught. These voyages from Portugal down through the South Atlantic and across the Indian Ocean were as dangerous as they were long. From 1499–1612, some 800 Portuguese vessels left Lisbon; nearly a 100 of these were never to be heard of again.

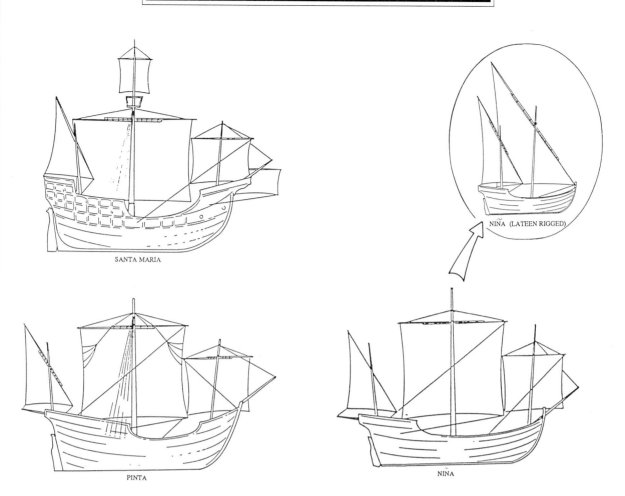

SANTA MARIA

NIÑA (LATEEN RIGGED)

PINTA

NIÑA

23 *Columbus' ships: the Rig. (after Martinez-Hildago, 1966)*

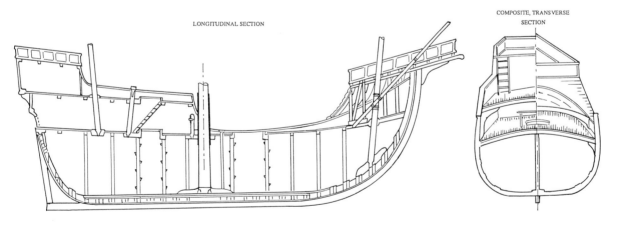

LONGITUDINAL SECTION

COMPOSITE, TRANSVERSE SECTION

24 *The Hull of the Santa Maria. (after Martinez-Hildago, 1966)*

25 *Spanish* carracks and galleons. *An engraving by Cornelius Van Yk in 1697. The forecastles show inboard-facing cannon and there are three- and four-masted ships. (Musée de la Marine, Paris)*

SPAANSSE CAR

EN OF GALIOENEN.

Some seven years prior to Da Gama's epic voyage to India, Columbus had chosen a Spanish *nao* and two caravels to make his famous westward crossing of the Atlantic and open up another important ocean trading route. One of his ships, the *Pinta*, had been converted from a lateen-rigged caravel to a typical carrack-style rig before the start of the voyage. *Niña*, another caravel, set out with main and mizzen masts lateen-rigged, but in the Canaries, and before crossing the Atlantic, Columbus also re-rigged *Niña* with square sails. *Santa Maria*, his third ship, was a classic example of the new three-masted ships. Its rig was described by Columbus in his log on 24 October 1492:

Then came a very good breeze and I set all the sails of the ship, one main course with two bonnets, the fore course, spritsail, mizzen and topsail.
(Hakluyt Society)

Throughout the sixteenth century, ships became long and thinner. Around 1450 the keel length to beam ratio was c2:1, but this had increased to c3:1 by c1600. From c1525 nearly all European ocean-going hulls were carvel-built (see p 40 ff). Galleons were carvel-built.

The galleon became the supreme sixteenth-century ocean trader and, by 1600, France, England, Holland and Portugal all had them. Well-armed galleons of rival nations clashed as the maritime nations continued their expansionist policies and fought and competed for control of the ocean trading routes. The English developed a galleon that was to play an important part in the failure of the 1588 Spanish Armada.

The galleon's origins remain obscure. Some authorities argue that it was developed by the Italians, other by the Spanish. Their windward sailing ability would have been much improved by bringing the large, overhanging forecastles, typical features of the carracks, back into the ship and even away from the bow. This reduced both weight and windage forward.

Platforms were built in the bows to help work the spritsails that were set from the bowsprit. The whole forward arrangement resembled the ramming beak of an oar-propelled galley (the Mediterranean warship for thousands of years), and no doubt due to this resemblance the platform was later termed the 'beak-head'. The beak led up from the bow and helped to create a more weatherly ship (meaning it went to windward more easily) by streamlining the stem and improving the bow's ability to cut through the sea. Galleons sometimes had four masts: two square-rigged fore- and mainmasts and two lateen-rigged mizzens, the second—smaller—mizzen mast being known as the 'bonaventure' mizzen. (Splitting down a rig by using more masts results in smaller sails which are easier to handle.) Extra square sails—topsails—were carried on both the fore- and mainmasts, above the large, square foresail and mainsail (or fore and main courses). A spritsail was set under the bowsprit and the largest galleons carried a topgallant, above the topsails on both the fore and mainmasts. Galleons would carry at least one row of cannon on each side and were longer and slimmer vessels, when compared with the carracks, which further made for improve seaworthiness and better sailing ability. (See Morton Nance's figures 5 and 6; 8 to 10).

Treasure galleons, with faster and less fuller-bodied hulls, were used by Spain to carry bullion back from its Middle and South American mines. They were continually harassed by French corsairs and later English and Dutch privateers. For protection, Spanish ocean traders sailed in convoys, or *flotas*, to the West Indies. There were two annual sailings, one in April, which sailed from Seville to the West Indies and New Spain and one in the late summer, which travelled to Panama where it loaded Peruvian silver. Both flotas would winter in the Americas before sailing back to Europe, and there might be as many as 40 or 50 ships in a flota. At first they sailed unescorted across the Atlantic, rendezvous off the Azores, and from there be escorted by well-armed galleons of the 'Indian Command' back to Spain. As hostilities increased, these galleons would escort the freighters from Spain to the West Indies and back. Often the flotas were made up of cargo ships that were not well suited for fast transatlantic voyaging: German and Flemish hulcs and carracks were often used instead of galleons.

The Portuguese, like the Spanish, used galleons for both traders and warships, but for their voluminous Eastern cargoes they used their enormous carracks.

Over 20 years of English piracy, privateering and exploring built up a considerable knowledge of what was required for a safe, strong, ocean-going ship. Invaluable knowledge that was used to some effect when the Elizabethan seamen fought the galleons of the Spanish Armada. Between 1562 and 1569 John Hawkins carried out three slave-trading voyages to Africa and the West Indies. He fought the Spanish at San Juan de Ulua in New Spain and the lessons he learned much have been invaluable when he became Treasurer to the Crown's navy in 1573 and helped develop a type of galleon instrumental in defeating the Spanish Armada in 1588.

In 1586 Matthew Baker (1530–1613), who worked closely with John Hawkins, produced an outstanding treatise on naval architecture. It was classified by Samuel Pepys (1633–1703), a naval administrator, as *Fragments of Ancient English Shipwrightry*, and today can be found at the Pepysian Library, Magdalene College, Cambridge. Matthew Baker

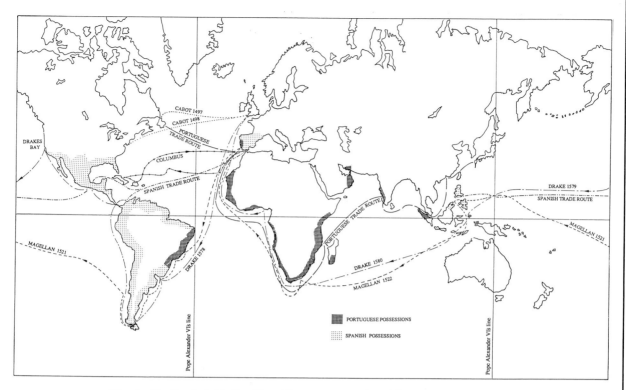

Map 5 *The Pope's divide: Spanish and Portuguese possessions. (after Moyse–Bartlett, 1937)*

(1530–1613) was the son of the shipwright, James Baker, who was partly responsible for the structural designs required for the heavy cannon carried on ships in Henry VIII's time. According to John Davis (c1550–1605), the Elizabethan Navigator, Matthew Baker's 'skill and surpassing grounded knowledge for the building of Ships advantageable to all purpose, hath not in any nation his equall.'

It is probable that between 1578 and 1588, Baker was responsible for building Elizabeth I's warships. In that decade some ten ships over 100 tons were built, the largest was the 800 ton *Ark Royal*. In his book, Baker described the underwater shape of an English galleon as best likened to a fish, even drawing a fish inside a hull to illustrate the point. Westcott Abell in *The Shipwright's Trade* states that in Baker's drawings of 1586 'there was broadly enough detail given to enable a ship to be built' and that Baker 'was the first of the English shipwrights to set down on paper the "lines" of a vessel'.

26 *A three-masted English* galleon, *c1586: 60 ft on the keel, 24 ft beam, depth of hold 12 ft—200 tons and 19 cannon. (from* Fragments of Ancient English Shipwrightry, *Pepysian Library, Magdalene College, Cambridge)*

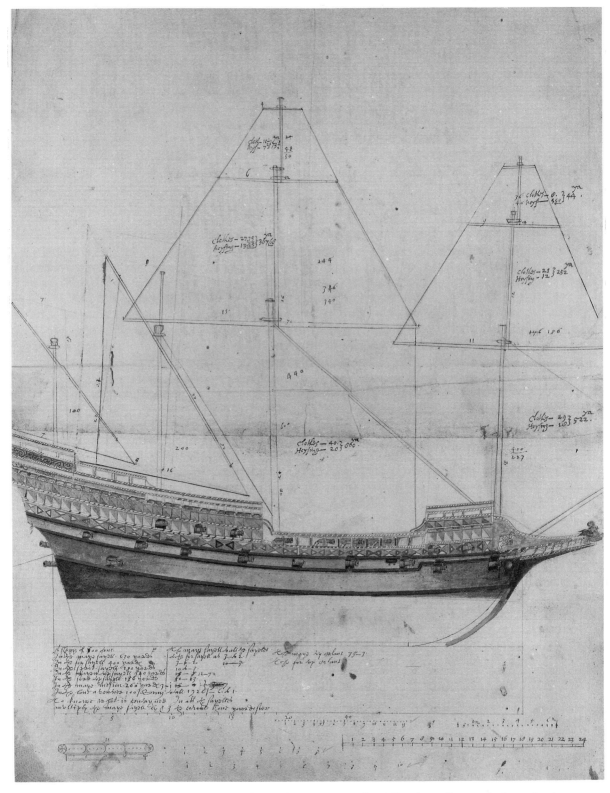

27 *Sail plan of a four-masted English galleon, c1586, showing lateen mizzens, and topsails and topgallants on the fore and main masts. 300 tons and 30–32 cannon. (from* Fragments of Ancient English Shipwrightry. *Pepysian Library, Magdalene College, Cambridge)*

English galleons, like the Spanish, had their forecastles built back from the bow, and their bows ended in beak projections. Sterns were 'square-tucked' (cut square across, that is 'square or transom-sterned') and hulls had a marked sheer, although the sheer was not nearly as marked as the 'banana-like' ships drawn by many contemporary artists.

Most English galleons at the time of the Armada were three-masted. Fighting at sea had changed: instead of grappling your opponent and then fighting a bloody hand-to-hand engagement, ships stood off and bombarded each other with cannon (see p 42 ff). The English were wary of being boarded by the heavily manned Spanish galleons. At the time of Spanish Armada, English galleons' main armaments were culverins, a gun that fired a smaller ball than the Spanish demi-cannon (17 versus 32 pounds) but twice the distance. English tactics were to fire from a distance at the Spanish ships, whose cannon, mounted on long, two-wheeled carriages, were difficult to manoeuvre and had a low firing rate. English galleons were less top-heavy, with lower forecastle and aftercastle, than the Spanish ships: their underwater hull shapes were more streamlined and they had flatter sails. Thus they could sail more easily to windward and fire at the exposed bottom planks as the Spanish ship was heeled by the wind.

By 1588 English galleons had the ability to 'strike their topmasts', that is lower their topmasts to the deck. In bad weather this decreased windage aloft and made a safer, more stable, ship. (It is unclear whether Hawkins or the Dutch were the first to introduce removeable topmasts.) Most of the ships in the English fleet that beat the Spanish Armada were armed, ocean-going traders—'defensible merchantmen'. Of the 180 or so ships that fought the Spanish, only 30 belonged to the English crown—although these were the ships that did the maximum damage to the Armada. Drake, Hawkins and many other Elizabethan seamen started their sea-going careers in merchant ships. In fact there was no true distinction at this time between royal and merchant seamen. As Laird Clowes wrote:

... Henry III (1207–1272) had hired out royal ships for merchant voyages, and within the limits this interchangeability of the role of merchantmen and man-of-war, as need arose, continued right up to the death of Queen Elizabeth.

During sixteenth century a gun deck, below the 'upper' or top deck, was often fitted to galleons. The deck ran from the bow and often dipped down in the stern to give head room for the cabins in the aftercastle. Similarly, the after end of the upper deck would rise at the aftercastle to form the castles' forward-looking face. Deck beams were supported by pillars stepped over the keel, one below each other.

Not all trade was carried by carracks and galleons. Smaller ocean traders, of around 200 tons, usually carried culverins and were three-masted. The sail plan was the usual six sails: spritsail under the bowsprit, a fore course and fore topsail on the foremast, main course and main topsail on the mainmast, and a lateen sail on the mizzenmast.

Elizabeth took an active part in developing and building the English galleon that helped bring about the failure of the Spanish Armada in 1588. Spain was seen to be vulnerable, and Spanish morale was damaged. The sixteenth century was to be followed by over 200 years of continued hostilities as Spain's maritime supremecy was challenged and nations continued the struggle to gain control of the sea. There was still a lot of wealth in colonies and ocean trade.

CHAPTER THREE

To Build, to Crew, to Navigate

Basic building methods, crew conditions and navigation techniques remained remarkably static from the Age of Discovery until the middle to late nineteenth century.

The disease, hunger and hardships experienced by the over-crowded crews in the early ocean traders of all nations changed little until the end of the nineteenth century. There was gradually less over-crowding, as rig technology progressed and shipowners realized it was more profitable to operate ships with smaller crews. Also, as trading companies sending ships to the Orient became wealthier, conditions aboard East Indiamen were generally better than those for seamen on most other merchantmen.

Many of the navigation techniques developed during the Age of Discovery are still taught today because modern sophisticated beacon and satellite navigation systems may sometimes fail. 'Latitude sailing', developed by the Portuguese in the early fifteenth century, was widely used by ocean trader captains until the 1840s.

Constructing an early trader

In 1711 one of the first books on wooden shipbuilding was published: *The Shipbuilders Assistant* by William Sutherland. (The book is summarised by Westcott Abell in *Shipwright's Trade*). In *Lords of the East*, Jean Sutton describes in some detail the building, in 1747, of a 620-ton Indiaman, 105 ft long and 33 ft 4 in. beam. It is remarkable how both methods are similar in principle and technique to those employed by a modern Devonshire yard that today builds some of the largest wooden boats in Britain.

From its peak around the middle of the nineteenth century, the number of shipyards building in wood rapidly declined, as iron, then steel became the

preferred shipbuilding material. Nevertheless ships are still built in wood throughout the world, and fishing craft are some of the biggest merchant ships built in Britain in wood. Many North Sea fishermen prefer wooden-hulled trawlers, since they believe that these hulls 'grip the water better than a steel-hulled one'.

Henry Hinks, the great grandfather of today's owner, Alan Hinks, opened a shipbuilding yard in Appledore, Devon, in 1844. Henry Hinks' methods were not greatly different from those used to build the 1747 Indiaman, nor did they differ much from those used by Alan Hinks when, in the 1980s, he built a 72 ft trawler for a Scottish fisherman, or when he built the *Nonsuch*.

Alan Hinks was chosen to build a replica of a seventeenth century ocean trader, the *Nonsuch*. (He has built other replicas, notably a Viking longship and Drake's *Golden Hind*, but not the one that sank in 1987!) To build *Nonsuch*, he was instructed to follow seventeenth-century methods as closely as possible. Thus in *Nonsuch* he used treenails (pronounced *trenels*), long cylinders of oak up to 1 in. in diameter and a foot long, to fasten the hull planks to the frames. They were made at the yard with a trenel mate (like a round spokeshave) and driven home with a special hammer, a 'pane maul'. *Nonsuch* was launched in 1968; Adrian Small was the captain.

Three hundred years previously on 3 June 1668, the original *Nonsuch* had set sail from London to her destination: Hudson Bay, Canada. The aim of the ocean voyage was to assess the possibility of shipping furs directly from the shores of Hudson Bay to Europe. This was a very lucrative trade, as furs were in constant demand, but much of the fur was going to Europe by a tortuous route along the St. Lawrence seaway. Aboard the *Nonsuch* as she left London was the captain, Zachariah Gillam, and a French trader, who had proposed the new trading scheme to

A SECTION and PLAN of the FALMOUTH Built at BLACKWALL Anno 1752

28 *Longitudinal section of the* Falmouth, *similar to the East Indiamen whose building was described by J. Sutton in* Lords of the East. *(National Maritime Museum, Greenwich)*

29 *Alan Hinks (right), builder of* Nonsuch, *and J. Heard, Shipwright. (M.W. Marshall)*

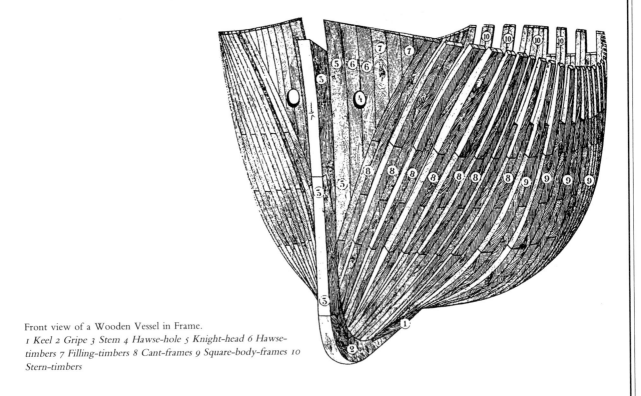

Front view of a Wooden Vessel in Frame.
1 Keel 2 Gripe 3 Stem 4 Hawse-hole 5 Knight-head 6 Hawse-timbers 7 Filling-timbers 8 Cant-frames 9 Square-body-frames 10 Stern-timbers

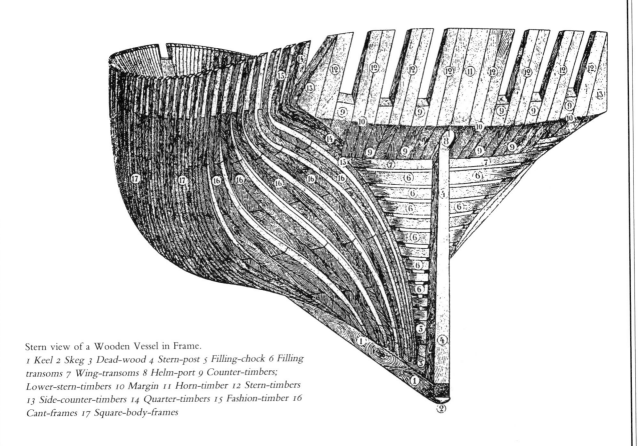

Stern view of a Wooden Vessel in Frame.
1 Keel 2 Skeg 3 Dead-wood 4 Stern-post 5 Filling-chock 6 Filling transoms 7 Wing-transoms 8 Helm-port 9 Counter-timbers; Lower-stern-timbers 10 Margin 11 Horn-timber 12 Stern-timbers 13 Side-counter-timbers 14 Quarter-timbers 15 Fashion-timber 16 Cant-frames 17 Square-body-frames

30 *A Vessel in Frame. (from Paasch, 1890)*

31 *The new* Nonsuch *running before a gale of wind under bare poles. (Devon Life)*

32 *Framing in a 17th-century ocean-going vessel. (Musée de la Marine, Paris)*

English merchants and speculators. Sailing around the top of England, the ship crossed the north Atlantic to arrive on 26 September 1668 in James Bay off Hudson Bay. The following year, loaded with beaver fur, *Nonsuch* made the return trip to London in October. Though the voyage was a commerical failure, a new ocean trading route was established and the investors approached King Charles II for a charter to set up the Hudson Bay Company.

The original *Nonsuch*, probably carvel-built, was likely to have been a two-masted, ocean-going cargo ship, a *ketch*–perhaps around 37 ft on the keel, 50 ft overall, some 15 ft in the beam and 45 tons displacement. *Nonsuch* would not have been much larger than a modern wooden yacht.

From scale drawings of such a ship, Hinks' yard drew full-scale 'formers' or 'moulds' to make the frames of the new *Nonsuch*. The frames, once set up, decide the final hull shape and sheer. The keel was laid first, a single piece of elm, and later, an elm 'false keel' was added to protect it. Elm was traditionally used as it lasted well under water and could replace oak, always in short supply. The rest of *Nonsuch*'s hull was built of oak, either seasoned, kiln-dried or air-dried. To the keel the stem and stern posts were added. The stem post was made up of two 'compass timbers'—the 'apron' and 'stemson'—while the stern post was a solid length of timber which ran up to the deck from the keel. The aft assembly, comprising of

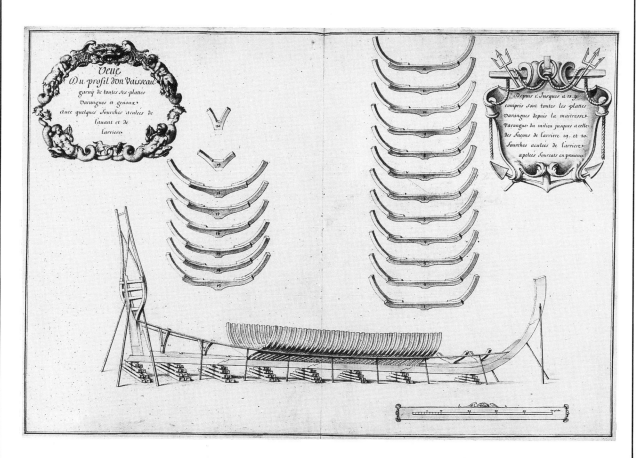

CHANTIER DE CONSTRUCTION DE VAISSEAUX

MARINES ET SVITE DES GALERES OV SONT REPRESENTEZ SAMBLABLES SVJETS DE VAISSEAUX
Presenté a Monseigneur de PHELYPEAUX chevalier Comte de Maurepas, Conseiller
du Roy, en tous ces Conseils Secretaire d'Etat et des Commandements de Sa Majesté
ayant le departement de la Marine et Commandeur de ses Ordres.

a Paris chez le Sr du Change Graveur du Roy.
Rüe St Jacques, et chez l'Auteur vis a vis dans la même Rüe

Avec Privilege du Roy.

Par Son tres humble et tres Obeissant
Serviteur. J. Rigaud.

33 *17th-century shipyard scenes. (Bibliothèque Nationale, Paris)*

stern post, horn timber and fashion pieces were all completed before framing started (for nomenclature see the drawing, 'A Vessel in Frame' in Paasch's *Illustrated Marine Encyclopedia*, 1890). The frames were bolted to the keel through their lowest sections or 'floor pieces'.

At first, in wooden shipbuilding, frames were made from naturally curved timbers, scarf-joined, and cut to shape using an adze. At a later date frame strength was improved by replacing the scarfed joints by overlapping the sides of the timbers over a number of feet, and then through-bolting the timbers together. The frames on Hinks' *Nonsuch* were about 6 in. thick, with 18 in. centres, and made up of five pieces: all were finally shaped using an adze. Each 'compound frame' was made up of a floor piece, which was end-butted against the next section, the 'foot-hook' (now 'futtock'), which in turn was end-butted against the 'top pieces'. The two timbers that overlapped the end-butts, and held the frame together, were known as 'butt straps'. The floor pieces were laid and bolted at right angles to the keel. A 'keelson', the same length as the keel, was put down on top of the floor pieces to help lock the frames into position. 'Deadwoods' were fitted at either end of the keel to allow for the 'rise' of the bow and stern.

Transverse deck beams connected the hull frames, supported the deck, and generally tied the two sides of the hull together. Square pillars, 6 in. by 6 in.,

supported the beams and angled 'knees' tied the beams to the vertical frames. Knees were fitted as one piece, and Alan Hinks searched all the local timber mills to obtain right-angled timber, or 'grown knees'. Massive strengthening, V-shaped pieces of timber, known as 'breasthooks' in the bow and 'crutches' in the stern, were fitted to run parallel with the keel. Frames and beams were joined by through-bolting with iron bolts or by the oak trenels, which were split at one end and wedged to create a tight fit.

Especially 'thick' hull planks (3 to 4 in.) were fitted first at the bilge, then at the 'sheer strake' and finally the 'garboard strake' (a run of planks nearest the keel), which was set into the side of the keel. (A strake is a complete longitudinal run of planks from stem to stern. 'Extra thick' hull planks or 'wales' (6 to 9 in. thick) were also used in the hull, the 'channel' wales were especially important as they carried the 'preventer' stays or 'chain plates' from the channel which carried the 'deadeyes'. The ordinary hull planks, 2 in. thick, were narrowed at the bow and stern and steamed into place, having been made pliable by sitting them in a 'steam box': two hours per inch thickness for oak. The planking was fastened to the frames and the gaps that were left between the planks caulked with spun hemp or 'oakum'. The last plank fitted was known as the 'shooter' and was a tight, wedge-shaped fit, having to be hammered into place. The inner hull planking, which contributed much to strength and known as the 'ceiling', was put on at the same time as the outer hull.

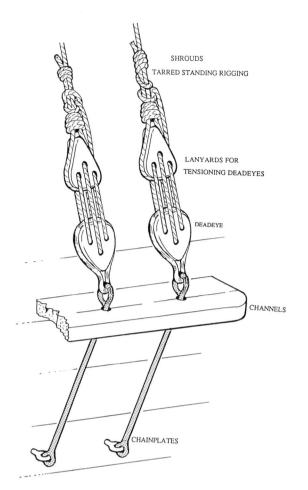

SHROUDS
TARRED STANDING RIGGING

LANYARDS FOR
TENSIONING DEADEYES

DEADEYE

CHANNELS

CHAINPLATES

The *Nonsuch* replica had Scotch pine deck planking, and all hull seams were 'stopped' after they had been caulked with a mixture of putty and white lead. Any hole created in the hull planking by a fastening was plugged with a 'round' of wood, a technique known as 'dowelling'.

Joe and Oswald Bennet, who had served their time rigging sailing ships, set up all the deadeyes and running and standing rigging. *Nonsuch* was rigged with a jib and staysail, as well as spritsail. On the first mast there was a course, topsail and topgallant, and on the second or mizzen mast there was a lateen mizzen and a square mizzen topsail (see p 99 ff for the development of this type of rig).

34 *15th-century dead-eyes and channels. (after Martinez-Hildago, 1966)*

35 *19th-century dead-eyes and channels on the* Joseph Conrad. *Launched in 1882, the* Joseph Conrad *is the iron-hulled, wooden-sparred, 400 Dead Weight tons, full-rigged ship that Alan Villiers sailed round the world in 1934. (M. Marshall)*

Life aboard

Life for ordinary merchant seamen in the Age of Discovery was usually brutish, violent and short. On a voyage of discovery there was something like a one in five chance of returning to port. These early ocean voyages often had a strong international flavour, as crowns of Europe hired foreigners to lead and crew their expeditions. For example, the Genoese Cabots were sponsored by England's Henry VII; Columbus was an Italian, Magellan a Portuguese, and both sailed under the Spanish flag. Even Portugal's Prince Henry the Navigator employed a Scandinavian to lead a voyage to Guinea.

In his article, *Vanguard of Empire*, Roger Smith described the three categories of the 'mariners of discovery'. In, for example, a Spanish ship there would be the captain and officers, the petty officers and the crew, a strict three-fold hierarchy that exists in today's merchant navy. Thus, in 1492 Columbus was the commander-in-chief of the expedition, since it was he who had raised money and lobbied the crown. Below him were the captains, or the commanding officers, each of whom was responsible for his own ship and crew. Often the captain would be a close friend or relation of the captain-general. Next was the skipper or master, often the owner of the vessels, who was in charge of the everyday sailing of the ship and was usually a good seaman. An important senior officer was the pilot, who was often employed by the crown, and who was responsible for navigation throughout the voyage. Next were the petty officers, of which the quartermaster, or boatswain, would be the head. An official crown voyage would have a paymaster and scribe. Other petty officers were the barber-cum-doctor; the steward, who had the key and controlled the storerooms; a carpenter; a caulker; and a cooper. Amongst the seamen were the experienced sailors, apprentices and ship boys. Artillery men, often mercenaries, would be carried to operate the cannon, and on some voyages there were priests and goldsmiths or silversmiths.

At the outset of an early ocean-trading voyage, ships were usually overcrowded because large crews were taken aboard in anticipation of losses; on the return voyage, sometimes there were insufficient men to work the ship into port. Cholera and typhoid would ravage a crowded ship or quickly kill men once ashore weakened by months at sea. Hygiene was almost non-existent. Toilet arrangements were extremely primitive; men would just grab hold of the rigging and relieve themselves over the side. In heavy weather, bilges quickly became foul with vomit, urine and stagnant seawater. Only later were rows of seats fitted into the bows of large ocean traders—they became known as 'the heads' by British

sailors and nicknamed 'el jardin' by the Spanish. Voyaging ships often had to be beached and cleaned out, as the stench became unbearable, and disease-carrying rats and lice made life intolerable. In wet weather or in a storm the men wore their everyday clothes; on English ships a brightly coloured hood, serge jerkin, loose fitting trousers and long woolen stockings. Seamen usually went bare-foot to grip the deck better: protective boots and clothing had yet to be invented. Officers might wear stockings and shoes. (see S.E. Morison's *European Discovery of America*)

Cooking was carried out in a large metal pot, situated on deck in a fire-box or in the hold on the rock or sand ballast. Smoke from the wood fire would escape up through open hatches or through a specially designed chimney. In the ashes of the fire-box unleavened bread was made from salted flour. Only the captain, master or pilot was housed in a narrow cabin. Other officers slept in the after castle on mats which they were buried in if they died at sea, while some officers slept on the quarterdeck near the tiller. Petty officers might sleep in the hold, but the ordinary seamen were often forced to sleep on deck, out in the open so as to be ready for emergencies.

Columbus wrote in his log on 17 October 1492, that he had seen hammocks in use by the San Salvador Indians, but they were not introduced into English ships until over 100 years later. Seamen's possessions were stored in sea chests: the higher the rank, the larger the sea chest. A captain would have his own chest, while ordinary seamen might have to share one between two and ships' boys one between four. Men died of disease, warfare and wounds and, above all, scurvy: the value of citrus fruits was not realised until much later. In the fifteenth and sixteenth centuries the basic shipboard food was heavily salted meat and fish, biscuits, cheese, chickpeas, wine and beer. A mid-sixteenth-century Iberian merchant seaman's basic daily fare might be: bread ($1\frac{1}{2}$ lbs), wine (2 pints), drinking water (2 pints) and washing water (1 pint). He was given salt pork, or fish, or beans or chick peas and occasionally cheese or salt beef. Olive oil was used for cooking. The officers might fare better with honey, rice, almonds and raisins, while freshly caught fish often supplemented the diet of both officers and crew. The officers ate at a table, looked after by a ship's boy and steward; the crew would eat where they could. The meat was tough, old and heavily salted, and ships' victuallers often supplied sub-standard produce in order to improve profit margins. Biscuits and meat became wormy, drinking water infected, the wine vinegary and beer sour.

Condemned criminals were carried for especially dangerous missions and shipboard mutinies were common. To maintain discipline captains hanged men from the yards; public floggings, chaining men to eye-bolts below deck and hanging them by their arms from the rigging were other means of maintaining order. Privateers, pirates and hostile natives were fought off. Cannons became increasingly powerful, and terrible wounds were inflicted by flying wood splinters as heavier cannon balls were developed to punch their way through the ship's planking. After a sea battle, with boarding and hand-to-hand fighting, the scuppers would literally run with blood. The men were jingoistic, violent and cruel—a reflection of the times. But chivalry existed: for example Drake treated his prisoners well, and once a ship had 'struck her colours' engagements were quickly terminated.

To understand the attitudes of the merchant seamen-adventurers it is revealing to read contemporary accounts of clashes between ships. This might be between armed merchantmen, privateer and ocean trader or crown warships, since until c1650 there was little distinction between privateer, well-armed ocean trader and crown warship, and all would be keen to take a prize. The 'Directions for Taking a Prize' was published in the *Seamen's Grammar* by Captain John Smith and is, in part, reproduced here:

'A sail!' 'How bears she (or stands she)? To wind-ward or lee-ward? Set him by the compass!' 'He stands right a-head (or on the weather-bow, or lee-bow).' 'Let fly your colours (if you have a consort, else not)! Out with all your sails! A steady man to the helm—sit close to keep her steady! Give him chase (or fetch him up!)—'He holds his own!' 'No—we gather on him, Captain!' Out goes his flag and pendants, also his waist-cloths and top-armings, which is a long red cloth about three-quarters of a yard broad, edged on each side with calico or white linen cloth, that goeth round about the ship on the outsides of all her upper works, fore and aft, and before the cubbridge-heads, also about the fore- and main-tops, as well for the countenance and grace of the ship, as to cover the men from being seen. He furls and slings his main-yard; in goes his sprit-sail. Thus they use to strip themselves into their 'short sails', or 'fighting sails', which is, only the foresail, the main and fore top-sails, because the rest should not be fired nor spoiled; besides, they would be troublesome to handle, hinder our sights and using of arms. He makes ready his close fights, fore and aft.

'Master, how stands the chase?' 'Right on head, I say.' 'Well: we shall reach him bye and bye. What! is all ready?' 'Yea, yea.' 'Every man to his charge! Dowse your top-sail to salute him for the sea: hail him with a noise of trumpets. Whence is your ship?' 'Of Spain: whence is yours?' 'Of England.' 'Are you a merchant, or a man-of-war?' 'We are of the Sea!' He waves us to leeward with his drawn sword, calls amain for the king of Spain, and springs his luff. 'Give him a chase-piece with your broadside, and run a good berth a-head of him!' 'Done, done.' 'We have the wind of him, and he tacks about.' 'Tack you about also, and keep your luff! Be yare at the helm! Edge in with him! Give

him a volley of small shot, also your prow and broad-side as before, and keep your luff.' 'He pays us shot for shot!' 'Well: we shall requite him!'

There is little mention of the carnage caused by the cannonballs in this romantic, but stirring, account of a seventeenth-century sea-fight.

Position finding at sea

To cross an ocean along a downwind sailing route is a beautiful, but often frightening experience. Even in the twentieth century the feeling of isolation is extreme: the boat appears minute in a sea that seems to go on forever. A hull, 36 ft long and weighing 10 tons, is lifted effortlessly by a unceasing Atlantic swell, which with the apparent gentlest of flicks, can send it flying down the face of a wave, spray shooting high and away from either side of the bow. Sounds, sights and sensations are different from those ashore: spray-rainbows at the bows, relentless creaks and moans as the wind drives its way through the rigging, the ominous hiss of the breaking top of a larger than normal wave as it approaches from behind. The louder than normal thump, as the big waves hits the stern, to fill the cockpit and swing the boat violently off-course. And always the rolling: minute by minute, hour by hour. Often the mast travels through 60 degrees of arc in less than 60 seconds: first, a lurch to port, a swing back to pause for a brief moment, vertical, and then over to starboard. The horizon is never still. At night the mast gyrates crazily around the fixed stars; by day the sun's steady east—west passage across the sky contrasts markedly with the plunging, rolling, forward motion of the boat.

My sail-boat, on its first transatlantic voyage, had the hindsight of nearly 600 years of ocean voyaging behind it: sextants, chronometers accurate to within seconds a year, electronic log, Admiralty charts and pilot books. The hurricane seasons were known, the sea currents understood and the path of the trade winds well-mapped. By comparison, the early ocean navigators had almost nothing. Their merchant ships were heavy, almost impossible to steer against the trade winds, over-crowded, difficult to handle and relied solely on wind power. Compasses and charts were primitive or non-existent, and almost nothing was known of the wind, weather or the sea. But it was these early merchantmen who opened up the trading routes on all the oceans and it was navigation that was the key.

In 1594 John Davis, the veteran English explorer of the North-West passage to the Indies and an exceptional Elizabethan navigator, wrote *Seamans Secrets*. The book ran to eight editions, the last being in 1657. In it, he argued:

For what hath made the Spaniard to be so great a Monarch, the Commander of both Indias, to abound in wealth and all natures benefites, but only the painefull industrie of his Subiects by Nauigation. Their former trade was only figs, orenges, and oyle, but now through Nauigation is brought to be golde, siluer, pearles, silkes, and spice, by long and painefull trade recouered.

(*Seaman's Secrets*, courtesy of the Hakluyt Society)

The early Portuguese and Spanish discoverers voyaged across oceans despite having only primitive means of finding their position at sea. They were unable to find longitude, and latitude was only obtained to within about a degree (60 nautical miles) with their primitive nautical instruments. Their compasses were crude, they had no idea how far they had travelled and the oceans and new lands were all uncharted. In 1545 the Spaniard, Pedro de Medina, published one of the finest treatises on navigation, *Arte de Navegar*, and its contents give a useful summary of the techniques then available: the use of the charts and compass, the Ptolemaic concept of the earth as the centre of the universe; time and tides in relation to the phases of the moon; latitude at sea from celestial navigation, which included tables of the sun's declination and the use of the astrolabe, quadrant and cross-staff for measuring altitude. These were the tools of the navigator's trade and they were always used in conjunction with the technique of 'dead reckoning'.

The art of dead reckoning

Dead reckoning is the most basic form of navigation—when navigators estimate their position at sea because they are unable to obtain a 'fix' by any other means, and involves estimating the course and distance run by the ship during a known period of time. Time was measured using sand-glasses (or sea clocks) which were turned every half-hour (or other interval) by the ships' boys. Later, it became possible to measure time at night by observing the relative positions of the pole star to the Guards of the Little Bear or Little Dipper. From time and the ship's speed, the distance travelled over the seabed was calculated, after making appropriate allowances for ocean currents and leeway. In Medina's book there was no mention of the use of a ship's 'log' for estimating speed and neither Columbus nor Vasco da Gama mention the use of it during their pioneering ocean voyages. Nor is the log mentioned in 1551 in one of the important books on navigation, *Breve Compendio de la sphera y de la Arte de Navegar com neuvos Instrumentos y Reglas*, written by another Spaniard, Martín Cortes, and later translated into English. But in 1574 the Englishman William Bourne's *Regiment of the Sea* was one of the first to discuss the use of a ship's log, variants of which were to be used from then up to the present day to measure speed through the water, or 'shippes way'.

Bourne wrote:

And to knowe the shippes way some doo use this which (as I take) is very good: they have a pece of wood, and a line to vere out over borde, with a final line of a great lengthe, which they make fast at one ende, and at the other ende, and middle they have a peece of a lyne, which they make fast with a small thred to stande lyke unto a crowfoote: for this purpose that it should drive asterne as fast as the shippe doth go away from it, always having the line so ready that it goeth out as fast as the shippe goeth. In like manner they have either a minute or an houre glasse, or else a knowne parte of an houre, by some number of wordes, or such other lyke, so that the line being vered out and stopt juste with that tyme that the glasse is out or the number of wordes spoken, which done, they hale in the logge or peece of wood again, and looke howe many fadome the shippe hath gone in that time: that being knowne, what parte of a league soever it be, they multiplie the number of fadome the shippe hath gone in that time: that being knowne, what parte of a league soever it be, they multiplie the number of fadomes by the portion of time or parte of an houre. Whereby you maye knowe justly howe many leagues and parts of a league the ship goeth in an houre, i.e., for an Englishe league doth containe 2500 fadome. And a Spanish or Portugale league dothe contayne 2857 fadome,

(Hakluyt Society)

The 'number of wordes spoken' means that by continuously repeating a word it is possible to estimate time (Mississippi is now often used by seamen to count seconds: one Mississippi, two Mississippi, ... During the Age of Discovery measurement of distance travelled was further complicated by the lack of universal standards of measurement. Bourne measured distance in leagues and fadomes (fathoms; 1 fathom today is 6 ft = 1.83 m).

In 1594 John Davis makes no mention of a ship's log, although he insists that the distance travelled should be carefully noted: 'a careful consideration of the number of leagues that a ship sayleth in every hour or watch, to the neerest estimation that possibly he can give'. He states that 20 leagues equals one degree of latitude which equals 60 nautical miles. He believed that for navigation a mile of 5000 ft. ought to be used. An English mile then equalled 1000 paces, and one pace was five feet, thus one land and sea mile equalled 5000 ft. (Nowadays, the standard nautical mile is taken as the average of one minute of latitude measured at the equator and one minute of latitude at the poles, which gives an average length of 6080 ft, because the distances of minutes of latitude are not equal as the earth is not a true sphere, but flattened at the poles.)

Dead reckoning, even with the crude instruments available to navigators in the fifteenth and sixteenth centuries, was reasonably effective; together with estimates of latitude from the sun and Pole Star navigators regularly crossed oceans to arrive at their destinations. They sometimes made mistakes: Columbus was at least 600 miles out on one of his return voyages!

John Davis brought dead reckoning to a fine art when sailing amongst the icebergs in the high northern latitudes in search of the elusive North-West passage, and his traverse tables are the basis of modern ships' 'log books'. Then, when going to windward, ships 'traversed' (or 'tacked' as it was called after the eighteenth century), and early ocean navigators recorded their compass courses and estimated their speed and distances with 'traverse boards' or 'traverse tables'. Traverse boards were used in the early part of the fifteenth century and pegs were inserted into the different points of a compass in order to record how long a ship had sailed on a given compass course. One peg might be equivalent to a half-hour's sailing on a given course. Every day the ship's position was estimated from the courses steered and the distances run over the last 24 hours and the noon position plotted on a special chart drawn by the navigator.

The final aim of navigation is to pinpoint the ship's position on the sailor's map or chart and important aids are pilot books and sailing directions.

Sailing directions and charts

Sailing directions were one of the first navigational aids and were used in the earliest sea voyages along the Black Sea and Mediterranean coasts. They were the means of passing information from navigator to navigator such as the distance between ports, tidal rips, prominent headlands, dangerous shoals. The Greeks and Phoenicians collected information on their coastlines, and c500 BC a navigator, Scylax, wrote a set of sailing directions known as a *periplus*, for the Black Sea and the Mediterranean. This was added to by other navigators and a twelfth-century periplus is still in existence. The peripli developed into the fourteenth century Italian *Portolanos* (in French *Portulans*), books of sailing directions illustrated with rudimentary charts. Few survive and those that do are usually well-thumbed and scribbled with pilots' calculations and notes.

The Portuguese produced their own sailing directions, *Roteiros* and were soon producing Ocean Roteiros. The Portuguese, under Prince Henry, established a school of navigation, as did the Spanish in 1503, and in charge of the schools was a *piloto mayor*, who was responsible for updating all the charts. Pilots on voyages of discovery had to report

back to the schools for navigation with all their findings, often having to defend their reports in the presence of the *piloto mayor* and his cartographers.

A Frenchman, probably Pierre Garcie, produced *Le Routier de la Mer* in the sixteenth century. The English translation of it was known as a *Rutter*. English Rutters were developed mainly for coastal navigating and were the forerunners of the Admiralty Tide Tables. *Portolans* rapidly proliferated in the Age of Discovery and by the end of the 1600s had gone as far as China.

Rutters would often describe the nature of the sea-bed, when ships approached land and got into soundings. The use of a heavy lead and a long line were extremely important in a voyage of discovery. When ships reached the end of a voyage, there were indications that land was approaching: the smell, the flight paths of birds, freshly broken branches in the water and the colour of the sea. Columbus carried lines up to hundreds of fathoms long for measuring depth. These lines were attached to lead weights of up to 70 lbs, and their bottoms were partially hollowed out and 'armed with tallow' to pick up particles from the sea bed. *Rutters* and later charts described the nature of the sea bed and often gave a reliable means of estimating a ship's position.

Early Mediterranean charts were surprisingly accurate and gave the discovery navigators confidence to cross oceans and construct new maps and charts (see Vaudrey Heathcote's interesting article, *Early Nautical Charts*). The origin of the first true charts remains obscure. One possibility is that they were developed from sea maps found in the first *Portolans* used to illustrate coastal routes. As ocean trade developed, it appears there was less and less text in the *Portolan* and an increasing emphasis on illustrations. Eventually, chart and sailing directions parted company and nowadays most maritime countries publish their own charts, pilot books and sailing directions for all the world.

One of the earliest surviving charts is from the atlas of Petrus Vesconte, dated 1313. The original leaves of vellum were kept between wooden boards that were smaller than the sheets. Hence the surviving charts are not well-preserved, but they still show the radiating lines that make medieval charts so bewildering to the modern eye. An interesting early chart of 1320 is cut as a circle with a compass placed in the centre. Lines radiate away from the centre of this compass and pass through the 'points' of the compass. (A point is $11\frac{1}{4}$ degrees and a modern compass 'rose' of 360 degrees will therefore contain 32 points.) For each of the four quadrants (north to east, east to south, south to west and west to north) there are eight points and north, east, south and west are known as 'cardinal points'.

Early coastal sailors knew from which direction the

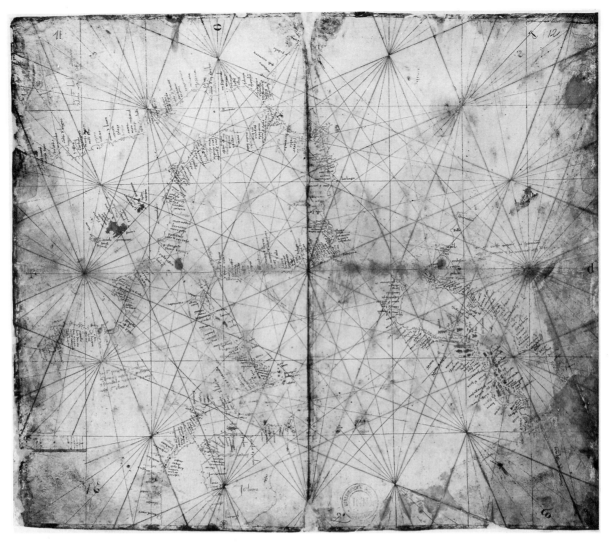

36 *One of the earliest charts: Petrus Vesconte's sea-map of western Europe c1313. (Bibliothèque Nationale, Paris)*

wind blew, as well as its seasonal variations, long before the compass became a standard navigational instrument. Mediterranean seamen named the principal points on early compasses after the prevailing winds, each point being known as a 'quarter-wind'. The cold wind from the north was known as the Tramontana; the warm south wind from the Sahara the Ostro; the west wind the Ponente and the east wind the Levante. On medieval charts the east point of the compass was generally marked with a cross, north with 'T', south with 'O' and west with 'P'. The north 'T' soon became elaborated, probably by the French, into a fleur-de-lys. The four other principal compass points were also named after prevailing winds, for example southeast was called 'S' after the Sirocco.'

The seamen in the Middle Ages only used points to steer by. In c1380 Chaucer made a reference to a compass being composed of all 32 points but it was not until the eigteenth century that the compass was divided into 360 degrees and not until the nineteenth

century that ships were steered to the nearest degree. Early English treatises on navigation talk about the 'Wyndis' to describe the breaking up of the compass rose into points and each point was known as a 'quarter-wyndis'. The French call a compass card, 'la rose des vents'.

In *Seamans Secrets* John Davis describes how the radiating compass lines of the early *Portolan* and Elizabethan charts were used to find the compass course between two places:

When there are two places assigned, the course betweene which you desire to know, set one foote of your Compasses vpon one of the places, then by discretion consider the lines that lead toward the other place, stretching the other foote of the Compasses to one of those lines, and to that part of the line which is neerest to you, keeping that foote still vpon the same line, moue your hand and Compasses toward the other place, and see whether the other foote of the Compasses that stood vpon the first place, do by this direction touch the second place, which if it doe, then that line wherevpon you kept the one foote of your Compasses, is the course betweene those places; but if it touch not the place, you must by discretion search vntil you finde a line, wherevpon keeping the one foote of the Compasses, will lead the other foote directly from one place to the other, for that is the course betweene those two places.

(Hakluyt Society)

Early *Portolans* ignored the curvature of the earth and were without latitude or longitude scales. But as the oceans were opened up and the technique of celestial navigation progressed, latitudes were marked at the side of the chart and measured north and south of the equator. *Portolans* assumed the earth's surface to be flat, but, because the earth is a sphere, when represented on a flat surface, the latitude scale should be increased as the poles are approached. In 1594 Mercator published a world map illustrating this principle, but is was not until the late seventeenth century that charts based upon Mercator's principle came into real use. John Davis was well aware that Portolan charts did not show 'proportionate agreements with the globe'.

The concept of defining a position by a lattice grid was not new to the Age of Discovery. Eratosthenes (276–196 BC) produced a map with rudimentary lines of latitude and longitude. Some 300 years later, Ptolemy (AD 90–168) proposed the fixing of locations by latitude and longitude. His other proposals of a spherical world and the earth as the centre of the universe are still used in modern navigation. And it was Ptolemy's erroneous calculation of the size of the earth at the equator that convinced Columbus that his discovery of the West Indies was in fact the Orient.

The prime meridian, the zero meridian from which longitude is measured, went, as cartography developed, variously through Ptolemy's meridian (which was two degrees west of the Canary islands), the Canaries, the Cape Verde islands, sometimes even through a port of departure, and London, before being finally fixed at the Greenwich Observatory in 1794. (There are a number of modern books dealing with the history of navigation and astronomy which deal with this, and other matters, in more detail; see, for example, C. Cotter and J. Hewson). In 1675 Charles II had set up an observatory at Greenwich to help solve the problem of finding longitude at sea, a problem that existed since the first voyage of discovery. In very early charts longitude lines were often left out, as they could never be reliably fixed, until the invention of the ship's chronometer by John Harrison in 1759. By the beginning of the eighteenth century, latitudes and longitudes were included on the charts as well as lists of the latitude and longitude of major navigational landmarks. Hessel Gerritsz' chart of the Pacific Ocean of 1622 or 1634 shows no lines of longitude. However, Jose Fernandez' chart of 1789 has both latitude and longitude (see Fig. 39).

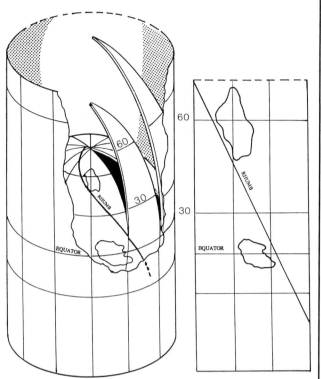

37 *The principle of Mercator's projection. (re-drawn from an illustration in Waters, 1958)*

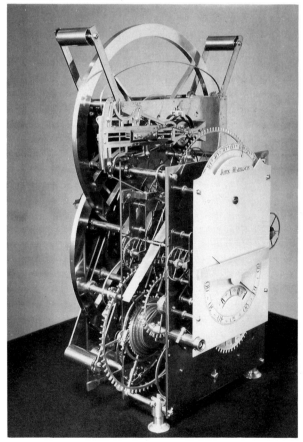

38 *Harrison's Third Marine Timekeeper Chronometer, 1757. It is signed by John Harrison and contains grasshopper escarpment, circular balances, compensation curb and remontoir. (National Maritime Museum, Greenwich)*

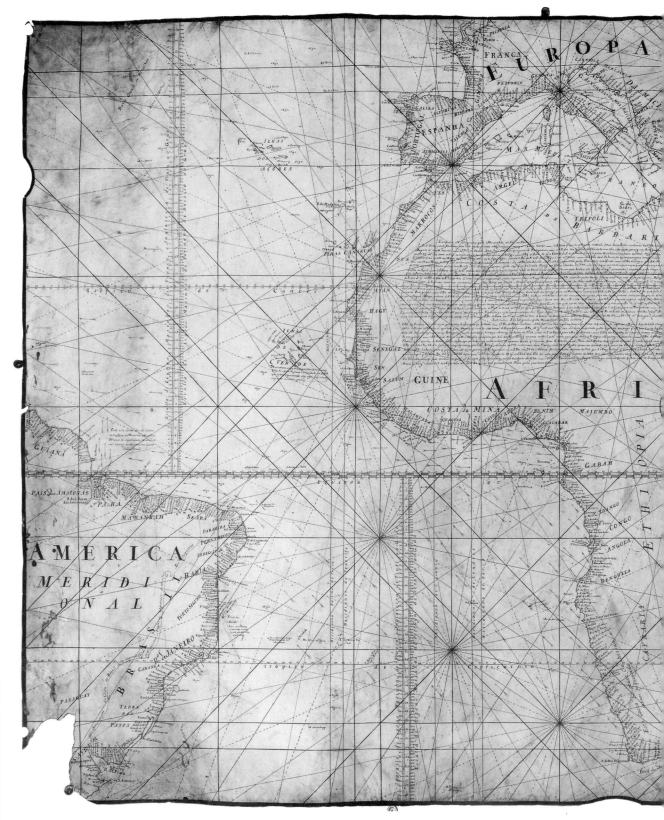

39 *José Fernandes' chart, 1789. One of the longitude 'meridians' on this chart passes through the Ilha do Ferro in the Canary Islands. He also drawns another longitude 'meridian' passing through Paris. (Bibliothèque Nationale, Paris)*

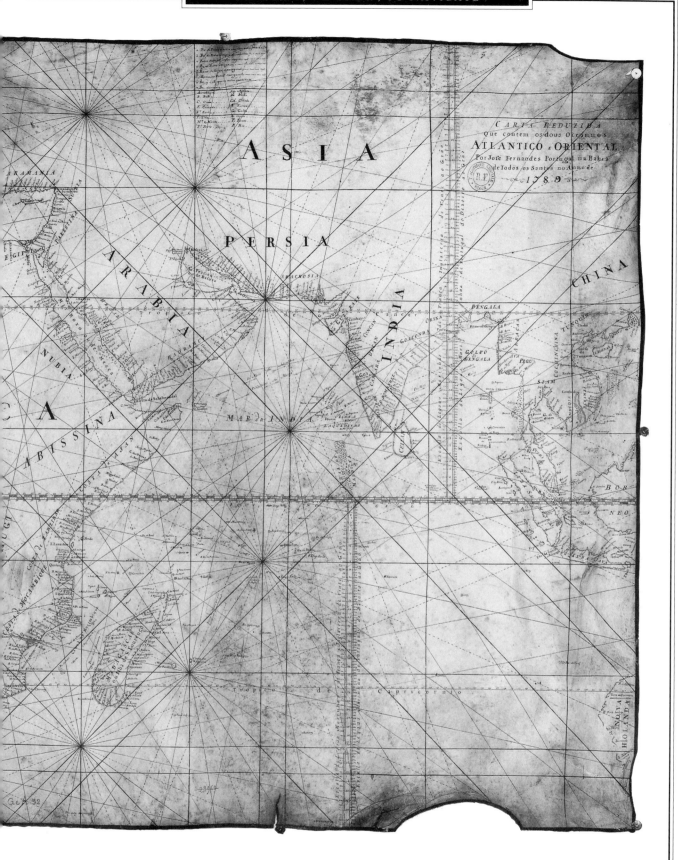

The compass

Once the ship was at sea and out of sight of land, *Rutters* and charts were of secondary importance and the compass was the most important navigational instrument in early ocean voyages. In 1269 Petrus Peregrinus, in his book *Epistle of Magnetism*, described the compass as being divided into four quadrants, each quadrant being 90 degrees. The Spaniard Martín Cortes, in his *Art of Navigation*, was well aware that 'true' and 'magnetic' north did not coincide and suggested that the magnetic pole was located somewhere in space! In 1600 the Englishman William Gilbert correctly concluded that the earth was a large magnet with two opposite magnetic poles. In the Age of Discovery the compass in a ship was mounted on a circular 'compass card'. Martín Cortes advises the card to be cut out of an old chart with a circle of ten inches in diameter. Underneath the card, lying along the north–south axis, an iron or steel needle was attached before being magnetised by stroking with a lodestone. The pilots of the sixteenth and seventeenth centuries thought that the best lodestones came from China and Bengalas, as they were particularly full of iron, which picked up the earth's natural magnetism. Lodestones were extremely valuable and often sold by their weight in silver. In the centre of the compass card a cap of brass-like material (latten) was fitted and mounted on a pivot. The mounted card was set in a glass-lidded, wooden box, gimballed within two concentric circles of latten. The compass was housed in a binnacle and a whale-oil lamp lit the compass at night. In a small ship, a single compass would be mounted on the upper deck and the officer would shout his orders down to the helmsman. On larger ships the helmsman would have a second steering compass mounted in a binnacle and set before him. The magnetic north and south poles do not coincide with the geographic poles and compass needles point towards magnetic and not True North. At any point on the earth's surface the angular difference between True and Magnetic North is known as variation and, because the magnetic poles are rotating around the geographical poles, variation changes annually. Columbus was one of the first ocean navigators to notice that the variation of his compass changed.

Celestial navigation

In 1400, the beginning of the Age of Discovery, it was still believed that the earth was the centre of the universe. The 'Columbus chart' of 1492 (see Fig. 12) shows a geocentric chart on the left hand side and it was not until 1543 that Copernicus showed that the earth rotated around the sun. Although the earlier belief was wrong it was a useful concept for navigators both before and after Copernicus; and modern celestial navigation still assumes that the heavenly bodies move relative to a fixed earth. In this theory of 'apparent motion', the earth is assumed to be the centre of an enormous celestial sphere and every other heavenly body moves relative to the earth. We know that the earth turns on its axis every 24 hours, tilts on its axis c$23\frac{1}{2}$ degrees, and orbits the sun once a year. The 24 hour rotation gives day and night, and the tilt and annual orbit give summer and winter. But when considering the 'apparent motion' of the *sun*, the earth, still assumed to rotate on its axis every 24 hours, is considered to be vertical and the sun said to travel around a celestial path, the ecliptic, which is inclined at some $23\frac{1}{2}$ degrees to the celestial equator, or equinoctial. Because the sun travels around the ecliptic once a year, its 'celestial latitude' or 'declination' is continuously changing. This is in contrast to the stars which, since they are so far away, have almost fixed positions defined by relatively constant declinations and celestial longitudes (a star's declination can be considered to be constant for periods up to about a month; see figure a).

Although the sun's (and planets') changing declination was undoubtedly known to the ancient Greeks, Prince Henry the Navigator, and his astronomers and mathematicians, were the first to draw up tables of the sun's daily declination; and by doing so pioneered the finding of latitude at sea (see figure a–d). With their latitude known, ships can sail either north or south to hit the latitude of their final destination, before turning to sail east or west, along the latitude of their final destination. This navigational technique, known as parallel or latitude sailing ('running your latitude down') was used by seamen until the late 1850s, even though, by then, the invention of the chronometer had enabled navigators to reliably fix their position by calculating both latitude and longitude.

At first navigators' instruments were fairly crude and based on the instruments used on land by astronomers. Navigational instruments for measuring a body's altitude were only really reliable when the use of Hadley's quadrant became widespread in the late eighteenth century. The earliest Portuguese pilots were said to measure the Pole Star's altitude by outstretching their hand and if the distance between the star and the horizon was the width of one finger the altitude was said to be 2 degrees, the width of a wrist 8 degrees, and a whole hand 18 degrees!

Not all the early celestial navigators used their hands, but instead carried quadrants and astrolabes. The marine quadrant, probably the oldest instrument used for measuring the altitude of a heavenly body, was a right-angled piece of wood marked in degrees, whose vertical was set with a plumb line. The quadrant could be used at night, but it had a major

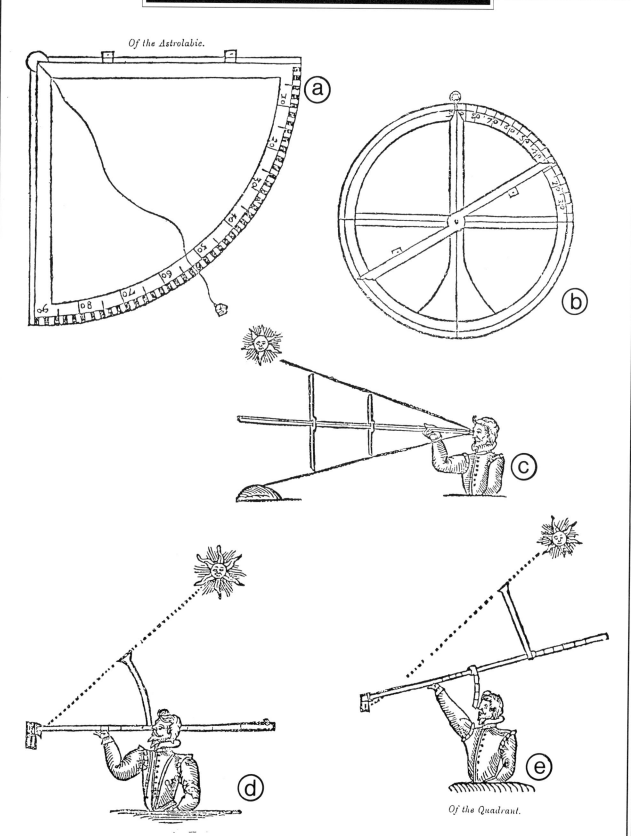

Of the Astrolabie.

Of the Quadrant.

40 *Early navigation instruments (a) and (b) astrolabes, (c) cross-staff (d) back-staff (e) quadrant for use ashore. (from John Davis'* The Seaman's Secrets. *The Hakluyt Society)*

disadvantage: because of the plumb line it was almost impossible to use on a moving ship's deck. Also two seamen were required to make a measurement; one observed the heavenly body through the sights, while the other noted whether the plumb line was vertical. In 1460 Diogo Gomes sailed to Guinea and marked on his quadrant its latitude from a measurement of the Pole Star, and soon the arcs of the early Portuguese quadrants were marked with the names of Portuguese coastal stations rather than with degrees. Marine quadrants were first used by the Portuguese for observing the altitude of the Pole Star so as to obtain their latitude, which was measured south of Lisbon (a measurement of the altitude of the Pole Star gives directly, after small corrections are applied, the latitude of the observer, see Fig. 41). It was easy to make mistakes as the Pole Star is not very bright. Columbus, using his quadrant to determine the latitude of Concepción in Haiti on 13 December 1492, made an error of some 855 miles. He found Concepción to be 34 degrees North after confusing the Pole Star with another star! When the Portuguese navigators first crossed the equator, c1470, they found they were unable to use the Pole Star for obtaining latitude and so had to rely on measurements of the altitude of the sun at noon. It was not until 1507 that they were able to use the stars of the Southern Cross to find the ship's latitude at night.

By c1480 the Portuguese had produced a navigation manual which had standardized methods for measuring latitude from the sun and Pole Star and contained tables of the sun's daily declination. Around this time astrolabes for measuring altitudes were introduced, which were at first made of wood but later were heavy metal circles, marked off in quadrants, and hung from the navigator's thumb by a small top ring. The altitude of the body was measured by the navigator, to about a degree of accuracy, by sighting along the pointer, the Pole Star at night and the sun at noon, when it was on the 'observer's meridian' (that is when the sun is at its highest point in the sky, above the observer). Martín Cortés described the use of the astrolabe in his *Art de Navegar*. Both the quadrant and the astrolabe were difficult to use, as Las Casas' reports for Columbus's voyage on 3 December 1492 show: 'The Admiral was unable to take the altitude [of the North Star] either with an astrolabe or a quadrant because of the rolling of the ship.' However, after three months at sea and out of sight of land, Vasco da Gama observed his latitude with a wooden astrolabe to within a league, when he arrived off the African coast east of the Cape of Good Hope.

The cross-staff was another important navigational instrument that came into use in the fifteenth century. It consisted of a three-foot long wooden staff, with small cross pieces (transoms) that could be slid along the staff. The end of the staff was rested on the cheek-bone close to the eye and one of the transoms, usually three, slid along the staff until the lower end appeared to coincide with the horizon and the upper end with the body being observed. The altitude was then read off the previously calibrated staff. Although more accurate than the astrolabe, altitudes being obtained to an accuracy of within 1/10 of a degree of arc, the cross-staff could only be used when there was a horizon and was difficult to use for measurements of the sun unless used in conjunction with a smoked-glass sunshade. John Davis invented the back-staff to overcome the problem of having to look directly into the sun to obtain an observation. He described his invention in *Seamans Secrets*, and, slightly modified, it became one of the principal navigational instruments for measuring altitude, until the invention of Hadley's quadrant. This quadrant allowed a measurement of altitude to be obtained by simultaneously viewing the celestial body and the horizon. In 1732, John Hadley's quadrant was tried at sea with the British Astronomer Royal, was deemed to be a success and was gradually adopted by navigators from many nations.

The principle of finding latitude by measuring the sun's altitude is fairly easy, provided that the sun's declination when it is at the observer's noon (i.e. at its highest point) is known. Because the Pole Star is not exactly at the geographical North Pole, corrections were made to take this into account. Its spatial relationship to a neighbouring star, Kochab, (and to a group of other stars) was noted, and this was used by early navigators as a means of correcting the discrepancy between the geographical North Pole and the Pole Star. With these corrections, measurements of the Pole Star's altitude gave the observer's latitude directly (illus. 41, figures a–d).

With these crude instruments for measuring latitude, with rough measurements of declination, with lead lines to measure depth and with guesses and crude log lines to measure the ship's speed, the early navigators opened up the ocean trading routes. Their courage, their tenacity and their ability to find their way, almost at will, across all the oceans were outstanding. The technique of arriving at a destination by running down a latitude became the most important deep sea navigational technique for over 400 years. When a measure is made of man's finest feats of exploration, the early ocean voyages must surely stand alongside the first manned journeys into outer space.

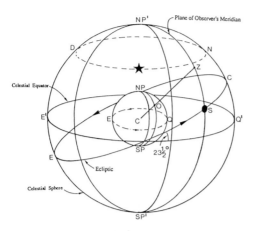

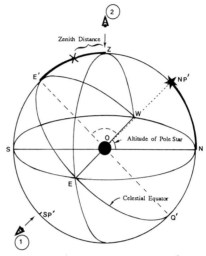

41a The earth is considered to be at the centre of an enormous sphere—the celestial sphere. Using the concept of apparent motion the sun, S, is assumed to travel around the ecliptic, EC, in an anti-clockwise direction once a year to give summer and winter. The ecliptic is said to be inclined at $23\frac{1}{2}°$ to the celestial equator, or equinoctial, E'Q'. The earth is considered to be fixed at the centre of the celestial sphere and to rotate anti-clockwise on its own axis, i.e. eastwards, every 24 hours. The celestial poles, NP', SP', are directly above the earth's north and south poles, NP, SP.

The declination, DN, of the star, X, is the celestial sphere equivalent to latitude on earth and is measured north or south of the celestial equator. An observer is situated at 0 on the earth's surface and the point directly above the observer on the celestial sphere is the oberver's zenith, Z. Noon each day is when the sun is at its highest point relative to the observer, i.e. when it is on the observer's meridian, NP', Z, S, SP' (it is the observer's noon in the figure).

41b Is drawn in the 'plane of the observer's meridian' of figure 41a, with Z now at the top of the figure. The observer is assumed to be in northern latitudes and the view of the earth (in this figure shown smaller, for convenience) and the celestial sphere is from the east. Z, the observer's zenith, is uppermost. NP', the celestial north pole, is 90° north of the celestial equator, E'Q'. A heavenly body, X, is on the observer's meridian (if X is the Sun it is the observer's noon on earth).

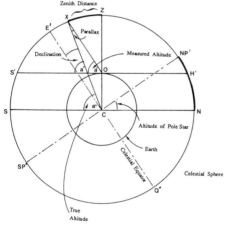

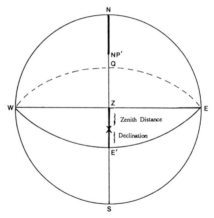

41c Is obtained by viewing figure 41b from the east at position 1, and the figure is said to be 'in the plane of' the observer's meridian. The 'measured altitude', a', of the body X is the angle measured between a horizontal plane passing through the observer's eye (sensible horizon, S'H) and the body. The 'true altitude', a", is the angle betwen the plane passing through the centre of the earth and SN and the body. After a few minor corrections (for refraction and the size of the heavenly body, etc.), a" = a' + ap, where ap is a small correction for parallax, due to the observer not being at the centre of the earth, but on its surface. The measured altitude, a', can be obtained with a nautical instrument, such as an astrolabe, or more accurately today with a sextant. Subtracting the true altitude of the body from 90°, the zenith's distance, ZX, is obtained. The declination of the body is E'CX, the angle the body makes with the centre of the earth, C, and the celestial equator, E'Q'.

41d Is drawn from figure 41b looking down onto Z from viewpoint 2. It is said to be in the 'plane of the celestial horizon', NWSE (for convenience the earth is not shown). NP' is 90° above the celestial equator, WE'E (E'Q' in figure 41a). The observer's celestial latitude is ZE', which is equal to the observer's latitude on earth. The principle of obtaining latitude when a body is on an observer's meridian (at noon-day for the sun at the observer's position) is as follows:

when the heavenly body, X, is on the observer's meridian, its declination is XE' (see figure 41c). The zenith distance, ZX, is calculated from the body's altitude which was measured with a nautical instrument (i.e. ZX is 90° minus altitude). If the body's declination is known for that day then from figure 41d, latitude can be seen to be the sum of the declination, E'X, and the zenith's distance, ZX. Latitude was measured from this fairly simple theory by early Portuguese discoverers and is obtained in the same way by navigators today.

Latitude, E'Z, is also obtained by measuring the altitude of the Pole Star. This is illustrated in figures 41b and 41c, with the assumption that the Pole Star sits at the true North Pole, NP'. From either figure, ZNP' + NP'N = 90° = ZNP' + ZE'. The ZNP's cancel one another (both on either side of the equals sign) so that NP'N (the true altitude of the Pole Star = ZE'—latitude of the observer).

CHAPTER FOUR

The Ocean Highways

By 1600 the Age of Discovery was more or less over and great progress had been made in opening up the trade-wind routes in the Atlantic and Indian Oceans. The period from 1400 to 1600 had been very much part of the Renaissance and led to the development of the carrack, galleon, cartography, celestial navigation and cannon. The seventeeth century was to see the continued development of the galleon as a fighting ship and of the ocean trader. As the century progressed, the nature of Atlantic and Indian Ocean trade changed. The early obsession with silver, gold and spices was replaced with a desire for coffee, tea, muslin, silk, sugar and slaves.

Ocean trade was to come to the Pacific much later than to the Atlantic and Indian Oceans. But the Pacific may have been crossed by the Chinese long before the Europeans arrived, and the Polynesians, around the birth of Christ, were exploring and settling hundreds of tiny islands. They sailed their ocean going, carvel-built, double canoes, without the aid of navigation instruments, on incredible voyages that were over 2000 miles long.

Europeans in the Atlantic and Indian Oceans (1600–1700)

In the seventeenth century powerful trading companies were working the Atlantic and Indian Oceans. In England, France, Sweden and Holland these companies developed private armies and navies (usually with government approval) and were able to conquer and control nations. The English government eventually used legislation to curb the power of the Honourable East India Company, which, backed by the company's private army and navy, eventually created a monopoly of trade with India and China.

Throughout the seventeenth century there were continuous blood struggles, ashore and on the oceans, between the competing empire-building nations: Portugal, Spain, France, Holland and England. Prizes to a victor were often paid for in colonies. England's Walter Raleigh well described the ideology of the new 'Age of Expansionism':

Whosoever commands the sea commands trade; whosoever commands the trade of the world commands the riches of the world, and consequently the world itself.

As one country fell another rose to take its place. China, the most technically advanced nation outside Europe, was content to sit back and watch, perhaps satisfied with its cultural and economic self-reliance. Portugal was the first to lose control to her overseas possesions and trade. In 1580 Portugal had come under Spanish domination and, although breaking away in 1640, Portugal found it difficult to maintain independence. A poor country with few resources and inhabitants, it was always short of man-power. Much of the wealth from Portugal's overseas trading had stayed with the monarchy, nobility and church. The country lacked a mercantile class; little of the wealth was made available for investment in the economy, and so the country stagnated. In contrast, the mercurial rise to power in the late sixteenth and seventeenth centuries by Holland, a small country, was partly due to its many active merchants who financed trading expeditions, re-invested their profits and were backed by a system of government which actively encouraged colonial growth, sea trade, investment and banking. But Holland's maritime power was soon to be severely tested in three Anglo-Dutch wars.

Ralph Davis, in *The Rise of the English Shipping Industry*, shows how, by the end of the seventeenth century, England began to overtake Holland and emerge as one of the most powerful maritime nations. But it was not to be an easy climb. Despite the failure of the Spanish Armada and the naval

42 *A 17th-century Dutch galleon from Joseph Furttenbach's* Architectura Navalis *(1629), showing a spritsail topsail set from the spritsil topmast and a square mizzen topsail. (Musée de la Marine, Paris)*

Disegno del modo, come si possano fabricare le Naui moltiremi, proposto, e publicato nell'
Accademia REALE, da GA Borelli Roma 5 Februaro 1675

43 *A 17th-century engraving of a Mediterranean galley with ramming beak and banks of oars. (Librairie Fontaine)*

supremacy of the Elizabethan galleon, Spain was still the major power in Europe in 1600. Phillip II of Spain, bent on conquering England, had severely curtailed English ocean trade. Holland, when still the Spanish Netherlands, had the monopoly of most of the trade in the North and Baltic Seas. By 1610 the Dutch fishing and merchant fleet numbered some 16,000 vessels, worked, it was estimated, by over 100,000 seamen.

Ocean trade for the Dutch started with voyages to both the West and East Indies. Ships from the newly formed Dutch West Indies Company soon challenged Spain's exclusive right to trade in the Caribbean and by 1600 Holland had made over a dozen expeditions to the Moluccas (Spice Islands), their ships travelling either westward through the Straits of Magellan or eastward around the Cape of Good Hope. Trading posts and companies were formed and in 1602 the Dutch government gave a large capital sum to enable the small trading associations to form the United East India Company or Dutch East India Company (VOC). The government gave the VOC as much support as it required, and encouraged the systematic ejection of the Portuguese from the Spice Islands. The VOC also challenged English traders in the Mollucas, and by diplomacy, stealth and force when necessary, the Dutch were soon masters of the Spice Islands.

During the seventeenth century Holland played a leading role in the development of two other emerging maritime nations: Sweden and Russia. A Dutch shipwright Henrik Hybertsson was employed by the Swedish King and in 1625 four new ships were commissioned for the developing Swedish navy.

One of these was the magnificent 1350-ton *Wasa*. Just after launching and kedging off-shore, the ship was caught by two strong gusts of wind. The *Wasa* heeled, water poured in through the open gun ports, and within minutes the ship had capsized and sunk in 100 feet of water. (In the 1960s *Wasa* was salvaged and brought ashore in her home port, Stockholm.) Dutch shipbuilders allowed Peter the Great, Czar of Russia, to actually work in the shipyards and gain experience in ship construction techniques. For two years the Czar toured European yards, including the Deptford yard in London. On his return to Russia he started a massive ship-building programme realizing, together with the other European nations, the importance of sea power for trade and national wealth.

Before the seventeenth century English merchants had realized that they had to become organized in order to take part in the new ocean trade. In 1599 London merchants formed a company to trade directly with India when the Dutch, then well-established in the Spice Islands, raised pepper prices from 3s to 6s a pound. In 1600 Queen Elizabeth I,

44 *An engraving of a Dutch East Indiaman with typical features of the 17th century—ornate stern and spritsail topmast. (Bibliothèque Nationale, Paris)*

who actively encouraged the formation of trading companies, granted a charter to the 'London East India Company' as 'The Governor and Company of Merchants of London trading with the East Indies' (EIC).

English trade to the Far East officially started in 1600–1601 when five ships sailed on the London Merchants Company's first voyage to Sumatra and Java. The largest trader was the *Red Dragon* at 600 tons; the four other vessels were *Hector* (300 tons), *Ascension* (260 tons), *Susan* (240 tons) and *Gift* (130 tons). On the second voyage, lasting from 1604 to 1606, four ships sailed, and the same number sailed in 1613, the first of the 'joint stock' voyages. In 1612 the EIC had created important trading stations at Bantam in Java (which they lost to the Dutch in 1683) and Surat on the west coast of India, and by 1616 they had begun to trade with Persia. By 1673 the EIC had developed the mid-Atlantic island of St Helena as a port of call for their homeward bound ships and by 1677, 30–35 Indiamen of between 300 and 600 tons were employed in the Indian trade.

Between 1618 and 1620 there was open war between the English and Dutch East India companies. By 1620 the Dutch had captured Jakarta and, after renaming it Batavia, the port became the centre of the VOC's empire. Not surprisingly the English objected to the Dutch take-over in the Moluccas. Resentment was further built up by the 'massacre' at Amboyna in 1623 when the Dutch accused 18 Englishmen of attempting to murder local Dutch residents; they tortured and finally executed 10 Englishmen.

Oliver Cromwell's Navigation Acts of 1650 and 1651 were indirectly aimed at reducing Dutch maritime power. The Acts stipulated that goods for Britain, Ireland and the English West Indian plantations had to be carried by British ships, or goods destined for England had to be carried by ships from the country of origin, if they came from Europe. The Acts mosly affected the Dutch, since they had few exports and relied heavily on their ability to carry cargo for other nations. Clashes over the Spice Island trade, the Amboyna massacre, disputes over fishing grounds, and resentment of English shipowners by the participation of the Dutch in the Newcastle coal trade finally caused a breakdown in Anglo-Dutch relations. War broke out in 1652 and, although no-one was the real winner, when Cromwell made peace in 1654 the Navigation Acts were not repealed, and the Dutch were forced to pay compensation for the Amboyna massacre. The English took over 1000 prizes, mostly unarmed merchantmen known as *fluyts*, which, according to Ralph Davis, in *The Rise of the English Shipping Industry*, supplied English traders with a cheap source of cargo vessels and was one of the wars most 'dramatic and important events'.

Cromwell allied England with France, against Spain, and obtained Jamaica in 1665; the same year that the first of two more Anglo-Dutch wars broke out (1665–1667; 1672–1674). More *fluyts* were taken, and they were now so popular with English traders that, according to Alan McGovan in Vol IV of *The Ship*, northeast English shipbuilders began building and adapting them to create an English version of the *fluyt*: the North-East *cat*.

Charles II (1630–1685) gave the EIC power to make 'peace or war with prince or people not Christian; to establish fortifications, garrisons and colonies and to return to England any English subjects trading without their licence.' The bulk of the Company's trade was pepper from the East Indies and saltpetre from north India, as well as drugs, silk, cotton and indigo, which took less hold space, and was far more valuable. Outward-bound, the Company ships carried brass, iron and bullion, which were used to buy their imports.

In his diary *Samuel Pepys* describes (for 16 November 1665) a visit to an EIC ship:

So I on board my *Lord Brouncker*, and there he and Sir Edmund Pooly carried me down into the hold of the India shipp, and there did show me the greatest wealth lie in confusion that a man can see in the world. Pepper scattered through every chink, you trod upon it; and in cloves and nutmegs I walked above the knees; whole rooms full, and silk in bales, and boxes of copper-plate, one of which I saw opened.

The EIC pushed northeastwards and in 1665 a trading post was established at Tonquin, in China, but the famous China tea trade had yet to start in earnest. Samuel Pepys wrote on 4 September 1660:

I did send for a cup of tee (a China drink) of which I never had drank before.

(From F. Bowman and E. Roper, *Traders in East and West*)

In 1664 tea was still so scarce that two pounds two ounces of it was presented to King Charles as a valuable offering. By the 1690s the china tea trade had begun to thrive: the European market was almost insatiable.

Tea trade was seasonal; EIC ships of around 200 tons would arrive off the coast of China in early autumn. To arrive too late might mean that other ships had picked up the cargo and, if the homeward passage was too long, the tea could be spoiled. The competition for cargoes and the race home was to become intense and lead to the famous nineteenth-century 'Tea Clipper' races.

In 1688 William III (1650–1702) incorporated 'The English Company trading to the East Indies' and as a result for the next 20 years there were two rival

ette Société qui prodigue sa vie
Pour nous combler des biens que produit l'Orient

Navires des marchandz
qui vont aux Indes
Orientales

Va les extremitez, le Monde mariant,
Et semble transporter en Europe l'Asie.

6

45 *A 17th-century engraving of French East Indiamen from the French East India Company. The inscription reads, 'This society which dedicates itself to fill us to overflowing with all the products of the Orient. Go to the extremities, make the world, one and seem to carry Asia to Europe'. (Bibliothèque Nationale, Paris)*

English companies. In 1708 both companies were amalgamated as 'The United Company of Merchants of England trading to the East Indies', generally known as the 'Honourable East India Company' or simply the East India Company (HEIC).

In 1664 the French formed the Compagnie des Indes orientales. Altogether the French formed five successive East India Companies and were able to establish trading posts at Pondicherry and Chandenagor. With their superb colonial administration they achieved a strong position in southern India and it was inevitable that they would clash with the interest of EIC.

In the West Indies, France had colonized Gaudeloupe, Martinique and Santo Domingo, all important sugar-producing islands. The English had Barbados, Antigua and St Kitts, as well as some of the Windward Islands. Barbados was the main English sugar-producing island, and the English planters, aided by the Dutch who had been ousted from Brazil, set up the large English sugar-cane plantations that exist today. By the 1660s sugar cane was the main crop of the Caribbean islands and formed part of an infamous trade triangle. Ships left England carrying manufactured goods, sometimes stopping in Ireland for beef and dairy products, or Madeira for wine, before arriving off the West

African coast to pick up slaves. By the mid-seventeenth century the slave trade had begun to boom, as the sugar-cane planters required more and more cheap labour. After crossing the Atlantic, slaves were sold and sugar cane loaded in the Caribbean islands for the return voyage to England, to complete the triangle.

The first English colonist had arrived in 1607 in America, at Chesapeake Bay, and by the 1650s there were colonies in Massachusetts, Maryland and Virginia. According to Ralph Davis, in *The Rise of English Shipping*, by 1713 English ships began to appear in Chesapeake, homeward bound from their Caribbean slave voyages. They would, on the last leg of the triangle, make a detour and call at England's new American colonies to load timber, tobacco and tar. The Royal Africa Company handled much of the slave trade between 1673 and 1713, and profits were highest from 1673 to 1689.

In 1669, at the height of its power, the Dutch VOC had a fleet of some 150 three-masted ocean traders, each with square sails on the fore- and mainmasts and a lateen-sailed mizzen course with square topsail. Despite losses of large numbers of merchantmen in the Anglo-Dutch wars, by 1670 the Dutch were well-established in Malaysia and had staging posts in Ceylon and the Cape of Good Hope;

they were trading with Japan and competing with the English in India, Persia and Siam. By 1700 Holland had complete control of Java, one of the main centres of the lucrative pepper trade and England had been forced out of the Spice Islands.

Royals, spritsail topmast, cherubs and whipstaff

Holland pioneered the building of cheap, unarmed merchantmen. And at the opening of the seventeenth century it was the Dutch, with their numerous, purpose-built merchantmen, who took the cargoes that had once been carried by the ships of the Hanseatic League. The Dutch *buss*, for example, was a specialized fishing craft that drift-netted most of the herring catch from the Baltic and North Sea. There were other specialized Dutch boats: *hoekers* (hookers) for line-fishing, and general cargo carriers, such as *boiers*, and *buyscarveels*.

It was at the end of the sixteenth century that Dutch *fluyts* (sometimes 'flutes' or 'fluits' and known to the English as 'fly-boats') first appeared, to become the coastal bulk-carriers par excellence. *Fluyts* cost

little to build, as they were lightly constructed. (They were light as they did not carry heavy cannon nor expect to be bombarded.) Large *fluyts* were three-masted, over 300 tons and some 100 ft long, with a long keel. Ralph Davis gives keel length to beam ratios of c4:1 and quotes a George Waymouth who in 1610 described Dutch vessels thus:

The ships in the Low Countries are built longer and according to bredth and depth, than our (English) Ships are. They bee built with broader and longer bottoms proportional to their length, than our ships bee.

Fluyts were also bluff-bowed and round-sterned, with such a 'tumble-home' (inward slope at the top of the hull) that it made them almost pear-shaped. They had shallow draughts, and the tops of their rudders were carried high, and often outside, their well-rounded sterns. Planking in the stern was carried right round to the stern post. Tillers were either led directly from the rudder head on to the poop or quarter deck, or through a specially constructed 'helm (or tiller) port' cut into the concave stern. Ocean-going *fluyts* were often 'short masted', with a simple three-masted rig which might be a square

Flute a l'ancre,

46 *A 17th-century Dutch* fluyt, *at anchor. (Bibliothèque Nationale, Paris)*

47 *Dutch* fluyt *drifting under lateen mizzen. (Bibliothèque Nationale, Paris)*

spritsail under the bowsprit, forecourse, maincourse
and topsail, lateen mizzen, or mizzencourse, and the
new square mizzen topsail. With short masts, the rig
could be easily handled by the small crews: it was
cheaper to arrive a day later than to pay for extra
hands. *Fluyts* were easily adapted and used variously
as colliers, timber carriers, general cargo carriers and
even, by strengthening the bows, as whalers in Arctic
waters. If anyone needed a cargo to be carried, the
Dutch would ship it cheaply and efficiently. *Fluyts*
not only coasted; the Dutch used large *fluyts* (up to
500 tons) on the Spice Trade route to the East Indies.

In the early seventeenth century much English
ocean trade was carried by merchantmen based on
the English galleon that had successfully defeated the
Spanish Armada. They were heavy ships, armed and
usually wider bodied than the warships, and
expensive to build. They were much used by the EIC

and also by the Levant Company. (The Levant
Company was formed from the amalgamation of the
Turkey Company and Venice Company and traded
in Mediterranean waters. In 1600 it owned 14 ships
and charted 15 others, all in the style of the English
galleon.)

In the ship-building tradition of the early part of
the seventeenth century the EIC built a number of
very large vessels in the Company's yards at
Blackwall and Deptford on the banks of the Thames.
Ships like the *Charles, Royal James*, and *Trades
Increase* were all over 1000 tons, while others, like
the *Elizabeth* and *White Bear* were over 850 tons.
(Around this period it was difficult to ascertain what
was meant by 'tonnage'—see p 97—as there was no
real standard measure of tonnage until 1773. It would
appear that these were tons 'measured', and not tons
'burden'.) None of these enormous ships sailed

48 *A late 16th, early 17th-century Dutch West Indiaman. There is no spritsail topmast, and the ship has a steep sheer fore and aft and a pronounced beak. (after a drawing in Culver, 1924)*

particularly well, and *Trades Increase*, of 1293 tons, was lost on the first Indian voyage. The EIC, realizing that losses were better minimized by building smaller ships, generally built vessels of between 300 and 800 tons for the next 150 years or so. Most were around 500 tons and much larger than merchantmen used on the trans-Atlantic West Indies, run, where ships averaged 150—200 tons. On this run ships only reached 300 tons in the mid-eighteenth century, when there was a need for larger ships to carry sugar from the Caribbean islands and timber from North America (see also J. Sutton's *Lords of the East*).

During the first 50 years of the seventeenth century, the design and structure of the largest ocean traders, the defensible merchantmen, were, as in the previous century, closely linked to warship development. Due to the keen interest shown by the English crown in building warships in the sixteenth century, the opening of the seventeenth century saw the new Crown yards moved from Portsmouth and Harwich to Deptford and Woolwich. Master Shipwrights of the Crown designed and built both war- and merchant ships alongside each other. Such was the close link between Crown ship and ocean trader that Edward Stevens (who later in 1603 was to

become the Crown's Master Shipwright) built the *Malice Scourge*. This ship was later bought by the EIC and re-named the *Red Dragon*, before becoming the EIC's flagship on its first venture to the Far East. William Burrell, the first Surveyor-General of the EIC, was also the Commissioner for the Navy and he designed and built the mighty *Trades Increase*.

In 1610 Phineas Pett (1570–1647), another Crown Master Shipwright, built the huge four-masted *Prince Royal*, and he was one of the first to build a ship from a scale model. These early, large warships were often important for the evolution of ocean traders as they often pioneered major advances in ship design. *Prince Royal* was the largest ship afloat, with a keel length of 115 ft, a 43 ft 6 in. beam, three decks, and armed with 50–58 cannon.

R. and R.C. Anderson, in *The Sailing Ship*, argue that the best available painting of the *Prince Royal* is a painting by Hendrik Vroom made in 1620. The painting shows a ship with a high poop, beautifully carved galleries aft, and a long, low beak forward. The Elizabethans developed quarter galleries on their ships and these 'walk-ways' were much liked by the officers who often used them as outside toilets! On the *Prince Royal* doors led out onto the galleries below beautifully carved porches. The bowsprit was

49 *The Deptford dockyard, c1660, where many East Indiamen were built. (National Maritime Museum, Greenwich)*

ORIGINAL SCALE-MODEL OF H.M.S. PRINCE ROYAL (1640)
in the T.S. Mercury Collection

50 *Scale model of the Prince Royal; rebuilt in Woolwich dockyard in 1641 and renamed* Royal Prince. *She was renamed* Resolution *between 1650 and 1660, and was burnt by the Dutch in 1666 when she went aground on the Galloper sands. (National Maritime Museum, Greenwich)*

THE TRVE PORTRAICTVRE OF HIS MA.^{tics} ROYALL SHIP THE SOVERAIGNE OF THE SEAS

PRÆGRANDIS ILLIVS ATQ. CELEBERR.^a NAVIS SVB AVSPICIS CAROLI MAGN: BRIT: FRA: ET HIB: REGIS AN.^o 1637 EXST

51 *J. Payne's contemporary print of Sovereign of the Seas, 1637.*
(Science Museum, London)

Tritons auspicious Sound usher Tagueique
Ore the curld billowes, Royal SOVERAINE.
Monarchal Ship: whose Fabrig rolls out fierce
The Pharos Colosse, Memphique Pyramide:
And seemes a moving Tower, when Streight comes
Quicken the motion, and embrace the failes
Wee haue heard of SEAVEN, now see EIGHT
Wonder at home: of Naual art the height
This Britain ARGO hath seen that of Greece
Be-Deckt with more then one rich Golden Fleece
Wrought into Sculptures, which Entertaine
Pregnant Conceipt to the more Curious eyes
Neptune is proud o'th burden: and doth wonder
To heare a Fourefold Tire out-rore loue's Thunder
Can tian Triumphal Arke with EDGAR's fame
To CHARLES his Scepter & Trident claime.
Tho: Cary.

INEATIO EXPRESSISSIMA ARCHINAVPEGO PETRO PETT jun: sculpsit: I.P.syne Cum priuilegio ad imprimendam solum.

longer than either of the mizzenmasts and the lateen topsails of the mizzens were now replaced by square topsails. A spritsail was set below the bowsprit and at the end of the bowsprit was a spritsail topmast which carried the new sail, the 'spritsail topsail'. The spritsail topmast was perched, rather precariously, at the end of the bowsprit. The spritsail topmast, used from the early 1600s to the early 1700s, was a typical feature of all large seventeenth-century ships (it was almost never rigged on small cargo ships). Like other masts, the spritsail topmast probably developed from a flag pole (on the bowsprit).

The Andersons point out that the *Prince Royal* shows another rigging change: the lateen topsails to the mizzens were replaced by square topsails. These square topsails, set athwartships, needed a new yard to hold out their lower corners, since the yard of the lateen course of the mizzen was set fore and aft. This was called the 'cross-yard' or 'cross-jack' (or crojack); the French named it the 'vergue seche' (barren yard) since it did not carry its own sail. The yards of the fore and main courses would take the bottoms of the fore and main topsails. Merchant ships took some time before they adopted the new square mizzen topsails. But a painting of the EIC yard at Deptford on the River Thames in about 1660 shows a ship with a crossjack yard.

The number of shrouds used to support ships' masts during the seventeenth century depended on the size of the ship. Typically an EIC ship such as the *White Bear* (900 tons) in 1618 might have had eight shrouds on the foremast, ten on the mainmast and five on the main mizzen. The number of shrouds tended to get less as the century developed. 'Chain-wales', pronounced 'channels', helped increase the angle that the shrouds made to the masthead and so improved the effectiveness of the shrouds in holding the mast vertical. Shrouds were tensioned with deadeyes and the lower deadeye was kept away from the ship's side by the chain-wales, before being made fast to the hull with a chain or a 'chain plate'.

The seventeenth century was the age in which ship decoration was to reach its height, becoming such an obsession with many shipbuilders that French captains were even known to cut away beautifully carved statues, cherubs and wreaths once the ship was at sea so as to reduce windage. In 1634 Charles I of England commissioned Phineas Pett to build another huge warship. Three years after being commissioned, the *Sovereign of the Seas* was launched, 126 ft on the keel, 46 ft 6 in. beam, and 1522 tons burden (old rule) or 1884 tons (new rule): a three-decked ship, and one of the first to carry 100 cannon, although they tended to make her top heavy. Decoration was so extreme that Pett became dismayed at the 'vain display of magnificence'. By now the stern galleries were covered-in, greatly carved and fitted with six decorated domes.

The *Sovereign of the Seas* was one of the first ships to set a square 'mizzen topgallant' sail, over the square mizzen topsail and lateen mizzen course. On the foremast and mainmast, new square sails were rigged above the topgallants—the 'royals'. Thus the sails on the mainmast would be, in ascending order, main course, main topsail, main topgallant and main royal. Royals, however, did not become standard rig for ships for at least another 150 years.

In light airs larger ships still fitted bonnets and drabblers on the fore and main courses. In strong winds reefing points were used to reduce sail area. They had been used some centuries before (see Fig. 6—La Rochelle seal) as a means of shortening sail, but had disappeared before reappearing in the seventeenth century in the topsails. As the force of the wind increased, a ship would lower its main yard and foreyard, detach the bonnet from the main course and fore course, if fitted, and depending on the strength of the wind, the courses would be furled. The topsails would be reefed by using the reef points (light lines attached to the sail) to tie off the lower part of the sail. As conditions worsened, the ships might be worked under reefed topsails alone or, under extreme conditions, with all the canvas

stripped off. Topmasts could be lowered to the deck to reduce windage.

The *Sovereign's* stern was no longer the square stern, common to all large ocean-going ships since about 1500, nor was it the fully rounded-stern of the Dutch *fluyt* boats. It was a compromise, where the bottom planks were brought out of the water before ending on a small square transom some 10 ft above the waterline. This 'modified round stern', introduced into English ships c1620, was very much a feature of English ships for about 100 years (see also p 99 ff).

A loss of the aft mizzenmast from large ships occurred in the early seventeenth century. *Prince Royal* had four masts, but *Sovereign of the Seas* had no bonaventure mizzen, nor did an English rigging plan of a large ship from Thomas Miller's *Compleat Modellist* of 1655. R.C. Anderson, in *The Rigging of Ships in the days of the spritsail topmast 1600—1720* writes:

How long one should go on fitting two mizzens I do not know. It would almost certainly be safe up to 1620 and I think it would be wrong to do so after 1630...

In the middle of the seventeenth century, the first clear break occurred between warships and defensible merchantmen as a result of changes in naval strategy: sea battles began to be fought by ships forming lines,

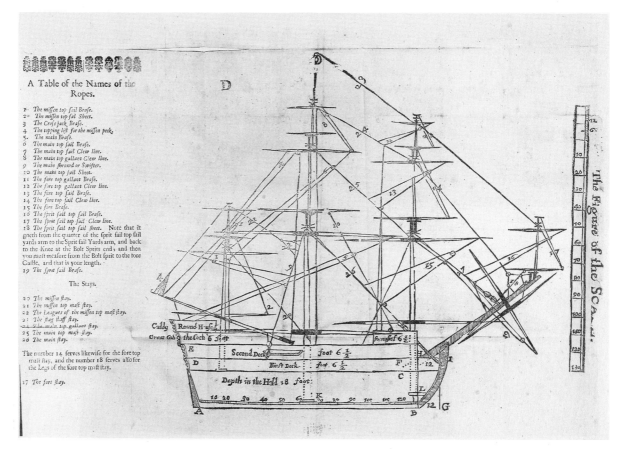

52 *Rigging plan from* The Compleat Modellist. *(Science Museum, London)*

and unarmed merchantmen began to sail in convoys protected by warships. A ship's cannon were mostly situated along its sides. When the ships formed lines, maximum use could be made of their fire power while vulnerable bows and sterns were relatively protected. In a battle, however, opposing ships had to be of a similar size and armament, otherwise it was almost certain defeat for the undergunned vessel. In 1652 Britain passed the Convoy Act, and in 1653 decided to keep ships with 50 guns or less out of the line.

Until the end of the seventeenth century the crowns and governments of the maritime nations still encouraged the building of large, armed merchantmen, that could not only act as auxillaries to the warships, but also, in times of need, fight alongside them. As a result large Dutch, French, Swedish and English East Indiamen continued the tradition of a close structural similarity between large trader and warship. Ships of the EIC never carried as many crew or arms as their warship counterparts but they were well built and reasonably well armed to fight off pirates and privateers; on occasion, they fought and defeated rival nations' warships. Thus, a comparison of English warship designs of the late seventeenth century with those of the late sixteenth is of interest.

The Master Shipwright of the English crown's navy in the latter part of the seventeenth century was Anthony Deane (1638–1721), who frequently copied French design when he saw fit. (French naval architecture was often more adventurous, and more advanced, than either the Dutch or the English.) Samuel Pepys was a contemporary of Deane's, and it is possible to compare the ship designs of Matthew Baker with those made some 80 years later by Anthony Deane, since Pepys, when Secretary to the Admiralty, collected an enormous amount of naval documentation, including Anthony Deane's *Doctrine of Naval Architecture.*

There are strikingly few differences between Baker's and Deane's ships. By the 1670s English ships had a modified rounded stern compared with the square stern found in Baker's Elizabethan ships; forecastles were lower and the long galleon beak was by then reduced in size (see R. Morton Nance, *The Ship of the Renaissance* and G.S. Laird Clowes *Sailing Ships*).

During the sixteenth and seventeenth centuries, as warships and ocean traders became large and poops became multi-decked, the tiller, attached as it was to the head of the rudder, came further away from the upper deck. As a result, communication between helmsman and deck officer was difficult and to reduce

53 *Rigging plan of an English three-decker or first rate from Anthony Dean's manuscript,* Doctrine of Naval Architecture, *c1761. (Pepysian Library, Magdalene College, Cambridge)*

WHIPSTAFF

GROMMET

TILLER SHAFT

54 *The Whipstaff. (after an illustration in Culver, 1924)*

this problem, 'the whipstaff' was developed. It was a peculiar and cumbersome arrangement: a pole was fitted over the end of the tiller and led up through the deck, perhaps inside a greased leather grommet; by pushing or pulling the whipstaff to starboard, not an easy movement, the tiller would be moved to port and the ship's head to starboard. There was friction to overcome and no great mechanical advantage to be had in using a whipstaff, and it had probably to be helped by tackles made fast to the tiller. In large ships, the helmsman was still well below the upper deck, but in a smaller merchantman his head might appear at deck level and have to be protected by a small cupola. A manuscript written c1625, entitled *A Treatise on Rigging*, describes the whipstaff under the section:

The meanes by wch the ship is turned, steered.

The Rother [rudder] hangs to the sterne post and is of the thicknes of the sterne post where it hangs, if it be broader it hinders her sterredge [steering] and makes it turne uneasely, from thence it growes thicker and thicker till it comes to the backe wch is the outter part of it, the thicknes ther makes the ship stere better: The Tiller is fastened to the heade of the Rother, and at the Helme porte [helm port] commes into the ship as far as the sterredge. The Whip is fastened to the ende of the Tiller with an ey of Iron it comes up at the 'whipscuttle' through the 'rowler' into the sterredge rome. [steering room]. The Whip moues the Tiller, the tiller the Rother, the Rother guides the ship. In the sterredge room is the Bitakle [binnacle] wch is a box madd of wainscott it has seueral particio[n]s [partitions], it serues to carrie the Co[m]passe, lights and Traineborde.

Towards the end of the century the size of the helm port on large ships was much reduced by bringing the head of the rudder inside the ship. The tiller was now inside the ship and the vulnerable opening in the stern much smaller, having only to accommodate the lateral movements of the rudder, and not the much larger arc swept out by a tiller. The smaller helm port could be more easily closed with the canvas rudder cloths which helped keep out dangerous following seas. Not all ocean traders would carry a whipstaff. In small ships, the rudder head might still end well below the ship's counter and tillers led in through large helm ports. Small, ocean-going merchantmen might have their tillers led out on deck.

Generally, small traders carried simple rigs that were operated by a few seamen, and only small numbers of cannon would be carried for protection against pirates and privateers. In 1620 the three-masted merchantman, *Mayflower*, set out to cross the Atlantic with a six-sailed rig that was common some 150 years before: spritsail under the bowsprit, forecourse and fore topsail, maincourse and main topsail, and lateen mizzen.

Throughout most of the seventeenth century, in small coastal vessels in Holland and England, seamen were experimenting with new fore and aft sails. The new sails were set on 'stays'—ropes that were part of the fore and aft standing rigging of the coasters. Later 'staysails' and 'jibs' were to play a major role in increasing the sailing efficiency of the ocean trader. R.C. Anderson, in *The Rigging of Ships*, wrote the following about the introduction of staysails and jibs into large sailing ships:

With regard to staysails, the first thing to be decided is which stays are to carry them. In a general way it can be said that there should (or might) be mizzen, main, main topmast and fore topmast staysails from 1660–1690 and that after that, mizzen topmast and main topgallant staysails might be added. From 1705, or a few years earlier, there might be a jib, though this was by no means universal.

The eighteenth century was also to see the development, and consolidation, of trading routes across three oceans: the Atlantic, the Indian and the Pacific.

Europeans in the Pacific Ocean (1500–1700)

Trans-Pacific Ocean trading routes only played a minor role in the sixteenth and seventeenth centuries. Other Pacific sailing-ship routes became increasingly important in the eighteenth and nineteenth centuries, when American British ships began to sail regularly round Cape Horn. Eventually the Pacific Ocean became a highway for a number of important trades: tea, fur, sandalwood, copra, whale oil, wool, wheat, nitrates, guano, and slaves, convicts and emigrants.

As in the Atlantic and Indian Oceans in the Age of Discovery, the initial main exploratory drive into the Pacific was Europe's craving for gold, silver and spices. The desire was twofold: an attempt to find an alternative route to the Spice Islands (west-about from Europe, via Cape Horn); and secondly a search for the fabled land of Ophir or 'Terra Australis Incognito' as it was then known. Ophir was mentioned in the Old Testament, where King Solomon's fleet was said to have carried off its riches. Marco Polo inspired the discoverers when it was believed that he had written about a 'southern continent rich in gold and spices'. In fact he never did; he was wrongly translated.

When Balboa plunged his sword into the Pacific Ocean in 1515 and claimed the 'South Sea' for Spain, the Portuguese had already rounded the Cape of Good Hope, crossed the Indian Ocean, passed through the Malacca Strait and loaded spices in the Molucca Islands. In 1520 Ferdinand Magellan, a Portuguese sailing under the Spanish flag, set out to find the west-about route to the Spice Islands. After one of the great, if not the greatest, voyages of discovery, he arrived in the Phillippine Islands only to meet his death in a futile skirmish. Only two of the five-ship fleet that had set out from Europe, left the Philippines to sail south to the Moluccas. Only one, the *Victoria*, made it back to Europe. The Spanish exploited Magellan's discovery of the Philippines and in 1564 sent an expedition from Mexico to colonize the islands. The outward voyage was easy, the ships running before the North-East trade winds, but to return they had to travel a long way north, to the latitude of San Francisco, before favourable westerly winds carried them back across the Pacific to the North American coast, where they could turn south for the return to Mexico. The expedition opened up the first European trade route in the Pacific. Spanish galleons would leave Mexico, loaded with silver, which they exchanged at Manila, which became an entrepot for Chinese silk and porcelain. The galleons then sailed into the north Pacific to search for the westerlies that would carry them back to Mexico.

Magellan's fleet, water-logged after thousands of sea miles, and decimated by worm, storm and scurvy, had almost failed to find a west-about route to the Spice Islands. Other Spanish Cape Horn expeditions followed, but none succeeded: the distances from Europe were great, the winds often contrary, Cape Horn seas enormous and violent, and sixteenth-century ocean traders not really up to the task. The route east around the Cape of Good Hope was in the hands of the Portuguese, and Spain soon sold its claim to the Moluccas to Portugal and allowed them the Spice Island trade, content with its vast and rich possessions in the New World and its Mexico-Manila run.

Magellan's voyage had not, however, discouraged the cartographers' belief in Terra Australis. They continued to draw a huge southern continent linked to the southern side of Magellan's Straits (Tierra del Fuego, land of fire, so named by Magellan, as he had been astonished by the local Indian habit of lighting numerous fires at night). So the search for Terra Australis continued. In 1567 Alvaro de Mendaña and Pedro Gamboa left Spanish Peru to search for its northern tip. After sailing almost a third of the way round the globe, they arrived at a group of islands just east of Papua New Guinea. They returned to Peru via the Philippines and the Northern Pacific route and called their find Solomon Islands, after King Solomon: Ophir had been found, or so they thought.

English attempts to find Terra Australis were behind Drake's circumnavigation in the *Golden Hind*. Devonshire merchants, who backed the voyage, hoped he would find Ophir, but Drake and Elizabeth I had other ideas. His six ships set sail in 1577. The largest, and Drake's flagship, was the 100–

120 tun ocean trader *Pelican*, later re-named by Drake, the *Golden Hind*. The *Elizabeth* was 80 tuns, the bark, *Marygold* was 30 tuns. There were two *pinnaces* of around 13 tuns, and a 50-tun *flute*, the *Swan*, was the storeship. Little is known of the size of the *Golden Hind*, but estimates (based on the size of a stone dry-dock that the *Golden Hind* was said to have been preserved in as a national monument following Drake's circumnavigation) put her as 75 ft length overall, 19 ft beam, and 10 ft draught. The hull was double-sheathed, with tarred horse-hair between the two layers of planking to keep out teredo worm. The ship was crowded, manned by a crew of about 80, and to give them more room the ship's boat was often towed. There were three masts, and the square sails set on the foremast and mainmast were lower courses and topsails. The mizzen was latten-rigged and there was a spritsail set below the bowsprit. There were 16 to 18 cannon on two decks, and the gun ports could be shut tight, made waterproof with caulking, and the cannon stowed below in heavy weather.

Off the coast of west Mexico in 1579, Drake knew he could not return southwards, back to England via Cape Horn, as Spanish warships would be waiting for him. So he sailed north up the west coast of present-day America. He then sailed west, across the Pacific, and in June 1580 rounded the Cape of Good Hope to arrive in England in September of the same year: a hero to the English, a pirate to the Spanish, whose galleons' bullion filled the hold of *Golden Hind* to over-flowing.

Thomas Cavendish, another Elizabethan adventurer, repeated Drake's capture of Spanish treasure, but his successor in 1594, Richard Hawkins, was captured by a strong Spanish squadron. By defeating Richard Hawkins, Spain felt less threatened by the English and sent out another expedition to search for Terra Australis. In 1595 Mendaña set sail, but he was never to see his Solomon Islands again. After finding the Marquesas Islands he sailed on to arrive at the island of Santa Cruz, some 200 miles east of the Solomons, where he died. His Portuguese pilot, Pedro Quiros, succeeded in returning to Spanish America by the North Pacific route.

In 1605 Spain sent out Quiros, with another Portuguese, Luis Torres, in charge of a second ship. They arrived at a group of islands just south of the Solomon Islands, the New Hebrides (nowadays Vanuatu), but there the two ships separated. Quiros returned to Mexico but Torres pushed on to make the last important Spanish Pacific discovery. He failed to weather the eastern edge of New Guinea and, sailing along the southern shore, discovered that New Guinea was not part of Australia, a discovery that was to remain virtually unknown until the time of Cook.

The Dutch quickly dislodged the Portuguese from the Spice Islands and it was a Dutch Commander, Willem Jansz, whose pinnace, the *Duyfken*, in 1606 was one of the first European ships to sight and land men in Australia. *Duyfken* sailed from the south coast of New Guinea and, without discovering the Torres Straits, sailed over 200 miles along the Australian coast before returning to Banda. This discovery was included in the Dutch East India Company's chart of the Pacific Ocean drawn by its cartographer, Hessel Gerritsz, in 1622. From about 1616 onwards captains of Dutch East Indiamen were not taking the Portuguese route to the Moluccas along the South-West trade winds that diagonally crossed the Indian Ocean; rather they rounded the Cape of Good Hope and sailed eastwards, between latitudes 30° and 40° South, on the top edge of the 'roaring forties' (the strong westerly winds that blow between 40° and 50° South) before turning northeast towards the Spice Islands. It was inevitable that they would observe the west coast of Australia and, although unimpressed by the barren coast, they named the country 'New Holland', even though they were unaware of the existence of the Torres straits, assuming that New Holland was connected to New Guinea.

In 1642 Anthony Van Diemen, the Governor-General of the Dutch East Indies, dispatched Abel Tasman to see if New Holland was part of Terra Australis Incognito. First Tasman sailed west from Batavia, Java, towards Mauritius, where he turned south and east to enter the strong winds and high swells of the roaring forties. After thousands of miles he saw nothing, until he arrived at what is now known as Tasmania, but which he called 'Van Diemen's Land'. He rounded its southern tip and after a voyage east for about 1000 miles arrived at New Zealand, the north point of which he called Cape Maria van Diemen: he assumed he was at the northern tip of Terra Australis. His two ships, *Heemskerck* and *Zeeham*, had also showed that New Holland or Australia was a separate continent.

European Pacific exploration was not re-awakened until 1697 when Dampier, an ex-buccaneer and round-the-world voyager, published his *New Voyage Around the World*. The book was so successful that the British Admiralty sponsored their first voyage of discovery when, in 1699 they gave Dampier a ship. He discovered the island of New Britain and the channel between it and Papua-New Guinea. The British Admiralty was also involved in one of the greatest feats of exploration of the Pacific, and its subsequent opening up to ocean trade, when, in the eighteenth century, they sponsored the three voyages of an ex-merchant seaman—James Cook.

55 Overpage *Map of the Pacific, c1622, by Hessel Gerritsz, official cartographer to the Dutch East India company from 1617 to 1633, when he died. He incorporated the discoveries of the* Duyfken, *and shows Dutch East Indiamen in the wild seas off Cape Horn. (Bibliothèque Nationale, Paris)*

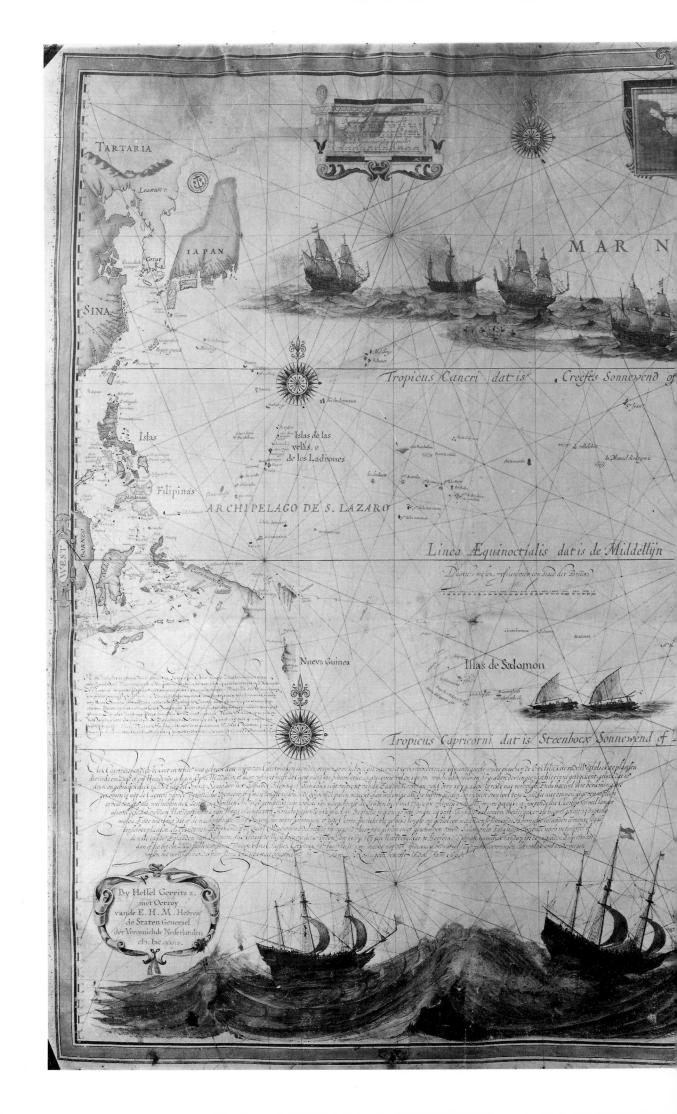

TARTARIA

SINA

IAPAN

Leequm r.

Corar

MAR N

Islas

Filipinas

Islas de las
velas, o
de los Ladrones

ARCHIPELAGO DE S. LAZARO

Tropicus Cancri dat is   Creeftis Sonnewend of

de Manuel Rodriguez

Linea Æquinoctialis dat is de Middellijn

Nueva Guinea

Illas de Salomon

Tropicus Capricorni dat is Steenbock Sonnewend of

By Heffel Gerrits z.
met Oectroy
vande E. H. M. Heeren
de Staten Generael
der Vereenichde Nederlanden
cb. bc xxxix.

BVTTONSBAY

QVIBIRA

LA FLORIDA

Balco Nuñez van
Balbao ontdecker
ende Adelantad van
de Zuydzee.

Hernand van Magal
lanes Portugeesch Rid
der ontdecker vande
Straet Magallanes.

Iacob le Maire Amsterdam
mer, ontdecker vande Pas
sage le Maire, ende Nieu
we Zuydzee.

Pueblos
de Moqui

Real del
Nuevo
Mexico

GOLFO DE
MEXICO

Governacion
de
Panuco

NVEVA
ESPANA

Iucatan

Honduras
Nicaragua

MAR DEL SVR

QVITO

PIRV

LIMA

COST

Sonnestandt

Sonnestandt

La primera que trocdava Magallanes
en este mar del Sur.

MAR PACIFICO

CHI
LE

OOST

CHAPTER FIVE

The Rig Develops

War at sea (1700–1800)

From 1689 to 1815 Britain fought seven wars which occupied 56 of those 125 years: five wars were started, and the other two ended, with France. It would appear that a principal cause of these wars was the competing interests of the empire-building nations as they struggled to gain control of the seas, ocean trade, and each other's colonies.

The Anglo-Dutch conflict ended when William of Orange (of Holland) became King of England in 1689. His succession to the English throne was one of the causes of the first English-French conflict. After every war, England became more powerful, gaining

56   *50-gun Dutch warship built in 1700 by 'an excellent master builder'. From* L'Art de Bâtir les Vaisseaux et d'en Perfectionner la Construction, *Amsterdam 1719. (Musée de la Marine, Paris)*

16th CENTURY/ 18th CENTURY

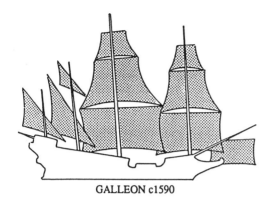

GALLEON c1590

GAFF MIZZEN c1750

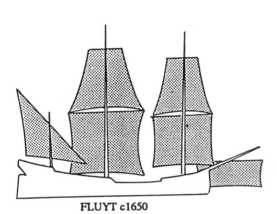

FLUYT c1650

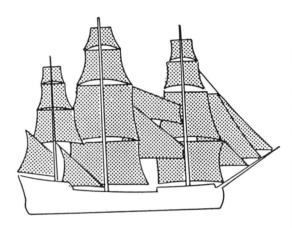

ROYALS c1790

LATEEN MIZZEN &
SPRITSAIL TOPSAIL
c1650

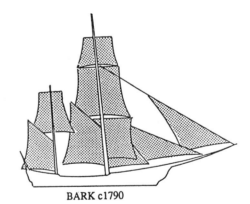

BARK c1790

SNOW c1790

57 *Sail Plans. (after Kihlberg, 1986)*

more overseas possessions from the nations which formed an alliance with France. After losing the Battle of Trafalgar in 1805, the French gave up the struggle, at least for a while, to become the major maritime power.

In England, during the eighteenth century, Cromwell's Navigation Acts were still in force whereby foreign ships were excluded from carrying English goods. In 1707 came the Act of Union with Scotland which allowed Scottish ships access to English trade and colonies. The Act of Union was the beginning of the climb that was to make Britain a maritime super power and to lead to Britain developing a huge colonial empire and adopting the title 'Great Britain'. The growth of English shipping in the eighteenth century was certainly phenomena: between 1686 and 1788 it quadrupled, increasing from 340,00 tons to over a million (see Ralph Davis, *The Rise of the English Shipping Industry*).

Of the other maritime nations at the turn of the eighteenth century, Holland still had almost exclusive rights over the Far East. France excluded all foreigners from her Canadian, Indian and West Indian colonies; Portugal was no longer a power; Spain prohibited trade with its vast Caribbean and American colonies, but was unable to control the enormous amount of smuggling that took place. Competing maritime nations—France, Sweden, Denmark, Holland and England—continued to develop their overseas trading companies, usually with government backing: some prospered, others crashed. Throughout the 1700s, the nations fought for control of the oceans and trade. As Ernest Fayle wrote (*A Short History of the World's Shipping Industry*):

It was a foolish game; but while everybody played it, those prospered most who could play it best. Every war left Holland, whether our [England's] enemy or our ally, a little more exhausted. Every war administered a check to the development of French commerce. Every peace treaty added to the markets open only to British traders and the ports open only to British ships. Canada and Newfoundland became British. The British East India Company found in the rapid growth of their possessions and spheres of influence in India a more than sufficient compensation for their exclusion from the Malay Archipelago [by Holland].

In India, the French and English East India Companies clashed. In 1751 Robert Clive of the HEIC took Arcot and in 1757, during the Seven Years War, he re-captured Calcutta. In 1763 the British had overrun the French trading post at Pondicherry and by 1769 the French East India Company was dissolved.

The Seven Years War (1756–1763) was a clear power struggle between France and Britain; fighting was mostly at sea with Britain usually the victor.

Britain gained Florida, part of Cuba, Manila in the Philippines and Canada. The only setback to Britain during the eighteenth century was the loss of her 13 American colonies and their important supplies of cheap timber. The colonies had almost unlimited supplies of fast-growing, softwood trees, and timber, forever in demand, was needed in enormous quantities to build Britain's evergrowing mercantile fleet. (It has been estimated that it took over a thousand trees to build a large HEIC Indiaman.) By 1776 about one third of the English merchant fleet was being built in the American colonies.

The American colonies revolted against the British Crown's authoritative rule and its attempts to tax the colonies so highly that they were almost unable to trade. Britain losing the American War of Independence (1775–1783) seems a foregone conclusion from historical hindsight, and her fate was sealed when England's old rivals, Spain, Holland and France, joined forces with America, to gain control of the English Channel and effectively blockade Britain. However, after the war Anglo-American trade continued, with Britain exporting manufactured goods, and exchanging slaves and gold from the Gold Coast in either the Caribbean or America for sugar, tobacco and timber.

After the French Revolution in 1789 Napoleon Bonaparte once again turned Europe into a battlefield and war continued at sea. But with the Battle of Trafalgar, where Nelson destroyed some two thirds of Napoleon's fleet before the other third could come into action, Britain's position as master of the sea was made secure for over 100 years.

Two unrelated events in the eighteenth century were to have important implications for the development of British merchant shipping in this and the following century. One, a new tonnage law, was to affect (adversely) ship-structure; the other, the creation of Lloyd's Society, was to have a positive effect on the development of the British shipping industry.

In the eighteenth century London coffee houses were the meeting place of intellectuals and merchants. Since Edward Lloyd's Coffee House was a gathering place of those involved in shipping, he took to posting up shipping intelligence. After Lloyd's death in 1713 his house continued to be the meeting-place of merchants, ship brokers and marine insurance underwriters. In 1734 the new owner of the coffee house published, for his clients, 'Lloyd's List', a weekly paper listing the movements of all ships involved in foreign trade that sailed in and out of the chief British ports. The 'List' was followed, in 1760, by a 'Lloyd's Register', a compilation of all ships insured by the underwriters. In 1774 many of the senior underwriters decided to move from the coffee house to the Royal Exchange where they set up a

Grave par F. le Gouaz d'après le Dessin de Mr Lescallier

58   *A 26-gun frigate from* Traité Pratique du Gréement des Vaisseaux et Autres Bâtiments de Mer, *1791. The spritsail topmast is here rigged below the bowsprit. (Musée de la Marine, Paris)*

new Lloyd's society. Ernest Fayle considers that Lloyd's played a crucial role in the development of British shipping:

It would be almost impossible to exaggerate the importance of these developments [the formation of Lloyd's] to the shipping industry. Without ample facilities for cheap, prompt, and safe marine insurance, and strict regulation of the underwriter's business, the vast commerce of Great Britain must have degenerated, especially in time of war, into a mere gamble, with the dice heavily loaded against both ship owners and shippers. (*A Short History of the World's Shipping Industry*)

Nowadays 'Lloyd's of London', the association of insurance underwriters, is quite distinct from 'Lloyd's Register of Shipping' which is one of the world's leading ship classification societies. First-class vessels are given the term '100 A1' (the 'A1' appeared in 1775) and a ship's classification acts as a guide to the underwriters.

The other event was the new tonnage law. Tonnage measurements had a history of being complicated and often confused, but were a necessary means of assessing a ship's size and cargo carrying ability. In the thirteenth century port dues were paid on the number of wine casks or tuns carried by a ship. England's Henry VII paid shipowners a gratuity (bounty) on vessels that were over 100 tuns in order to encourage cargo ship expansion and to have a pool of 'defensible merchantmen' he could call upon in time of war. Ships were then classified as 'tuns burden in merchant goods' (based upon the vessels' wine carrying capacity), or 'deadweight tunnage', which was burden plus a third. In 1582 the experiments of the Elizabethan shipwright Matthew Baker, with a ship's known cargo capacity relative to its measured volume, led to a bizarre formula for calculating burden tunnage:

$$\frac{\text{keel length} \times \text{depth} \times \text{breadth}}{97\frac{1}{2}}$$

It was never clearly stated where the hull's plank thickness was to be incorporated into these measurements, or from what points the length of the keel was to be taken (also a problem in the 1773 Act). By the seventeenth century 'tuns' had become 'tons'. In 1628 the divisor $97\frac{1}{2}$ became 100, but in 1642 it was changed to 94.

In order to rationalize tonnage measurements an Act of Parliament was passed in 1773. The burden (or burthen) tunnage, which was later known as Builders Old Measurement (BOM, BM or OM: 1773–1836), was defined in the 1773 Act as:

$$\frac{\text{'keel length factor'} \times \text{maximum beam} \times \text{a 'hold depth factor'}}{94}$$

'Keel length factor' (my terminology) was obtained by measuring, on deck, from the foreside of the stem to the aftside of the stern post and then subtracting 3/5 of the maximum beam. The 'hold depth factor' was obtained by halving the maximum beam $\frac{\text{Beam}}{2}$, the rationale for this was to avoid measuring the hold of a laden ship. The Americans followed the 1773 British Act of Parliament with a similar law in 1789, but used a divisor of 95. BOM stayed in use until a new Act of Parliament in 1836, although many shipbuilders continued to use it.

New Measure (NM: 1836–1854) defined tonnage in terms of an estimate of a cargo ship's internal capacity. Internal capacity was not very accurately measured since it was obtained from transverse sections taken at only three points along the length of a ship. A divisor of 92.4 replaced 94 to give the number of registered tons. New Measure stayed in force in Britain until a new Act of Parliament was passed in 1854.

George Moorsom, the Secretary of the Royal Commission, studied the problem of ship's tonnage before the 1854 Act was passed. The system of measurements became known as the 'Moorsom System', and is the basis of the tonnage measurements used today by the maritime nations of the world. The Americans passed a law in 1864 that followed the Moorsom system.

Today a ship's 'tonnage' has four different meanings:

Displacement tonnage, which is the weight of water displaced by the ship, in tons, where one ton equals 2240 lbs: it is the total weight of ship. A 'metric tunne' (1000 kg) has recently replaced the ton (2240 lbs).

Deadweight tonnage (DWT), is the difference in weight expressed in tons (i.e. the displacement tonnage) between the ship when it is loaded to its maximum and when it is empty.

Gross tonnage, which is expressed in units of 100 cubic feet, is a measurement of the enclosed, watertight volume of the ship.

Net tonnage, is also expressed in units of 100 cubic feet, and is the total enclosed volume (gross tonnage) minus that volume not used for carrying passengers or cargo—it is a measure of the carrying/earning capacity of the ship.

The important outcome of the 1773 Act was that a ship's depth was not taken into account when calculating tons burden, but was assumed to be half the breadth. In 1786 an Act was passed which stipulated that all ships over 15 tons had to be registered. Cargo dues, harbour fees and so on, were paid on tonnage measurements. Since hull depth was not penalized in the 1773 Act, shipowners built ocean traders to obtain maximum advantage when paying tonnage fees. The result was deep vessels with bluff bows and sterns. They were as unwieldy as they were slow, but they could carry cargoes well in excess of their registered tonnage: good for British shipowners' profit, but bad for the development of ship design.

Even British owners who wanted faster, more weatherly ships were almost forced, if they wanted to remain competitive, by the 1773 Act to operate slow, deep ships. These types of ships were common until the 1850s, when the NM and Moorsom system began to have an effect on ship design, and longer, faster, sleeker vessels were built. British shipowners were also safe from any faster, better designed foreign ships because Cromwell's Navigation Acts kept the competition at bay (see p 78).

Although warships and merchantmen had begun to diverge structurally since the middle of the seventeenth century, when ships with over 50 cannon began to fight in lines, differences between large ocean traders and warships were not great. Warships were more massively framed and planked than their merchant ship counterparts, as they continued to develop into floating gun-platforms: the 'wooden walls' of Nelson's navy. Warships had an open waist with light gangways running from aft to forward while, by 1744, most merchantmen needing to store and protect their cargoes, had a completely covered-in upper deck. HEIC ships, however, continuing to resemble warships, retained an open waist until almost the end of the century.

While the structure of large ocean traders, like the Indiamen of the HEIC, is well documented, there is less information on the smaller, more numerous ocean traders but they were undoubtedly lighter built, rounder bilged and carried fewer cannon than any similar-sized warships. A small merchantman in the early 1700s, such as the 170-ton *Mary Galley* which sailed to the East Indies, would have carried a six-sail rig on three masts, similar to the rig carried by the *Mayflower*.

Large HEIC ships were lighter built than any similar-sized warships: smaller Indiamen were built

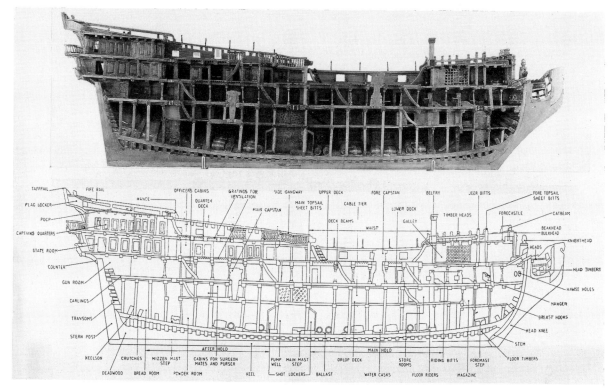

59 *Longitudinal section of a 69-gun ship c1750. (Science Museum, London)*

like 'frigates', a class of ship carrying between 20–44 cannon, while larger HEIC ships approximated 'two-deckers'.

Three masts: square sails and Indiamen

There were no major changes in hull structure during the eighteenth century, although hulls gradually shed the expensive, elaborate carvings that had been so popular in the large ships of the seventeenth century. There was an increasing shortage of timber for building merchantmen and, towards the end of the century, the use of iron caused some changes in hull construction. Large ships became larger, and all traders tended to become straighter and more U-shaped, although tumble-home still existed. Hull structure continued to be influenced by the successful Dutch *fluyts*, as well as (adversely) by the 1773 British tonnage acts.

During the eighteenth century there were major developments in the rigging of ships, which led to more efficiency and smaller crews, much to shipowners' liking. Shipowners could increase profits by operating larger ships with larger holds and smaller crews—the most expensive recurrent cost of operating a ship. By 1700 most traders over 60 tons were three-masted, but by 1750 three-masted ships were usually only those above 200 tons. By 1725 most three-masted traders carried the new fore and aft sails. By the end of the century ships of over 400 tons would carry many fore and aft sails and often

square 'royals' above the topgallants on all three masts (see D. MacGregor's *Merchant Sailing Ships*).

To the landsman the rig of a square-rigged sailing ship appears as a mass of ropes, blocks, spars and sails, but there was a structural simplicity, which is elegant in both form and function. A merchant seaman going from one ship to another would quickly learn the position of the sheets, tacks, braces and halliards. Each square sail has a basic set of ropes and one or more yards, and the set is repeated as the numbers of square sails increased.

(Today the term 'ship' usually implies any sea-going or coastal vessel and that is how the term is generally applied throughout this book. However 'ship' can be more specifically used to mean a vessel that is square-rigged on all its masts. Hence there are terms like 'rigged as a ship' or 'ship-rigged' or a 'full-rigged ship', all of which mean a vessel with square sails on all three (or more) masts. Falconer's Marine Dictionary of 1769 states that 'ship' was particularly applied to a vessel with three masts, each mast composed of lower, top, topgallant and royal masts.)

Since the late sixteenth century masts had had removable topmasts which resulted in the mainmast being called the 'lower mast', and the mainsail being sometimes referred to as the 'lower sail'. In the eighteenth century the mainsail, like all square sails, was attached to its yard with light ropes known as 'robands' (also 'robins or rope-bands') that went right round the yard and, when furled, the sail was kept in place by rope lashings or 'gaskets' that also went

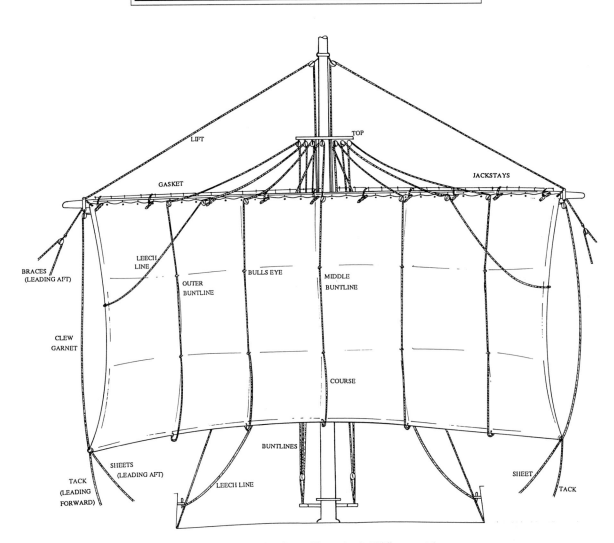

60 *A square sail. (after an illustration in Kihlberg, 1986)*

round the yard. A yard was fixed to the mast at its midpoint by a 'parrel' which was designed to allow the yard to be angled when pulled by the 'braces' that were attached to both ends of a yard. When trying to drive a 'square-rigged ship' to windward, the braces are used to swing the yard into the wind, and the leading edge of the sail is flattened by tensioning the 'bowlines'. Bowlines were used from the earliest days of square sails, and are attached to the middle of the leading edge of the sail, via a number of light ropes known as 'bridles'. The bowline is led forward to a block on the end of the bowsprit, which allows the leading edge of the square sail to be pulled into the wind. The longer the bowsprit, the further the sail can be pulled towards the fore and aft line of the ship, and the closer the ship would sail to the wind.

By hanging square sails from yards, and setting yards transversely across the ship on a number of masts, thousands of square feet of sail can be set: the 'square sails' of a square rigger are the most efficient downwind sailing rig yet devised. On a three-masted ship, the yard of the foremast's lower sail is known as

the 'foreyard', and on the mainmast it is the 'mainyard'. On the mizzen, where the lateen topsails had been replaced by square topsails since c1650, the lower mizzen topsail yards were known as crojacks or crossyards (see p 103). 'Lifts' are used to support the ends of yards, and yards are hauled up the mast by the 'haulyards' or halliards.

From the lowest corners, or 'clews', of the square sail, 'sheets' are led aft, while 'tacks' are led forward. Sheets and tacks are used to control the lower corners of the sail. To reduce sail in strong winds, sails are pulled up to the yards by the 'buntlines', which travel over the forward face of the sail, and by 'clewlines' or 'clew garnets' which pass to the clews of the sail.

A spritsail, when set below the bowsprit, had the same rigging as other square sails, except that the yard would be pulled out along the bowsprit by a halliard (rather than up a mast). The spritsail yard was attached to the bowsprit by a parrel, supported by lifts and controlled by braces. There were no tacks, as there was no place to lead them to, but the sail did have sheets, clewlines and buntlines. The

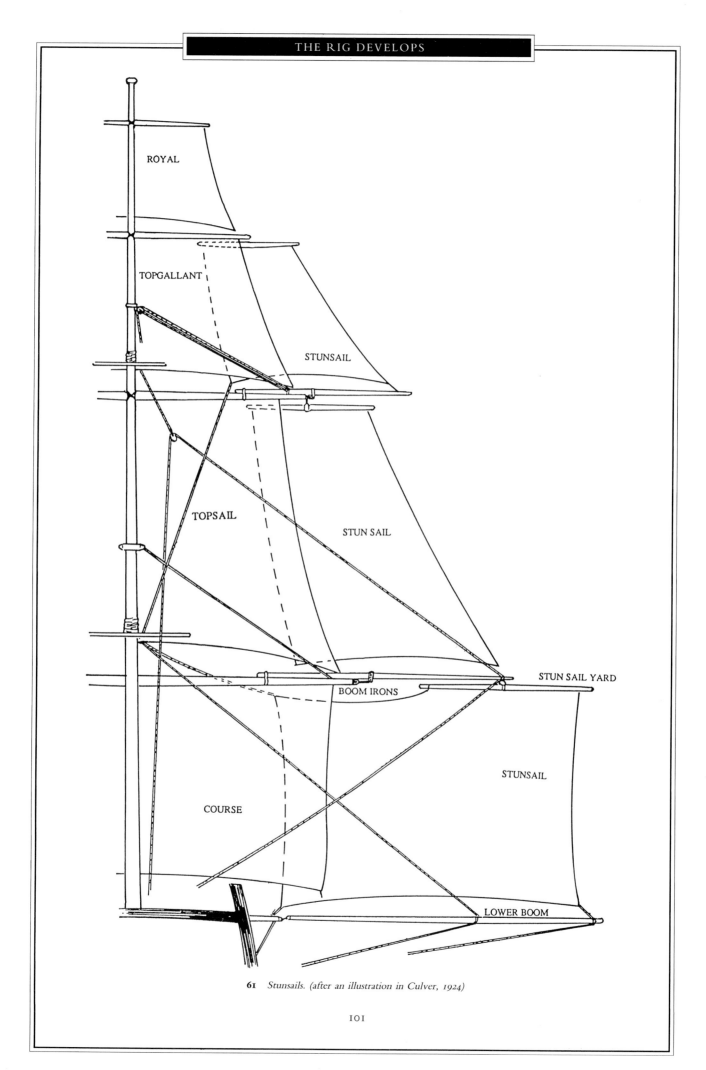

61 *Stunsails. (after an illustration in Culver, 1924)*

spritsail topsail would have been rigged like any other square sail and set on a spritsail topmast—the peculiar seventeenth and early eighteenth century mast set at the end of the bowsprit.

In the eighteenth century 'studding sails' or 'stunsails' began to be used more frequently than in the previous century. They had been employed at least from the middle of the sixteenth century, and are mentioned in *A Treatise on Rigging*, published c1625, as 'Studing sayles wch ar set on ether side of yor fore and mayne sail'.

Stunsails were enormous square sails carried beyond the edges ('leeches') of the largest square sails to increase sail area when winds were light. 'Stunsail booms' were connected to the front, or the rear, of the yards by 'boom irons', which supported the stunsail booms and allowed them to slide in and out. The lowest stunsail sheets were made fast to a 'bumkins' (small booms) that projected from the ship's side at deck level. By the end of the eighteenth century stunsails were carried from at least the foresail yard, and the fore and main topsail yards. (R.C. Anderson's *Rigging of Ships* has further details).

Models are a great help to the maritime historian when studying ship evolution, (for example, C.S. Laird Clowes' book *Sailing Ships* is based on ship models at the London Science Museum), and model making from 1650's onward became a fine art. The earliest model in the Greenwich Maritime Museum, London, is dated 1655. But historians treat ship models with caution, as the builders, often sailors, were sometimes more concerned with nautical aestheticism than historical accuracy! Nevertheless, ships models from 1650 onwards are an important primary source for observing ship evolution, and are often used in conjunction with contemporary paintings and treatises on naval architecture. From these sources it can be seen that one of the most important rigging changes that occurred during the late 1600s and early 1700s was the increasing use of fore sails, and aft sails, jibs and staysails on the large three-masted ocean traders. Jibs and staysails improved enormously a ship's ability to sail to windward and have a further advantage in that steering is easier, as the trader becomes better 'balanced'. In addition, when compared to square sails, fore and aft sails were easier to handle: men did not always have to go aloft as jibs and staysails could be worked from the ship's deck.

In the early eighteenth century staysails were laced to the stays with light lines that crossed the lay of the rope and hauled-up by halliards. Ship models of this and later periods show staysails set on topsail mast stays (the fore and main topmast staysails), the lower mast stays of the fore and mainmasts (lower fore and mainmast staysails) and on the mizzenmast stays

(mizzen staysails). About 1760, staysails not set from the foremast were frequently converted from their original, triangular shapes to four-sided, but still fore and aft, sails. A 'bobstay', which was led from the end of the bowsprit to the ship's stem, appeared in the late seventeenth century, and acted as a counter-force against the upward pull exerted by the forestay, the fore topmast stay and the fore topgallant stay, as well as any sails rigged on these stays. To obtain efficient, well-set staysails, ships' stays have to be well tensioned.

In the early eighteenth century, the bowsprits of large traders were rigged with a jib, two fore staysails, a spritsail and a topmast spritsail. The rigging must have been indescribably complicated to operate and soon, by c1720, large vessels were sailing without the awkward spritsail topsail set on the spritsail topmast. The sail was still kept, however, but moved below the bowsprit and set from a yard attached to a new spar—the 'jib boom'.

Foremast staysails were then made fast to the bowsprit, but the jib was attached to the new jib boom. At first the jib was set 'flying', that is without being laced to a jib stay, as the 'flying jib'. But a jib stay was soon permanently rigged and, on large ocean traders, a second jib, an un-stayed flying jib, would be set off the end of the bowsprit. The tack of the flying jib would be attached to an extra-long jib boom or, sometimes, on an additional forward-leading spar, the 'flying jib boom'. About 1795, in order to counteract the upward pull of the jib(s) on the jib boom, a 'martingale' rope (later chain) was led down, and through, a small, seaward-pointing spar which was attached to the end of the bowsprit and known as the 'martingale boom' or, more arrestingly, the 'dolphin striker' (see below, David Steel's 20 gun ship, Figs. 64–66).

Another major technological development that occurred around the middle of the eighteenth century was when the lateen mizzen sail, or mizzen course, that had existed on three-masted ships for some 300 years, was replaced by a 'gaff' sail. A spar, the 'gaff', extended the head of a rectangular fore and aft sail, while the bottom edge (or 'foot') of the sail was without a spar or boom. The part of the long spar which went forward of the mizzen mast of the laten-rigged mizzen sail was, at first, retained on some ships, where it could be used for damage replacement, especially in warships. Contemporary paintings of large ships, c1760–70, show a long lateen yard with the luff of the reduced sail lashed to the mizzen mast (see Fig. 63). But a long yard, swinging around on the mizzen mast must have been very cumbersome and, by c1800, it disappeared from most ships.

Ocean traders, if sailing in light airs, or downwind for long periods, would often increase the size of the

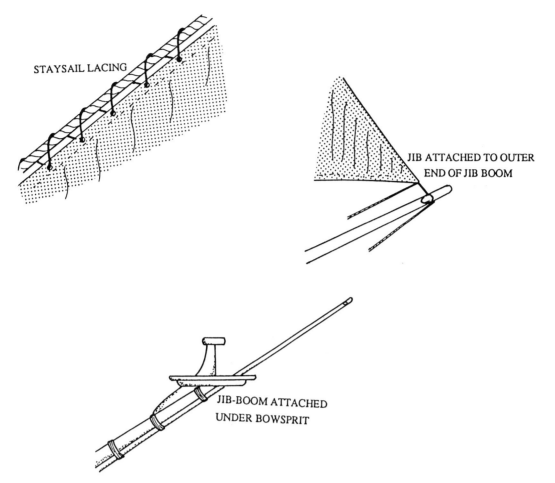

STAYSAIL LACING

JIB ATTACHED TO OUTER
END OF JIB BOOM

JIB-BOOM ATTACHED
UNDER BOWSPRIT

62   *Staysails and jibs. (after illustrations in Anderson, 1927)*

gaff sail by extending the gaff with a small spar, and then flying a 'ring-tail' sail off the spar. Later the boomless-gaff mizzen sail could be completely replaced by a larger, fair-weather sail, the 'spanker' (known as the 'driver' in a British warship). This sail was set on a boom and the foot could then be pushed out over the ship's side ('boomed out') so as to catch more wind.

Thus, at the beginning of the eighteenth century, typical large ocean traders had a spritsail and a spritsail topsail on the bowsprit. There were up to three square sails on both the foremast and mainmast: courses, topsails and topgallants. On the mizzen there might have been a lateen course, but the seventeenth-century lateen-mizzen topsail would have been replaced by a square mizzen topsail and a crojack yard. By the end of the eighteenth century three-masted traders had developed into fully-rigged ships: the spritsail topmast had disappeared; there were staysails on the stays, jibs on the jib boom and perhaps on the flying jib booms, 'gaff sails' on the mizzen mast, and square sails on all three masts. 'Royals' made a reappearance c1780 and were found even on small traders, set above fore and main

topgallants and sometimes about the square, mizzen topgallants. It was often the job of the youngest and lightest crewman to go aloft and furl these.

In 1794 David Steel published his *Elements and Practice of Rigging and Seamanship* and, although a treatise on naval architecture, his drawings showing the rigging of a 20-gun warship would also apply to a well-found ocean trader.

One of the great classes of three-masted, eighteenth-century ocean traders were the ships of the East India Companies (e.g. HEIC and VOC)— the East Indiamen. They resembled warships and were often mistaken for third and fourth rates or frigates. Throughout the eighteenth century, HEIC ships increased in size (see J. Sutton's *Lords of the East*, appendices). At the beginning of the century, company ships were between 300–400 tons; but by 1755, although ships were actually bigger, they were only recorded as 499 tons; because if they exceeded 500 tons they were required to carry a chaplain! When this rule was relaxed, 18 years later, ships suddenly increased in size and were recorded at between 750–800 tons.

During the eighteenth century, the HEIC gained a

63 *A rig of a merchant ship taken from Falconer's* Shipwreck, *c1769. The luff of the mizzen sail is lashed to the mizzen mast. (Science Museum, London)*

monopoly of the India (and eventually China) trade. Company ships became larger as trade expanded and traders pushed further eastwards to China to load the new exotic freights: tea and porcelain. In 1793 there were 40 ships of 800 tons designated for the India trade and 36 over 1000 tons for the China trade. Some giant 1200 and 1400 ton ocean traders were also built for the China trade.

64 **Opposite top** *Square sails and driver (the driver is set from a boom on the mizzen mast), from David Steel's* Twenty Gun Ship. *(University of Newcastle upon Tyne Library)*

65 **Opposite bottom** *Fore and aft Sails, from David Steel's* Twenty Gun Ship. *(University of Newcastle upon Tyne Library)*

66   *HEIC's East Indiaman,* The Earl Balcarras, *with starboard stunsails set, and spanker on the mizzen. (Science Museum, London)*

Although HEIC ships looked like warships, it was company policy never to carry more than 30 cannon even on their largest ships. The largest, 1000-ton plus Indiamen very much resembled two-decker warships, and the Crown, when hard-pressed, stood them in the line as third or fourth rate warships. But company ships were lighter-built, had larger holds with flatter floors, and were less well armed.

By the end of the century HEIC ships, and most large merchantmen, had planked in the waist to form a continuous deck running from forecastle to quarter deck. The deck had evolved from a temporary connecting walkway, built between forecastle and quarter deck. In British warships, however, the top gun-deck was left open from the 1750s until around the 1830s.

As the century developed an acute shortage of timber, especially of oak, was felt by British shipowners and builders, due to the constant increase in the size and number of ocean traders, and to continued war-losses. Besides importing both ships and softwoods from the North American colonies, owners moved from oak, and experimented with elm, ash and fir. The HEIC also began using ships built in Indian shipyards with a wood that was far superior to most European hardwoods: teak. By 1775 the Bombay shipyards were as good as, if not better than, any in Britain. The Parsee yard built the *Earl Balcarras*, launched at Bombay in 1815, and this ship was considered to be one of the largest and finest traders ever built for the HEIC. Although the painting (Fig. 66) shows the trader as 1488 tons, David MacGregor, in *Merchant Sailing Ships*, quotes the *Earl Balcarras* as being 1417 tons BOM, with a keel length of 176 ft 8 in. and breadth of 43 ft 3 in.

In 1804 David Steel published *Elements and Practice of Naval Architecture* and illustrates a 1257-ton East Indiaman which has, like all large HEIC ships, the upper deck covered-in between the forecastle and the quarterdeck. Aft, there are two tiers of windows and no galleries, while there is a

small raised forecastle forward. Steel describes the 'Force In War' of the Indiaman as twenty-six 18-pounders on the middle deck, ten 18-pounders on the upper deck and, in the after ports, two eight-foot as stern chasers. The ship resembles a two-decked warship but, as Steel's engraving shows, there are no gun ports on the lower deck. However, it was a company policy to paint dummy ports on the hull (no doubt to frighten off would-be adversaries) as seen in the contemporary painting of the Earl Balcarras.

Smaller East Indiamen, of c500 tons, were like naval frigates. British frigates probably appeared around the 1750s; they were speedy and ideal for attacking, as well as protecting, merchant ships, and probably evolved from a two-decked ship which, on its lower deck, had only a few cannon but was oar-powered through special ports. The ports were sealed and frigates soon only carried guns on their continuous upper deck; they never stood in the battle line.

In Stockholm in 1768, Fredrick af Chapman published a magnificent portfolio of ship designs and attempted to classify contemporary merchant ships into five classes (see below). One of his classes was based on the frigate, and he gives an example of an 'English East Indiaman'. Laird Clowes (*Sailing Ships*) has also written: 'In all essentials of design the East Indiamen of 1773 were—and the smaller ones remained until the end of the century—frigates with increased passenger accommodation.' According to Laird Clowes, Chapman's 676-ton East Indiaman was very much like a 32-gun frigate of the period, 'with the addition of a short poop, with its accompanying second tier of stern and quarter-windows and stern-walk'.

West Indiamen were always smaller than East Indiamen—they had less far to go and kinder seas. In the 1770s they averaged c400 tons, about half the size of the average East Indiaman. Chapman shows a West Indiaman in his portfolio, which is not at all

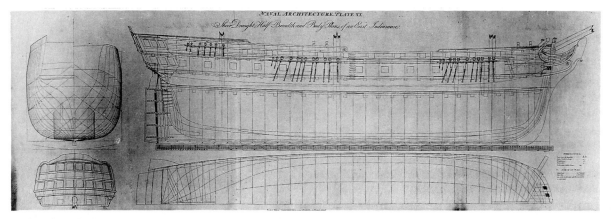

67 *David Steel's lines plan of an East Indiaman, 1804: length between the perpendiculars—165 ft 6½ in.; length of keel for tonnage—134 ft; breadth extreme—42 ft; depth in hold—17 ft; tons burthen—1257. (University of Newcastle upon Tyne Library)*

ENGLISH EAST INDIAMAN

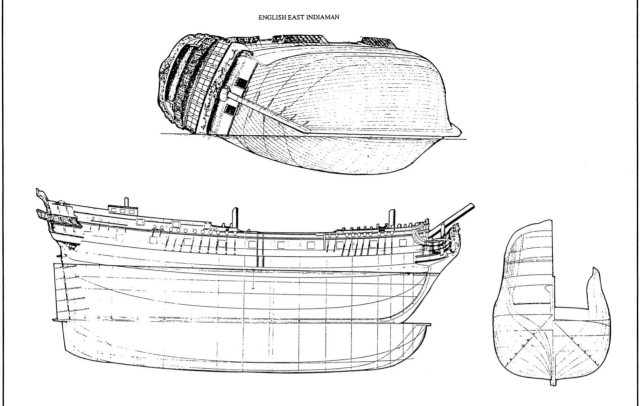

68 *Fredrick af Chapman's lines plan of an East Indiaman, dimensions: length between perpendiculars of stem and stern post—129¼ ft; breadth moulded—33¼ ft; draught of water—19⅓ ft (i.e. 129¼ × 33¼ × 19⅓). (University of Newcastle upon Tyne Library)*

ENGLISH WEST INDIAMAN

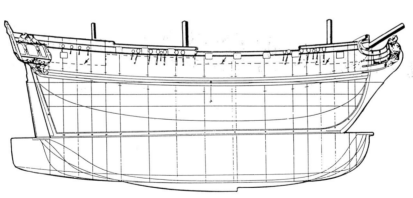

69 *Fredrick af Chapman's lines plan of a West Indiaman, dimensions: 97 × 27 × 15¼. (University of Newcastle upon Tyne Library)*

like the naval frigates, having an irregular upper deck at four different levels. Later in the century, in line with all merchant sailing vessels, West Indiamen became larger, although probably never exceeding 600 tons, with a continuous upper deck, and at this time also resembled small frigates (eg. the 544-ton West Indiaman depicted in Steel's 1804 *Naval Architecture*).

70 *The West Indiaman,* Medina, *1811. Setting the starboard stunsails; a spanker on mizzen; and, like* The Earl Balcarras, *royals are set on all three masts. There is an entry in Lloyds Register for 1812 under 'Medina': ship-rigged, hull sheathed with copper, 469 tons and working between London and Jamaica. From an oil painting formerly in the Science Museum. (Science Museum, London)*

Both West and East Indiamen were three-masted and rigged with the new fore and aft sails. Although these fore and aft sails were one of the major steps forward in ship technology, the main downwind power units for all ocean-going merchant ships remained their square sails. Along the trade wind routes, with the wind aft of the beam, square sails are the most efficient. As ocean trade evolved and the wind systems of the world became better understood, the sails of merchant sailing ships became highly sophisticated engines capable, by the 1850s, of powering traders up to speeds of 20 knots and driving them over 300 miles in 24 hours.

Other important technological advances which improved eighteenth-century ship efficiency—and shipowners' profitability—were the invention of the the round-headed rudder, the ship's steering wheel and copper sheathing.

In 1757 Gabriel Snodgrass was appointed the HEIC's Surveyor in England. He was responsible for many innovations in HEIC ships that were later used in British warships. In 1779 he introduced round-headed rudders into company ships, and in 1791 iron knees, and diagonal ties to increase longitudinal strength.

Round-headed rudders were a particularly important innovation, and were formed by building up the forward part of the rudder top or 'head' and bringing it through a cut-away stern post. The round-headed rudder was a clear advance in ship design as it required a smaller helm, or rudder, port (see p 89) which could be more effectively closed by the rudder cloth, or the rudder cloth dispensed with altogether. Thus ships were less prone to being swamped by following seas and the rudder and tiller were more protected.

The ship's wheel quickly made its appearance in large, three-masted ships in the early part of the eighteenth century (see also R. and R.C. Anderson, *The Sailing Ship* and A.McGowan, *The Ship* Vol. 4). An English ship model, dated 1703, has a winch barrel positioned athwartships on deck. The barrel has a handle at each end and ropes, which run around the middle of the barrel, are connected to the ship's tiller. There are other models of a similar period where the barrel winch is absent, but which have a position for a whipstaff and a ship's wheel. It could not have been long before it was realized that a more efficient steering system could be made by turning the winch barrel 90 degrees. Removing the handles at each end, compressing the barrel, and adding spokes to the rim, would give the familiar ship's steering wheel. Steering ropes running from ships' wheels, which appeared in models in 1706, were connected to tillers in the same way as they had been for the early experiments with barrel winches. The ship's wheel, although still requiring relieving blocks and tackles to be attached to the tiller in heavy weather, could now be placed on deck. This was a huge advantage: the helmsman could now directly communicate with the deck officer, anticipate danger, see the sails and know from which direction the wind blew. In rough seas more helmsmen could be used on the wheel to help control the rudder and do some of the work of the relieving blocks. (It must have been difficult to get more than one man on a whipstaff, or two on the fore and aft barrel winch.) On Britain's first ironclad, *HMS Warrior*, as many as 16 men could hang on to the spokes of its enormous wheels. And above all, with a ship's wheel in his hands a helmsman could 'feel' a ship. The spokes gave fine control over rudder movements and soon copper-sheathed ships were making even faster passages for they deviated less from their compass courses. (also see R. and R.C. Anderson, *The Sailing Ship*; and A. McGowan, *The Ship*, Vol. 4)

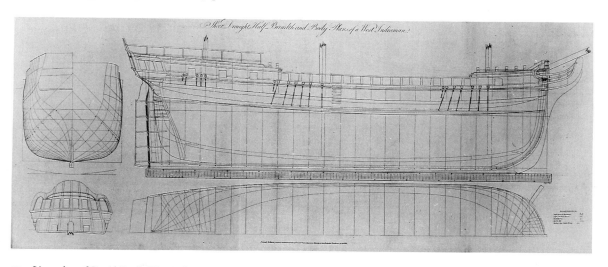

71 *Lines plan of David Steel's West Indiaman, 1804. Dimensions: length between perpendiculars 129 ft 9 in.; length of keel for tonnage 100 ft; breadth extreme 32 ft; depth in hold 14 ft 9 in.; tons burthen 544. (University of Newcastle upon Tyne Library)*

72   HMS Warrior's wheels. (M.W. Marshall)

A

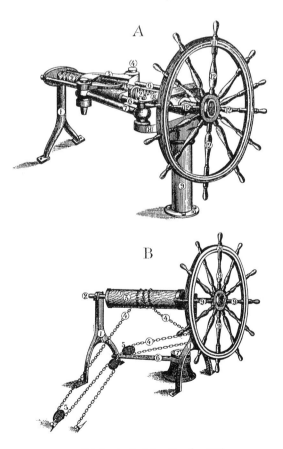

B

73   Ship's wheels. (after Paasch, 1890)

Sheathing the underwater section of ships' hulls with copper allowed ships to stay longer at sea and make faster passages. The thin copper sheets kept hulls free longer from marine growth and protected their underwater planking against attacks by the boring worm, *teredo navalis*: in the tropics, captains were more frightened that their ships would be literally eaten by the teredo worm, than they were of sailing into the eye of a hurricane. The problem became particularly acute as traders spent more time in warm waters: English ships were particularly vulnerable because the worm appeared to have a preference for Sussex oak! Early attempts to resist attack and prevent the build-up of marine organisms, such as laying a mixture of hair and tar on the hull before over-planking, were never really effective. Metallic copper poisoned marine growth and was a barrier to worm attack, but galvanic interaction between the iron fastenings and the copper plate created serious corrosion problems and the copper sheets would sometimes even detach themselves from the hull. Better attachment to the planking was obtained by using heavy-duty paper to insulate the iron fastening from the sheath but this was only partially effective. But by then the efficiency of the copper sheath had been clearly demonstrated, and successful attachments were soon obtained using nails made of hardened copper or copper-zinc mixes. By 1778 all British warships had copper clad bottoms, and it was not long before merchantmen were also clad.

Two masts: brig, snow, bilander and schooner

The eighteenth century was the age of the 'two-masted ship'. These ships were far more numerous than three-masted traders and carried most of the ocean trade. Their bluff bows and sterns, and U-shaped hulls maximized cargo space, and their new fore and aft rigs, requiring smaller crews, resulted in increased economies for their owners. As the century progressed, and sail handling became easier with the new rig, it was found that two masts could do the work of three on ships up to 200 or even 300 tons. (see D. MacGregor, *Merchant Sailing Ships*)

This new class of single-decked, two-masted ships were known as *sloops* and were classed, in size, below frigates. Two types of sloops were the 'snows' and 'brigantines'. Snows, which appeared in the 1670s, were square-rigged on both masts but had a gaff mizzen known as a 'trysail' set on a special

74 *Snow-rigged sloop, c1720. The second mast has a square sail; behind this mast is the gaff-rigged snow mast. (Science Museum, London)*

'trysail, or snow mast' placed just behind the main mast. They also had a square sail which could be set on the mainmast in front of the snow masts. Snows were to be seen more often on the ocean routes than brigantines, which appeared c1700. Initially, brigantines were square rigged on two masts but it was not long before the square mainsail on the mainmast was replaced with a boom-footed gaff sail. Around the middle of the eighteenth century the term brigantine was being abbreviated to 'brig'. Throughout the century brigs and snows, in keeping with most ships, gradually increased in size. Around 1710 they were c60 tons, but by the 1770s brigs and snows of 150 tons were common.

The term 'brigantine' gradually went out of use in the eighteenth century, replaced by its diminutive 'brig'. 'Brigantine' returned in the nineteenth century but was often used loosely. Nowadays it is usually applied to a two-masted ship, square rigged on the foremast and fore- and aft-rigged on the mainmast— sometimes referred to as an 'hermaphrodite brig'.

Another two-masted ship was the *bilander*, but it is probable that this ship, mainly a coaster ('by-lander') was extinct, at least in Britain, by the beginning of the nineteenth century. The bilander had, on its mainmast, a trapezoidal, fore and aft mainsail set from a long yard which went forward of the mast.

The *schooner* was another two-masted ship that carried gaff sails on both masts, and later these vessels were built with three, four, five, six and even seven masts. The huge gaff sails carried by these massive, multi-masted schooners were too heavy to be worked by men alone. They needed steam power to drive the hauling-up winches, and so only appeared in the nineteenth century. Early schooners, gaff-rigged with one or two headsails, appeared in Holland in the 1650s and in England c1700. They were used much in England's American colonies, brought there from Holland and England, as they were smaller, cheaper to build and required fewer men to crew than traditional three-masted, square-rigged ships. Beautiful, fast ships, with fine hulls and fore and aft sails, they could sail closer to the wind than any square rigged ocean trader, which could probably only manage to sail with the wind a point or two forward of the beam.

An interesting variation in schooner rig was the 'topsail schooner', where square sails were carried above gaff mainsails. The rig's origins remain obscure, but the topsails were probably left over from a square-rigged, three-masted ship when the new fore and aft gaff sails replaced the square sailed courses. Topsail schooners were employed on the transatlantic routes as the square topsails were better suited to the downwind trade wind passages. Schooners without square topsails were coastal traders, used where winds were less steady and predictable than on the open seas.

Chapman's merchantmen

In 1768 the Swedish Master Shipwright, Fredrick af Chapman published his famous *Architectura Navalis Mercatoria* in Stockholm. A beautifully drawn portfolio of mid-eighteenth-century ship designs, it is an outstanding primary source of the form of ocean traders. He included a page showing a number of ships under full sail, including a three-masted frigate with the new gaff mizzen, a two-masted snow with its snow mast, and a two-masted brig. A bilander shows the mainmast with its long yard (sometimes known as the 'crossjack') and above this a barren yard to hold out the clews of the topsail; it has a foresail, and topsails and topgallants are carried on both the foremast and mainmast. The schooner shown has a topsail on the foremast.

Chapman identified five classes of merchant ship: frigat(e) built, hagboat, pink, cat(t) and bark. Within these classes, merchantmen could be either 'ship-rigged' or rigged like a brigantine, snow, schooner or sloop. During most of the eighteenth century ships were classified according to the structure of the hull and it was only in the next century, with the marked increase in numbers and types of sailing ships on the ocean routes, that the rig was used to identify a class of ship. David MacGregor, in his *Merchant Sailing Ships* (1775–1815), compares and extends Chapman's five hull classification to include a sixth class, the flute, 'although it is not yet clear if, for example, all British merchant hull types will fit into these six classes'. (David MacGregor, personal communication).

In the eighteenth century a ship's stern and 'tuck' were useful for hull identification and therefore its class. There were round and square sterns, and tucks. A tuck was the way in which either the ends of the bottom planks or the lower whales were ended at the ship's stern. A 'round tuck' was a classic feature of Dutch *fluyts,* (see p 80 ff) where the planks and whales curved right round to the sternpost. A 'square tuck' was where the bottom planks and lower whales ended on a transom.

Laird Clowes wrote in *Sailing Ships*:

At the beginning of the seventeenth century all English ships were built with the square tuck, or transom stern, which had been introduced in the early part of the previous century. This method of constructing a stern remained in general use amongst Dutch and other continental nations for many years but in England it was gradually replaced by the round tuck, in which the planking was curved round the quarters and carried right into the rabbet of the stern-post.

BRIG

FRIGATE OR SHIP

BILANDER

SNOW

SCHOONER

KETCH

75 *Chapman's traders under sail. (University of Newcastle upon Tyne Library)*

Early in the seventeenth century British ships had developed a tuck that was more round than square, the 'modified round tuck'. This form of tuck allowed sterns to be constructed more easily and was eventually used by the other maritime nations. But not all ships had round tucks; many were still built with square tucks.

In the early part of the eighteenth century, the term 'ship-rigged' was usually applied to vessels which had square sails on all (three) masts: snows were considered to be more 'ship-rigged' than the brigs. Before c1750 the term 'bark' was the general name for a ship, as 'vessel' is today. But in the latter part of the eighteenth century bark (or 'barque' as it was later written), increasingly meant a three-masted vessel with no square sails on the mizzen mast (that is the fore and main masts were still 'square rigged', while the mizzen mast has a gaff sail, the spanker, and perhaps a gaff topsail). 'Ship-rigged' or a 'full-rigged ship' continued to be applied to vessels with square sails on three (or more) masts. A full rigged ship would still carry jibs, staysails and a gaff mizzen sail, below its square mizzen top sail.

There is a useful table in D. MacGregor's *Merchant Sailing Ships, 1775–1815*, summarizing in more detail the main features of Chapman's classification.

Class 1
Frigate. These three masted ships showed many of the advances in rig technology that had taken place by the 1760s: jib boom and flying jib, staysails, and lateen mizzen replaced by a gaff sail. Frigates were ships with a square tuck, and the 'counter' (the inwardly curved part of the stern) overhung the rudder, allowing galleries—favourite walking places for the ships' officers. They had beak-heads (the small platform at the fore part of the upper deck) and figure-heads—ornamental figures on the continuation of the ship's stem. They were fast and were used as privateers as well as merchantmen. Plate XXXI of Chapman's *Architectura Navalis Mercatoria* shows a frigate which was a 40-cannon privateer.

76 *Frigate. Dimensions: $156\frac{1}{8} \times 39\frac{1}{4} \times 18$. A 40-gun privateer. 'Frigate rigged'. Chapman's Plate XXXI. (University of Newcastle upon Tyne Library)*

FRIGATE

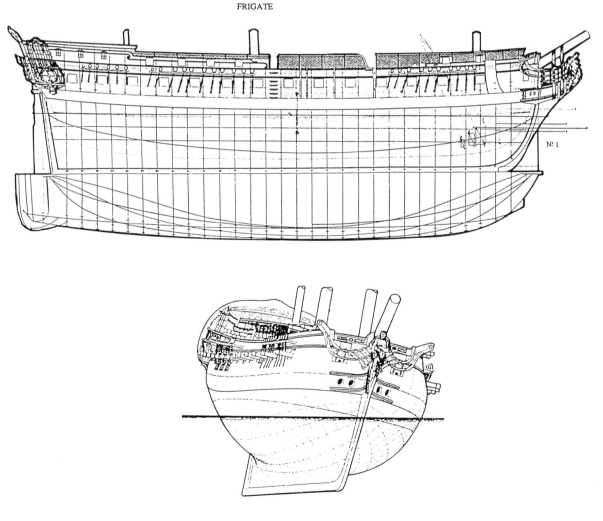

Class 2

Hagboat. These were probably developed from *fluyts* and, like the fluyt, had a round tuck stern. But, apart from their sterns, they were more like frigates and generally had beak-heads and figure-heads. Plate 66 shows a frigate and a hagboat compared. Apart from their sterns, these two classes of ships can be seen to be very similar, the hagboat showing the more developed U-shaped hull of an ocean trader.

Class 3

Pink. Like the hagboat, pinks were probably developed from the Dutch fluyts, and kept the fluyt's bluff-bow and round-stern. They differed by being generally slimmer and by having beak-heads. English ships were sometimes described as having 'pink-sterns'.

Class 4

Cat. These were probably also developed from the fluyt and showed the typical eighteenth-century evolution from the fluyt by having a reduced tumble home (the hulls were less pear-shaped) and broader stems and sterns. They lacked a beak-head and figure-head and their quarters often projected. (The quarter is the part of the ship's side which lay towards the stern, ... [between the] aftermost end of the main chains and the sides of stern, where it was terminated by the 'quarter pieces'. Falconer's *Marine Dictionary*, 1769.) Chapman's Plates XV and XVI show two cats, one viewed from the starboard quarter and the other lying on its side, out of the water. Plate XV clearly shows the cat's full, round stern with its quarter piece running forward from under the stern windows, before reversing and ending at the sternpost. There is a small, square, double-tiered stern above the the rudder port. Plate XVI shows a ship with very bluff bows. Both of Chapman's Plates show how cats were designed to carry the maximum possible amounts of cargo. Cats were probably the eighteenth-century ship that was most like the seventeenth-century fluyt and they were much used by the Danes. Scandinavian *katschip* were pole masted (single mast), so topsails and their yards could be hauled up from the deck.

Class 5

Bark. Chapman's barks had similar square tucks to his frigates, but British barks probably had the modified round tuck. Barks, unlike frigates, were not generally fitted with figure-heads and beak-heads, and were more U-shaped in cross-section, with flat floors designed to dry out at low tide when they were beached to load and unload cargoes. Northeast English barks made ideal colliers, and these ships were used by James Cook in his extensive explorations of the Pacific Ocean.

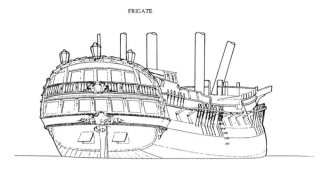

FRIGATE

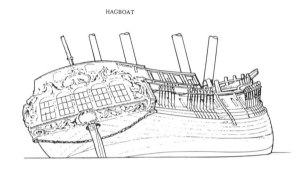

HAGBOAT

77 *Frigate and Hagboat. Upper: Frigate, Chapman's Plate III. Dimensions: 136 × 36 × 19, 761 tons. Lower: Hagboat, Chapman's Plate X. Dimensions: 132½ × 34¼ × 18¼, 716 tons. Both ship-rigged. (University of Newcastle upon Tyne Library)*

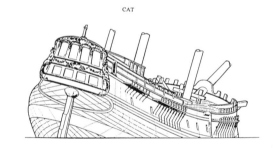

CAT

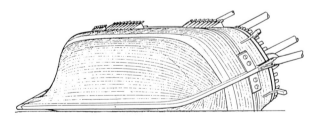

78 *Cat. Upper: Chapman's Plate XV, stern view of a Cat. Dimensions: 151¼ × 37½ × 19⅓, 1097 tons. Lower: Chapman's Plate XVI, Cat viewed from the bow. Dimensions: 141 × 35½ × 18¼, 833 tons. Both ship-rigged. (University of Newcastle upon Tyne Library)*

BARK

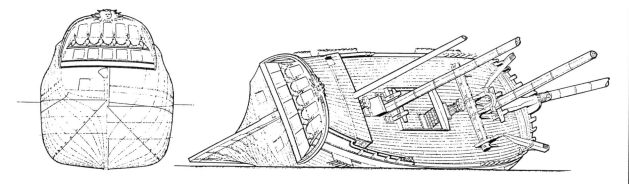

79 Bark, Chapman's Plate XXI. Dimensions $150\frac{1}{4} \times 38 \times 20$, 1257 tons. Ship-rigged. (University of Newcastle upon Tyne Library)

Chat

80 Cat with three pole masts, engraved after the design of M. Lescallier, c1790. (Musée de la Marine, Paris)

Cook, colliers and Pacific trade

Outside the Pacific Ocean, during the first half of the eighteenth century, the European wars of expansionism continued unabated: it was not until the 1760s that the British and French were ready to contest the South Seas trading routes. Almost simultaneously both colonized the Falkland Islands, seeing them as a good departure point for their Pacific explorations and searches for Terra Australis. In 1764 Louis Bouginville landed a colonizing party and, unaware of the French presence, John Byron landed a party at Port Egmont whilst on his way, unsuccessfully, to find a Pacific opening to the North-West Passage. (Attempts to find a passage from the Atlantic side had almost ceased following the failure of the explorations of Luke Foxe and Thomas James).

At first, minor French and English expeditions were carried out, resulting in Samuel Wallis finding Tahiti, but the fabulous gold and spices of King Solomon's southern continent had yet to be discovered. Ophir's fate was to be decided by one man of humble parentage, James Cook, and by a cargo ship that had been designed to carry coal.

Magellan's 85-ton *Victoria* crossed the Pacific Ocean, on its way to become the first ship to sail around the world, and was followed by another small merchantman destined to play a crucial role in opening up the Pacific for ocean trade. This vessel was a collier, given to James Cook by the British Admiralty. Cook was born in Yorkshire in 1728 and did not go to sea until he was 18. He served as an apprentice in colliers on England's east coast, and his first ships the *Freelove* and *Three Brothers* were typical coal-traders of between 300 and 500 tons. As

81 *Contemporary model of a collier bark, c1750. These ships were replaced by the collier brigs and were said to have pink sterns and no keel. There are no square yards on the mizzen and the model represents a vessel of about 98 ft long and 28½ ft breadth. (National Maritime Museum, Greenwich)*

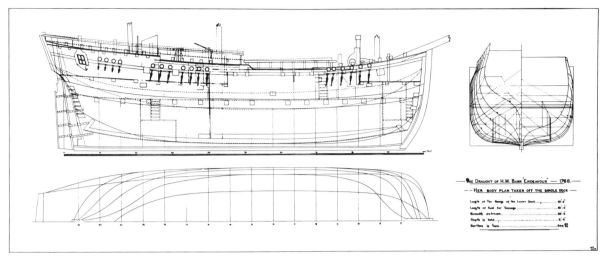

82 *Lines plan of H.M. Bark* Endeavour. *Length of the range of the lower deck—97 ft 6 in.; length of keel for tonnage—81 ft; breadth extreme—29 ft 2 in.; depth in hold—11 ft 4 in.; burthen in tons—366 49/94. (Science Museum, London)*

mate on the *Friendship* he gained invaluable coasting experience as he worked the dangerous waters of the Wash and the Thames Estuary, little realizing that these skills would be later used to explore the Great Barrier Reef on Australia's east coast.

James Cook came to the attention of the Admiralty after carrying out surveying in Newfoundland, following the military successes of General Wolfe in Quebec. In 1768 he was given command of H.M. bark *Endeavour* and left England for Tahiti, via Cape Horn, to take possession of the Society Islands for Britain. Another aim of the voyage was to take scientists to Tahiti to measure solar eclipse. On board with Cook was Charles Green, assistant to the Astronomer Royal. To find Tahiti Cook had first arrived at a longitude well east of the island and then carried out the traditional method of 'running down the latitude' to arrive. He did not carry one of the newly invented Harrison chronometers and found his longitude by lunar observations, measuring the angular distance of the moon from a fixed star, no doubt ably assisted by Charles Green. With this method Cook recorded his discoveries to an accuracy of about a degree.

After attempting to measure the eclipse, Cook went in search of the southern continent. After travelling to latitude 40° South, he made no landfall and so sailed west until he reached New Zealand. There, carefully working his way along the coast, he showed that there were two separate islands. Travelling west he crossed the Tasman Sea to arrive on the east coast of Australia at Botany Bay. He sailed north, charting New South Wales before running aground on the inside of the Great Barrier Reef. Only a collier could have survived a grounding on coral so sharp that it punched its way through the

thick hull planking. Undeterred, by jettisoning cannon, food and water, Cook refloated the lightened ship. He spent six weeks up a river repairing the hull, before continuing northwards to eventually show that New Guinea and Australia were separate when he travelled through the Torres Strait. Finally, he sailed to Batavia to complete repairs and returned to England in 1771 by way of the Cape of Good Hope.

The Admiralty, more than satisfied with his first voyage, sent him again to search for the southern continent. He left England in 1772 travelling east with two more colliers, *Resolution* and *Adventure*. After rounding the Cape of Good Hope he sailed to nearly 67° South before his way was blocked by ice. On this remarkable passage he carried a Harrison chronometer, enabling him to obtain his longitude with a far greater degree of accuracy than on his first voyage. By the beginning of 1773 Cook had crossed the Antarctic circle. He continued eastwards, sailing hundreds of miles in heavy seas, rigging and decks slippery with ice, always under constant threat from icebergs and the chance of being entombed in pack-ice. For the first time in the history of ocean voyaging, even though months had been spent at sea, scurvy was prevented. Cook, realizing the advantage of fruit and vegetable extracts, kept his crew under a strict discipline: regular doses of extract, dry quarters and changing wet clothes.

Bad weather forced Cook north, and as he continued eastwards he thrust south whenever he could, but saw no land. He lost contact with *Adventure*, and the ships failed to meet at a pre-arranged rendezvous in New Zealand. Setting out again, he travelled towards Cape Horn, reaching 71° South before once again being stopped by ice. He turned north, visiting more islands in the South

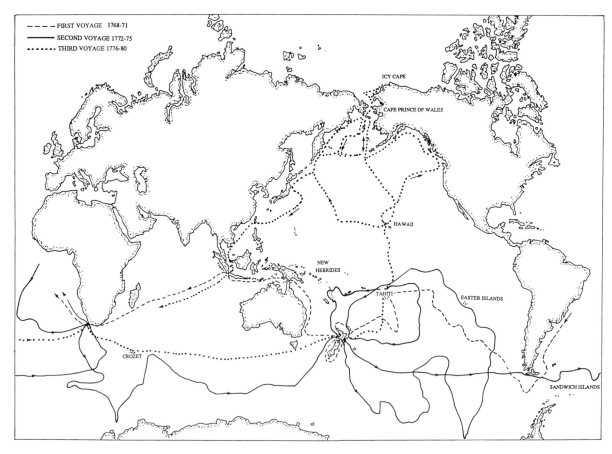

- - - - FIRST VOYAGE 1768-71
———— SECOND VOYAGE 1772-75
• • • • • THIRD VOYAGE 1776-80

ICY CAPE

CAPE PRINCE OF WALES

HAWAII

NEW
HEBRIDES

TAHITI

EASTER ISLANDS

CROZET

SANDWICH ISLANDS

Map 6 *Cook's explorations in the Pacific. (after Moyse-Bartlett, 1937)*

Pacific, then east to the Atlantic, once again to take possession of South Georgia before returning home to England in 1775. He had sailed an incredible 60,000 miles, all without losing a man to scurvy, and became the first European to cross the Antarctic circle.

James Cook never found the Spice Continent, and the existence of Terra Australis Incognito was finally disproved. He did assume that there was a southern land but realized, 'There must be some [land] to the South behind this ice; but if there is, it can afford no better retreat for birds, or any other animals, than the ice itself, with which it must be wholly covered' (*Journals*).

On his third voyage, in 1776, he went via the Cape of Good Hope to look for the Pacific entrance of the North-West Passage. After stopping at his favourite anchorage in New Zealand, he set sail northwards for the Sandwich Islands (Cook's name for the Hawaiian Islands). He then sailed to the west coast of North America and coasted northwards, along the Alaskan coast, surveying as he went. Once through the Bering Strait he was stopped by an ice barrier at $70\frac{1}{2}°$ North. Unable to find an opening he returned to the Sandwich Islands. At Kealakekua Bay, on the west side of Hawaii, Cook was killed,

like Magellan, in an unfortunate skirmish with the local people. So died one of the greatest maritime explorers, a man like his collier ships: modest and practical. Man and ship opened up the Pacific to ocean trade in a manner that was both steady and sure.

Cook used Whitby colliers because he held that 'the ship must not be of great draught but of sufficient capacity to carry a quantity of provisions and stores for the crew, and of such construction that she will bear to take the ground, and of such a size that she can be conveniently laid on shore if necessary for repairing any damages or defects, and these qualities are to be found in North Country-built ships, such as are built for the coal trade, and in none other' (quoted from J.A. Williamson, *Cook and the Opening of the Pacific*).

In searching for a vessel to undertake the Pacific explorations the British Admiralty went in search of a 'cat-built vessel of 350 tons'. They needed a sturdy ship, with a large hold to take all the provisions needed for a long voyage. After surveying a number of ships they settled on the *Earl of Pembroke*, a collier built in 1764 at Thomas Fishburn's yard in northeast England at Whitby. The ship was fitted-out at Deptford, London, and Figure 82 shows the

83 'The head of a New Zealander with a comb in his hair and ornament of green stone in his ear and other of fish tooth around his neck,—an illustration from Cook's first voyage, by S. Parkinson who accompanied Cook, first published in 1773. (National Maritime Museum, Greenwich)

modifications that were made (dotted lines). There were two decks and a deep hold, and an almost flush deck, with the forecastle and quarter-deck rising only a few feet above the upper deck. Thus the floors of the aft cabin and forecastle were sunk to increase headroom. There were five windows right aft, and like all colliers, the hull was U-shaped and the bows bluff. It is interesting to compare Cook's bark with Chapman's.

In the *Earl of Pembroke*, the beams of the lower deck would have been left uncovered so as to leave a large hold for the coal, and there were ports, caulked when at sea, through which coal was shovelled. A wheel was placed forward of the mizzen mast (behind the companionway), but the tiller ran from the tiller-head to behind the mast. The collier was not 'cat-sterned', at least as defined by Chapman, as it lacked any forward projecting quarter pieces (see D. MacGregor).

The 366-ton collier, re-named H.M. bark *Endeavour* to avoid confusion with the warship, was handed over to Cook in 1768. *Endeavour* was ship-rigged with square sails, gaff mizzen, two spritsails and often a set of stunsails. With all sails set, maximum speed was around seven knots. In the next century colliers lost a mast and became known as 'collier' or 'Geordie' brigs.

Endeavour carried 94 crew, a ratio of almost 1 man to 4 tons of ship, much higher than the sixteenth-century ratio of 1 man to 2 tons (see also Conclusion)—the improved efficiency from the advances made in sail, rigging and ship technology in the eighteenth century. After *Endeavour's* return in 1771, she made several voyages to the Falkland Islands before being sold in 1775. There is some doubt as to her final history: she probably returned to trading as a collier in the North Sea before being brought by the French. Cook's ship could have then crossed the Atlantic to end her days in Newport, Rhode Island.

For Cook's second voyage the *Endeavour* was replaced by two more Whitby colliers, the *Drake* (462 tons) and the *Raleigh* (366 tons), but in order to placate the Spanish crown they were renamed *Resolution* and *Adventure*. They were crewed by 118 and 83 men respectively and were almost new when bought: the Admiralty spared no expense in fitting them out, outlaying more than their initial cost. Against Cook's advice *Resolution* was fitted with increased upper works, and became so top-heavy that the river pilot refused to take her out of the Thames, thus delaying departure until *Resolution* was turned back in to a collier.

On Cook's last voyage there were again two colliers. The *Resolution* and another Whitby-built ship of c229 tons burden, the *Discovery*. *Discovery*

was built at George and Nathaniel Langborne's Whitby yard in 1774 and bought by the Navy for £2450. The *Resolution* had a re-fit. But worn-out, and with the work done badly by the then inefficient Naval yard at Deptford, the ship leaked badly for most of the voyage. When Cook was killed in 1779, he had explored more of the world than anyone before him or since. After Cook's death George Vancouver, who had sailed with Cook, and others, quickly charted the remaining part of north-west America.

The British Admiralty sponsored another famous Pacific voyage when, in 1787, they purchased the 230-ton, 91 ft long, 24 ft 10 in.-beam merchantman, *Bethia*. Although only two years old, the ship was refitted: the bottom was sheathed in copper and the aft section of the lower deck fitted-out to take 1000 breadfruit plants. In 1787, *Bethia*, renamed *Bounty*, set sail for Tahiti with orders to load a cargo of Tahitian breadfruit plants for the West Indies. After battling against westerly gales, the ship failed to round Cape Horn, and so turned east, to reach Tahiti by way of the Cape of Good Hope, a voyage of ten months and 27,000 miles!

The *Bounty* was commanded by William Bligh, and the first mate was Fletcher Christian. When most of the crew mutinied, Christian set Bligh and 18 non-mutineers adrift in a 23-ft open boat which the undaunted captain, who had once sailed with James Cook, navigated some 3,600 miles to the Dutch colony at Timor—with the loss of a man. Fletcher sailed the Bounty to the Pitcairn Islands and deliberately sank her by fire.

At the end of the American War of Independence in 1783, Britain obtained the right to travel through the Dutch East Indies, which resulted in an increase in the trade with China. Soon British merchants were shipping furs from Alaska across the Pacific to pay for Chinese goods, especially tea. In 1788 convicts were sent to form a colony at Sydney, and soon ocean traders from Australia were voyaging across the Pacific Ocean, supplying China with sandlewood, sea-slugs and eggs from many tropical islands. By the nineteenth century, copra from many Pacific islands played an increasingly important role in the China trade.

In the early nineteenth century Spain's hold on its American colonies, stretching from San Francisco to Cape Horn, was loosened. Britain blockaded the sea-link with the mother country and, in a series of bloody revolutions, the colonies declared themselves independent nations. Chile developed the nitrate trade, Peru the guano trade to meet the world's demand for fertilizer.

In 1840 the Pacific Steam Navigation Company

came into operation, the first to fit compound steam engines into its ships. Steam had seriously begun to replace sail on all the oceans of the world: quite soon the merchant sailing ship would be no more.

CHAPTER SIX

The Rise and Fall of the Sailing Trader

The nineteenth century saw the greatest, most rapid shipping revolution the world has seen. In Britain the industrial revolution, Victorian free-enterprise and the triple-expansion steam engine brought about the death of the sailing ocean trader. By the end of the century sails were replaced by steam engines, wind energy by coal, and wooden planks for timber frames by steel plates and girders. The end of the sailing ocean trader perhaps started as early as 1807 when, on the Hudson river, the *Clermont* became the first steamship to work commercially, and in 1819, when the American ship *Savannah* crossed the Atlantic with the aid of steam-driven paddle wheels. But the end of the sail was a long time coming. The sailing trader flowered throughout most of the nineteenth century, and only after c1885 did it really start its decline. The invention and widespread use of an efficient steam engine, employed in a large iron hull, and the opening of the Suez Canal in 1869, caused sail traders to finally yield to steamers. But towards the end of the century, sailing ship technology reached its peak and produced some of the largest, most beautiful merchant sailing ships that ever travelled the oceans in search of trade. Then, after over 5000 years of use, the sailing trader took only 20 years to all but disappear. There was a brief resurrection of the sail-powered ocean trader from the middle of World War I, which only lasted 10 years before steam finally emerged as the victor.

For a while, steam engines even aided the development of sailing ocean traders. At the beginnings and ends of voyages, steam powered tugs towed sailing ships in and out of harbours: vessels no longer had to be built small and manoeuvrable for the shallow, coastal-water parts of their voyage. Designers could concentrate on the ocean passage and produce large, safe, fast sailing ships operated by fewer and fewer seamen. Auxiliary steam-driven capstans replaced the work of dozens of men when they lifted anchors and heavy yards, and special winches tensioned halliards and braces (see also C. Ernest Fayle and B. Greenhill in *The Ship*, ed. B. Greenhill, vol. 7).

Great Britain and Pax Victoriana (1800–1910)

Before the opening of the century, in 1793, Britain and France had begun fighting the familiar war of two competing empire-building nations. In 1795 Britain had Ceylon (Sri Lanka) under its control and began occupying the Cape of Good Hope. In the same year the Dutch East India Company was disbanded, and many Dutch possessions were handed over to the British to prevent them from going to the French. After losing the Battle of Trafalgar in 1805, France may have lost control of the sea, but still retained much of Europe. On land Napoleon attempted to bring about the commercial strangulation of Britain by banning British goods from his empire. At sea French ships went privateering and were effective in forcing British merchantmen into huge convoys. The convoy system also did little to encourage radical thinking in British merchant ship design, with the slowest ship dictating the speed of the convoy and the emphasis being on cargo capacity rather than speed. In this period competitive trading, and experiments with ocean trader design by British shipowners was almost non-existent.

In 1807 Britain, as the world's most powerful maritime nation, attempted to avoid France's commercial strangulation by passing a law that forced all neutral vessels wishing to trade with Napoleon's Europe to first unload their cargoes in a British port. They then had to pay the British government a due before reloading and setting sail. America, as a neutral, found its trading position

84 *Model of the American paddlesteamer,* Savannah, *c300 tons. (Science Museum, London)*

intolerable, and went to war against Britain in 1812. Mutual war-weariness led to the Treaty of Ghent in 1814, restoring the territorial situation of 1812.

From 1815 until the end of the century, Britain's power and expanionism were unstoppable. The industrial revolution had started in Britain c1750, some 100 years before any competing nation. In 1750 Britain's agricultural revolution was also well under way: improved agricultural methods helped bring about a rapid increase in the population. By 1800 Britain had the technology, an expanding population, the manufactured goods and the desire to create and find markets all over the world. Britain was strategically positioned in the North Atlantic, had numbers of well-protected harbours, enormous reserves of coal and low-grade iron ore and a skilled workforce. The rapidly developing industries were driven by laissez-faire economics and the Protestant work ethic. Britain quickly took the industrial revolution to sea, and soon controlled a huge empire that was to peak in the 1860s. Throughout the

nineteenth century Britain made the goods and ships that other nations wanted. During the Napoleonic wars, smuggling thrived between Britain and France, and it was said that despite Napoleon's attempts to ban the importation of British goods, he was forced to dress his armies in British cloth!

The more enlightened attitudes of the nineteenth century brought an end to the slave trade, but international legislation took a long time to come into effect, and illegal slave trading continued into the 1860s. In 1808 Britain abolished the slave trade throughout its territories. France abolished slave trading in 1818 and Spain followed two years later. In 1833 slaves were set free in all British colonies, but it was not until 1836 that Portugal banned the export of slaves (although it had forbidden its citizens to participate in slave-trading in 1820): the originator of the slave trade and the last country to ban it. From 1807 no more manufactured goods were loaded in England into ships known as 'Guineamen', which then sailed to the West African coast for slaves and

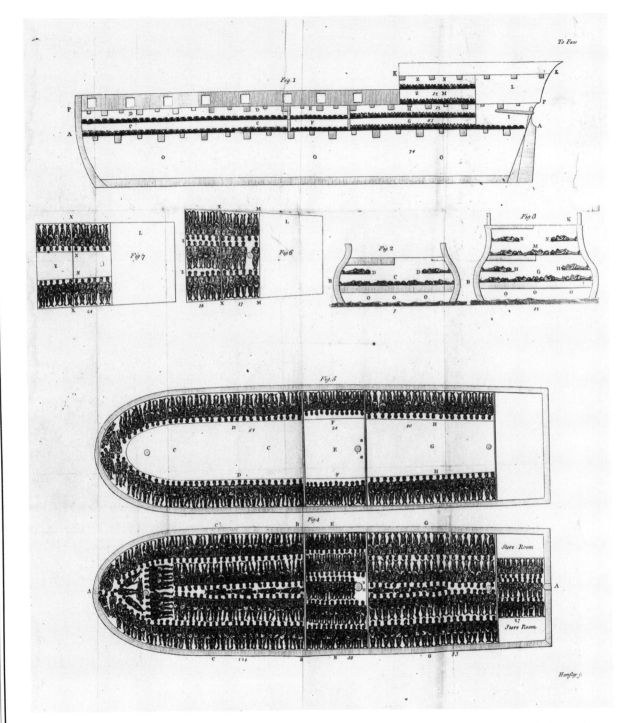

85   *Late 18th-century slave trader: length of lower deck—100 ft; beam of lower deck—25 ft 4 in.; depth of hold—10 ft. (National Maritime Museum, Greenwich)*

gold: the slaves that survived the infamous 'middle passage' across the Atlantic were exchanged in the Caribbean and North America for sugar, tobacco, tar and lumber.

The loss of the American colonies forced British merchants to seek markets elsewhere. It was not long before all the powerful maritime nations realized that their colonies wealth was not only there to be syphoned off, but that they could also provide markets. Britain rapidly developed its textile industry: cotton from America and later, in the 1870s, wool from New Zealand and Australia were efficiently transformed into cloth by Lancashire looms. The cloth was not only exported back to the suppliers, but also to the rest of the British colonies and to many other countries.

British merchants especially wanted to obtain access to the huge Chinese markets. China, after receiving the Portuguese, Spanish and Dutch, in that order, was visited by HEIC ships in 1635 and only carried out a limited trade with Britain, while merely observing European power struggles. However, British expansionism in the nineteenth century had other ideas, and it was not long before China was embroiled in the Opium Wars.

British HEIC ships arriving in China to collect tea were forced by the Chinese to pay for their cargoes in silver; but British merchants were always short of silver. Many Chinese were addicted to opium, whose supply the authorities were trying to control by banning its importation. Fast British 'opium clippers' manned by young adventurers, supplied the Chinese demand. Firms like Jardine, Matheson & Co., and Dent, bought opium in India and smuggled it into China, making huge profits which the Chinese paid for in silver. The smugglers sold their silver to the HEIC and other British merchants, who then used it to pay the Chinese merchants.

In 1834, by Act of Parliament, the HEIC lost its monopoly of the China trade and other British merchants were eager to compete for the new markets, especially the Lancashire cotton manufacturers. The Manchu Emperor, however, only allowed trade between foreign and Chinese merchants to take place at Canton. In 1839 Britain went to war against China, on a pretext that some British-owned opium had been burnt. In reality the aim was to force open the China markets. After successes by British warships and troops five Chinese ports were released for trade and residence in 1842: Amoy, Canton, Foochow, Ningpo and Shanghai. Hong Kong was ceded to the British. A second Opium War started in 1856 when Chinese officials boarded a British ship to search it. When the war ended in 1860 further gains had been made for British trade.

Since the 1770s, the British government had been eroding the commercial and political power of the HEIC in India, which had reached a peak a decade earlier (see p 103 ff). Driven by the spirit of 'free trade' (or the desire to find more markets for British goods!) the British government had opened up the Indian market to all countries. After 1834 the HEIC ceased all commercial activities: with its Eastern trade monopoly cancelled, it restricted itself to administrating its Indian holdings. In 1858 the government of India Act transferred administration to the British Crown. In 1874 the HEIC's final charter expired and one of the world's most powerful ocean trading companies died.

In China, after the cancellation of the HEIC monopoly, American ocean traders were soon on the scene, and for a short while they dominated Chinese trade. After the War of Independence, America's shipping industry was in disarray, but it quickly recovered. It had a vast supply of soft-wood timber, skilled shipwrights, and a number of well-placed shipyards. It also had several brilliant designers, and soon its yards were turning out fast, seaworthy ships. In 1818 the American Black Ball Line started regular, lucrative runs across the Atlantic, carrying passengers, parcels and freight in fast 'packet ships'. Other packet shipping companies followed, such as Red Star Lines and Swallow Tail, and by 1855 there were 56 packet ships, driven hard by their captains making regular runs across the Atlantic, forerunners of the great ocean liners.

Even by 1830 American merchant shipping was booming, and American ocean traders had special privileges under Britain's Navigation Acts: most of the cotton arriving at England's mills was carried by American ships. By 1860 Britain and America had the world's largest merchant fleets, each country having over five million tons of shipping, over two million of which were ocean traders.

The years between 1810 and 1840 are now considered to be one of the greatest periods of American maritime history. In London, capital was raised for its rapidly expanding merchant fleet, and between 1830 and 1860 America's ocean trader tonnage increased some five-fold to over two million tons. Like the British, Americans actively searched out new markets and, if necessary, created them by force. In 1853 Matthew Perry led a naval expedition to Japan, a country that since the beginning of the nineteenth century had resisted outsiders and only carried on a limited trade with the Dutch. Perry compelled Japan to open diplomatic and trade relations with the USA. From 1810 to 1840, 90% of American trade was carried by American ships, but by 1860 this figure had decreased to two thirds; and the American Civil War (1861–1865) heralded a fall so complete that by 1900 the figure was down to less than 10%. During the American Civil War half a million tons of shipping went to Britain and, after 1865, America turned inwards, content to develop its own enormous resources rather than ply the world with her shipping industry (C. Ernest Fayle, *A Short History of the World's Shipping Industry*).

In 1847 gold was discovered in California, and the European potato crop failed. Grain was desperately needed from America. Immigrants poured into America and everywhere there was a shortage of tonnage. The California gold rush created a huge demand for fast ships to round dangerous Cape Horn for San Francisco. Ships, almost anything that could float, were soon pounding around the Horn in droves, the fastest driven by hard skippers and crewed by British and European seamen—Americans could earn more money ashore! In 1849 some 800

86 *The Gold Rush fleet in San Francisco harbour in 1851. Yerba Buena Cove contained over 800 ships, many of them abandoned.*

ships and 90,000 men sailed from the east coast to California gold fields. Some of these were clipper ships and, if the crew had not deserted for gold fields, these 'Californian Clippers' loaded gold dust, and sailed west across the Pacific to buy tea in China before returning to America. By 1850 San Francisco harbour was becoming choked with abandoned ships.

In 1851 gold was discovered in Victoria, Australia, and British shipowners turned to Canadian and American-built clipper ships, over 1000 tons and built from softwoods, to make fast, reliable passages out to Australia. The Boston shipbuilder Donald McKay (see below) built some outstanding clipper ships for the British and the 1462-ton *Lightning*, launched in 1854, made the return run from Melbourne to Liverpool in 69 days, a record that was never beaten.

In 1849 Britain had repealed the Navigation Acts. As a result, British-built ocean trade to China and Australia was, for over a decade, almost entirely carried by faster, larger American-built clippers. But British shipowners had been warned. A government report in 1847 complained that British owners and designers were not responding to foreign competition and were becoming complacent, their trade protected by the Navigation Acts. And the repeal was not an entirely selfless act, in keeping with an 'international free trade' philosophy. British merchants required further markets for their manufactured goods, and

Britain's expansionism was being stifled by other nations copying the Navigation Acts: Britain needed 'free trade' to get at other countries markets. Repealing the Acts was not too great a sacrifice: they had become almost unworkable with half of Britain's trade governed by exemption clauses.

British shipbuilders responded to the American challenge. In 1836, 1854 and 1867 British Acts of Parliament were passed to bring about a rationalization of the tonnage measurements. Under the old tonnage laws (BOM, prior to 1836), British shipowners built hulls that were deeply U-shaped and slow: 'tonnage cheating ships'. Ship's dues were paid on registered tonnage, and cargoes carried in these hulls might be twice that of the ship's registered tonnage. By the 1850s, with the Navigation Acts repealed and the tonnage laws changed, British shipowners no longer had an advantage in producing tonnage cheaters and yards began experimenting with design. British-built hardwood clippers of this period were fast and lasted longer than the American softwood ones, and Britain recaptured the China tea trade. By 1860 the total British merchant fleet was some six million tons while the American fleet was down to two and a half million. This, along with the Civil War and the completion of the railway line connecting the east and west coasts in 1869, were key factors in bringing about the downfall of the American sailing ocean trader. American

(National Maritime Museum, San Francisco)

merchantmen disappeared from the ocean trading scene for a short while: Britain reigned supreme.

The British Empire was at its height by 1860, during the reign of Queen Victoria (1837–1901), and Pax Victoriana created a period of world peace and prosperity—especially for the British. Laissez faire was the economic philosophy: many businessmen resented any interference from government, while government's main concern was maintaining Britain's commercial empire rather than in running industries. One result was that sailors were often badly treated and ships were unsafe. Although ships were insured, this often worked against the seamen: when a ship went down with all hands, it could still make a profit for its owner from the insurance money! From the middle to the end of the nineteenth century there was an enormous number of shipwrecks, as ships were often undermanned, overloaded and coming apart at their seams: not surprisingly many ships became known as 'coffin ships'.

From 1850 the British Board of Trade, established in 1786 'for all matters relating to trade', slowly introduced rules to improve the competency and conditions of the officers and men as well as the safety of merchant ships (see S. Foreman's *Shoes and Ships and Sealing Wax* for a history of the Board of Trade). A Member of Parliament, Samuel Plimsoll, wrote about the appalling safety record of British ships, much to the chagrin of some Victorian

shipowners, and in 1873 a map was published that showed the incredible number of shipwrecks on the British coast alone. A year later a commission on 'Unseaworthy Ships' supported Plimsoll's claim, and in 1876 the British Parliament passed an act that enabled the Board of Trade to survey ships before passing them as seaworthy. Ships also had to be marked with a load line—the Plimsoll line—below which they could not be submerged.

Canada also played an important role in the development of ocean traders in the nineteenth century. After losing the War of Independence, Britain had to turn to Canada to supply timber for ship-building. Between 1812 and 1865 Canada was an important source of both softwood and ships (peaking in the periods of the Crimean War, 1853–1856, and the American Civil War). Even as early as 1840 nearly half of the registered tonnage in Britain was built in Canada. Canadian merchantmen were operated along the American lines with skippers who part-owned and sailed the ships. Canadian ships, like American softwood ships, were large. Softwood ocean traders, of up to 2000 tons, appeared in the 1850s, and in the 1860s Canadian yards began supplying British shipowners with these large craft, almost twice the size of the largest British merchantmen.

Although between 1850 and 1860 British steamship tonnage was on the increase, sailing ships were still

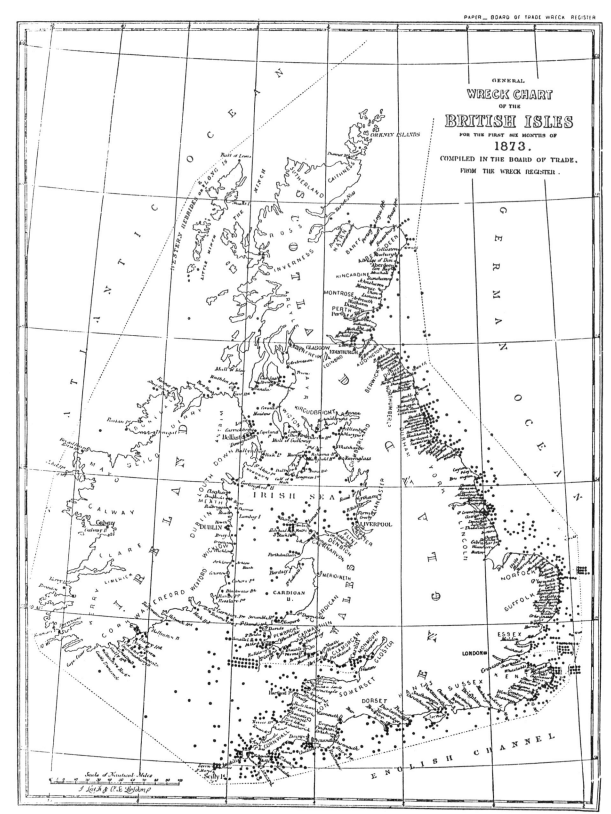

SIX MONTHS' CASUALTIES ON THE COASTS OF GREAT BRITAIN AND IRELAND
EACH DOT ON THE MAP REPRESENTS A WRECK WHICH HAS TAKEN PLACE WITHIN THE SPACE OF HALF-A-YEAR

87   Board of Trade 'Wreck Chart' for the first six months of 1873. (Board of Trade Wreck Register)

the supreme ocean traders, such that during this period sailing tonnage increased by about a million tons, to over four million tons. During most of the nineteenth century the bulk of ocean trade was carried by wide-beamed, plodding merchantmen, despite the disproportionate amount written about the 'clipper age' of the 1850s and 1860s.

But as the nineteenth century progressed, Britain became less dependent on wooden and Canadian-built ships, as iron, and later steel, replaced wood. 'Composite' ships of wood and iron had been built since 1839 and were much liked by clipper ship owners. And from c1870 the industrial revolution was having a profound effect at sea: steel-hulled steamships were about to take over from sail. (See Basil Greenhill's 'The industrial revolution goes to sea', in *The Ship*, Vol. 7).

In the last quarter of the nineteenth century large iron- and steel-hulled, square-rigged sailing traders (also American and Canadian wooden-hulled sailing ships) continued to work the long-haul, bulk ocean routes, where coal and water were in short supply. The long haul routes were to be the last bastions of the sailing ocean traders.

Other factors also speeded up the demise of the sailing ship. In 1850, the international electric telegraph had come into being, and this marked the beginning of a world freight market. Ships could now be moved from port to port at a day's or even an hour's notice; they could be ordered to search for new cargoes and reject others, depending on the world commodity markets. Steamships were far more flexible than sailing ships. In 1869 the Suez canal was opened, shortening the route to India and the Far East. The compound steam engine, the iron hull and a world-wide, coal-bunkering network largely set up by Britain, quickly killed off the merchant sailing ship. Paradoxically the steamer coaling stations had often been created, and fed, by sailing ocean traders.

By the end of the nineteenth century, Great Britain, with her empire, metal-hulled steamers, advanced industrialization and large reserves of coal and iron ore, prospered mightily. Pax Victoriana reigned supreme, but not for long—World War I was not far away.

The tonnage cheaters

Until the 1850s most classes of British, Canadian and American ocean trader were wooden-hulled, registered-tonnage cheaters known as 'kettle bottoms' in America: heavy, slow, deeply U-shaped vessels. And the HEIC's very large, 800 registered-ton ships for the India trade, or 1000-plus ton ships for the China trade, were no exception. Although still built to resemble warships superficially, they were slab-sided and barrel-bowed: but they could carry over twice their registered tonnage of cargo. David Steel's 1257-ton East Indiaman, published in *Naval Architecture* in 1804 (see p 108) would have been typical of an early nineteenth century HEIC ship, like the *Reliance*, which could carry some 2000 tons of cargo.

When the HEIC lost its monopoly of the China trade and ceased trading, there was no longer a requirement for East Indiamen. Prior to this, many HEIC ships had been built at the Blackwall yards on the River Thames; in fact building Indiamen at Blackwall had begun in 1611, when the *Globe* was launched and sailed on her maiden voyage to India. Throughout its long history the Blackwall shipyard had turned out some of Britain's finest ocean traders. HEIC ships were nearly always well-built and well-designed, with the result that innovations sometimes appeared in Indiamen before being taken up by the British Admiralty. For example, by 1800 large HEIC ships were using the new type of 'round-headed' rudder (see p 112) before British warships. By 1811, HEIC ships had developed a different way of setting up the 'futtock', or 'foot-hook' shrouds—shrouds that led up to the 'tops'. Since c1720 tops had lost their large circular appearance to become more stream-lined—rectangular with a rounded, forward-facing edge. Ropes were stretched between the futtock shrouds to form ladders so that the crew could climb easily to the sides of the tops. In Indiamen the futtock shrouds, instead of being attached to the lower shrouds, were now attached to an iron band that went around the mast. British warships copied this, but used chain instead of the iron hoop. (see Darcy Lever's *Young Sea Officers Sheet Anchor* for many details)

The widespread use of iron in sailing ship and steamship construction began to take place c1830. But in the late 1700s, HEIC ships were already using iron knees, iron brackets and pillars to strengthen their ships; and iron hoops were being used to strengthen main masts and replace rope lashings or 'wooldings'. One other important technological advance as far as the seamen were concerned was the fitting, in the early part of the century, of iron 'jackstays' to ships' yards. Sails were made fast to these, rather than with robands that went right around the spar. Men working aloft no longer had to stretch their arms around the yard, to bend on or furl a sail, it was now safer, and much easier, to attach the rope lashings, or 'gaskets', to the jackstays.

Following the loss of the HEIC trading monopoly in the East, ships continued to be built at Blackwall but were owned by the new firms that took over the HEIC's trade. The new ships also looked like warships, and became known as 'Blackwall Frigates'. (Many are described by Basil Lubbock in *The*

Blackwall Frigates.) Blackwall frigates were some of the largest wooden vessels ever built in Britain, exceeding 1500 tons, although more usually between 500 and 1500 tons and owned by firms such as Richard and Henry Green (owners of East Blackwall yards) and Money Wigram (owners of West Blackwall yards), firms that were then household names.

The *Seringapatam* was built at East Blackwall by the Greens. Launched in 1837, at 818 tons it was similar to contemporary naval frigates, and was without the double-tiered stern and galleries typical of the HEIC's Indiamen. There was an increase in the length to beam ratio, and generally Blackwall frigates were sleeker, faster vessels, especially when compared to their high-sterned HEIC predecessors. Other Blackwall ships followed, based on the *Seringapatam*, but the London monopoly of 'Blackwall frigates' was challenged when many fine 'Blackwallers' were built in the northeast of England, at Sunderland and Newcastle upon Tyne. Thomas and William Smith of Newcastle built two flush-decked Indiamen in 1846 and 1848, the *Marlborough* and the *Blenheim*, which, when presented at the Great Exhibition in 1851, were said to be the finest merchant ships afloat. They had no poop decks or raised sterns, and looked very much like 50-gun naval frigates. The Pile yard built nearly all of Richard Green's Blackwall frigates

at Sunderland, one of them, the *Malabar*, launched in 1860. After the 1860s, flush-decked ocean traders appeared to go out of fashion, no doubt the lack of a protective forecastle making them wet, uncomfortable ships in any sort of bad weather.

The powerful freight and passenger transporting Blackwallers were very different from the fast clipper ships that were being developed by both America and Britain for the China tea trade. The Blackwall frigates followed a separate, more stately line of ship evolution, rooted in the grandeur of the HEIC's past and the HEIC's close association with the Crown and the Royal Navy. In 1863 Richard Green died, and in 1875 the last of Green's Blackwall Line sailing ships, the 1857-tons, 269.8-ft. long, iron-hulled *Melbourne* was launched. It was the beginning of the end of the Blackwallers.

The majority of early nineteenth century merchant sailing ships were not Indiamen or Blackwallers. Most traders were small, under 300 tons, built of wood and two-masted: brigs, brigantines and schooners abounded. These two-masted vessels, often less than 60 ft. long, accomplished many remarkable ocean passages. Larger ocean-going ships from c250 to 800 tons were three-masted and either rigged as ships (square sails on all three masts) or barques (fore and aft sails on the mizzen).

88 *The Blackwall frigate* Malabar, *1860. Registered length—210.3 ft; breadth—36.6 ft; depth—22.6 ft; 1219 tons. (Science Museum, London)*

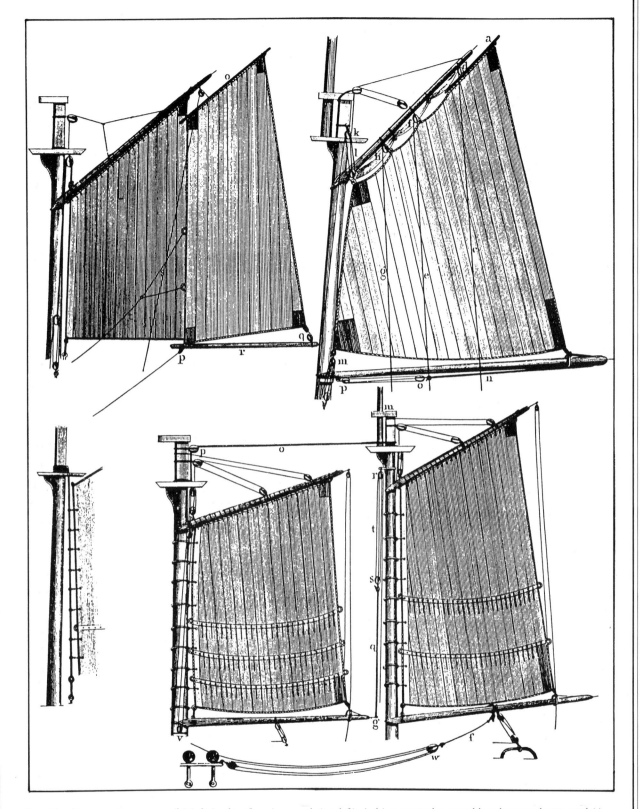

89 *The driver, as a temporary sail (o), hoisted to the mizzen peak (top left). A driver or spanker spread by a boom and extra yard (a), (top right). Fore (bottom left) and aft (bottom right) mainsails. (from Darcy Lever's* Young Sea Officer's Sheet Anchor)

In 1830 Peter Hedderwick published his *Treatise On Marine Architecture containing the Theory and Practice of Shipbuilding*. He showed similar, deep-draughted, medium-sized traders (347, 400, and 500 tons) to David Steel's West Indiaman. The deeply U-shaped ocean traders prior to c1850 needed to set enormous amounts of canvas to sail at five to six knots, especially in light airs. Hedderwick shows the full mast and rigging plan of a 500-ton ocean trader which has a continuous upper-deck and is rigged with a full set of square sails: from royals down to courses. Just aft of the foremast and mainmast there are 'gaff sails', set on 'trysail masts' which end below the fore and main tops. These gaff sails had already effectively replaced the less efficient main and middle staysails in warships, sometime after 1815, and became common on ocean traders around the middle of the century (Laird Clowes), although there was a tendency to loose the fore trysail mast. Darcy Lever, in his second edition of *Young Sea Officer's Sheet Anchor* (1819), describes them as 'fore and aft mainsails'. The gaff sail, set on the fore trysail mast, was known as the 'fore trysail' or 'Spencer', and the gaff sail set on the main trysail mast was the 'main trysail' or 'Yorkie'.

Around 1815, 'spanker' became the common term used to describe the mizzen mast's boomed-gaffsail, and a fore and aft 'gaff topsail' was set above the spanker on some ocean traders c1820. By the early nineteenth century the dolphin striker allowed the setting up of a permanent jib-stay. Spritsails were not used on ocean traders much after c1830, and although the spritsail yard was at first used as a lead for the bowsprit rigging, it was slowly moved further and further aft, eventually to disappear. Around the middle of the century steel wire was replacing hemp on the standing rigging, with the great advantage that it did not stretch as much as rope and, strength for strength, was half the diameter of rope, with the resulting reduction in windage aloft.

An interesting feature of a Peter Hedderwick ship of 1830 is the large windlass forward, used for lifting the anchor, and situated at the break of the forecastle, which, according to Laird Clowes was a 'typical distinguishing mark of all merchantmen of the period—other than East Indiamen'. At first a handspike operated windlass was often found aft of the foremast, but with the invention of a vertical stroke, pump-handled windlass, by 1840, the foremast was moved abaft of the windlass and the windlass often situated inside the forecastle, or under a shelter deck, to protect it from sea-water that came aboard in bad weather. The pump handles were worked by seamen on the fore-deck. (For this and discussions of much else of the period, see David Macgregor's last two vols. of *Merchant Sailing Ships*.)

The adverse effects of the British tonnage laws on ship design also applied to America, and no class of ocean trader was exempt. However, there was one type of vessel where the law's effect was not so disastrous—the whalers.

The whalers

An American whaler, the *Charles W. Morgan*, built in 1841 at New Bedford, Massachusetts, had the typical hull shape of the American kettle-bottomed cargo ships. For a whaler a deep draught was an advantage: ships put to sea for years at a time and needed deep holds to carry the vast amounts of supplies and spares. If the voyage was successful, large quantities of whale oil could be carried in the U-shaped hulls. Whalers also relied on the skill of the harpooners and the stealth of their whaleboats, rather than the speed of the mother ship, to catch their quarry.

In 1844, the *Charles W. Morgan*, a typical American whaler, embarked upon a working life that was to last 37 voyages, span 80 years, and to cross and re-cross the seven seas continually in search of sperm whales, described in detail in J. Leavitt's *The Charles W. Morgan*. At the end of her first voyage the American whaling fleet was at its height. Most whalers worked out of New Bedford and Nantucket, and the total American whaling fleet numbered over 700 vessels, with a combined tonnage of 235,000 tons. But from 1844 onwards whaling everywhere was on a slow decline, unable to compete with the growth of the petroleum and plastics industry.

Long before the *Morgan* was launched, whales had been pursued for commercial gain. Since 1610, and throughout much of the seventeenth century, the Greenland Right Whale had been caught by the Dutch, who dominated the whaling off the East Greenland coast. In the next century the Dutch had penetrated through to the Davis Strait of West Greenland, and were returning to Holland with large hauls of whalebone and blubber. The British, challenging Holland's maritime power throughout the rest of the world, decided in 1732 to pay a bounty (subsidy) of 20 shillings (£1) a ton on whalers over 200 tons; payment to be made after a voyage had been completed. In 1749 the government doubled the bounty. Merchants in British northern ports like Aberdeen, Leith, Peterhead, Dundee, Newcastle, Sunderland, Whitby, Lynn and Liverpool set about creating whaling fleets. By 1769 the British government had paid out over half a million pounds in its attempts to break Holland's control of the Greenland whaling. And they were successful. Twenty years later, in 1789, the British ship, *Emelia* became the first whaler to sail round Cape Horn and kill a whale in the Pacific. At that time, some 200 whalers, of around 300 tons, were sailing annually

90   *The* Charles W. Morgan *at Mystic seaport. (M.W. Marshall)*

91   *The* Charles W. Morgan, *looking aft, starboard side: tryworks and cutting-in tackles. (M.W. Marshall)*

92   *The* Charles W. Morgan: *look-out position on topgallant mast. (M.W. Marshall)*

from British ports. Voyages were sometimes three or four years long, and the ships needed to be deep, bluff and roomy to carry the stores and captured whale oil. By 1813, whale oil was fetching £50 per ton, its price having doubled since 1803, but British whalers, so successful at first, were in turn overtaken by American whalers: one of them was the *Charles W. Morgan*.

The *Morgan* was launched as a three-masted, full-rigged ship, setting square courses on the fore- and mainmasts, and the standing rigging being made of good-quality hemp rope. There were topsails, topgallants and royals on all three masts; a spencer and yorkie on the fore and main mast; and a spanker on the mizzen, which could be pulled in ('brailed') toward the mast. For the headsails there was a flying jib, jib, fore topmast staysail, and fore staysail set from a flying jib boom, jib boom and bowsprit. Topmast and topgallant staysails were rigged between the masts. Studding sails were set from the fore and mainmasts. This rig was to change during her working life.

A new tonnage law was passed in America in 1864, similar to the British Moorsom system of 1854 (see p 98). When registered in 1853, the *Morgan* was 106 ft 6 in. (some 111 ft stem to stern) x 27 ft $2\frac{1}{2}$ in. × 13 ft $7\frac{1}{4}$ in. which gave a registered tonnage of $351\frac{31}{95}$. After re-measurement in 1864, when the new tonnage laws had come into effect, the *Morgan* was 105.6 ft × 27.7 ft × 17.6 ft to give 313.75 tons. (The differences in depth being due to the 'hold depth factor', half the beam, not being used in the calculation.)

In 1867, the yards were removed from the mizzen mast and *Charles W. Morgan* was now registered as a bark. In 1881, for ease of handling, the topsails were doubled (split in two for easier handling) on the main and foremasts and the ship sailed for the rest of her working life as a 'double-topsail bark'. Wire was used to replace some of the hemp rope standing rigging.

The *Morgan* carried four double-ended whaleboats—each was around 25 ft long, clinker-built and launched from davits. Whales were looked for by men stationed aloft in waist-high iron hoops mounted on an extra set of cross-trees on the topgallant mast head. The royals were sent down when in whaling grounds, as they interfered with the lookouts' views. Once a whale was sighted, the double-ended whaleboats would be launched off the davits. They carried masts and sails and were steered by a rudder. When approaching a whale, the rudder was replaced by a 20-foot steering oar mounted in the stern. Often, but not always, the sails were lowered and the whaleboat rowed, one man to an oar, three oars on the starboard side and two on the port. In the bow the harpooner braced himself

against a leg-notch cut in the most forward seat. Two harpoons were joined together in tandem, the second 'iron' some 20 ft from the first. Both irons were attached to the whale line, a long fibred, best quality $\frac{3}{4}$ in. manila rope that had been carefully coiled down into tubs: once the harpoons were into a whale, the line ran out at tremendous speed and it was essential that it did not kink or become tangled. Whale line was kept in two tubs, each containing 150 fathoms (900 ft), which were stowed towards the stern of the boat. The whale line was led out of the tubs, around a vertical stern post and then taken foward to the bow, to be led over a deep groove cut in the stem. The groove was fitted with a peg to stop the line from jumping out once the harpoons were in a whale. If he was quick, and lucky, the harpooner would obtain a hold with both irons. The whale men waited, back-watering slowly with their oars, for the whale to do one of three things.

It could sound, diving deep towards the sea-bed, causing the line to run hissing out of the tubs. The men tried to slow the line's progress by snubbing it on the upright post, the 'loggerhead', wetting it with sea-water to prevent it from singeing. Alternatively, the whale might stay on the surface and swim at high speed, dragging the boat on a 'Nantucket sleigh ride': it was not uncommon for whaleboats to be towed for miles on a wild, exhilarating ride. But there was always the chance that the whaleboat would lose sight of the mother ship, then, as was often the case, boat and men might never return. Finally, the whale might turn on the boat, smashing it with its powerful flukes or crushing it in half with its lower jaws. On all whaling ships, many a man was maimed or lost from fighting harpooned whales, and the *Morgan* lost its fair share of seamen.

The whale was played like a fish, the whalemen using the weight of the boat as a heavy drag to exhaust their prey. Once exhausted the whale would lie quietly on the surface and the men, hauling in the line as they went, carefully approached the dying animal. Its lungs were sought for the death-blow, given with a specially sharpened killing lance that was thrust into them and twisted from side to side. This also was a dangerous period, whaleboats were sometimes destroyed during the final death throes, as huge flukes were smashed down on the surface of the sea or the animal reared out of the water to fall back on the whalemen. To make sure the whale was finally dead, a killing lance was thrust into its eye. A hole was then cut in the head and the whale towed back to the mother ship by the whaleboat.

Once alongside, always the starboard side on American whalers, a 10 ft section of the ship's rail was removed, and a cutting stage lowered overboard. This was a three-planked staging, rigged with a waist-high rail on the side nearest the ship which the men leant against as they worked with long-handled cutting spades, stripping off the blubber, a fatty layer that lay just below the surface of the skin and varied from a few inches to a foot in thickness. The men tried to avoid falling to the sharks which were often in attendance, excited to a frenzy of feeding by the blubber and whale's blood. First the head of the whale was cut off and made fast to the ship's side or, if small enough, brought abroad and lashed down. A hole was cut into the blubber to take a large metal hook. This was attached to a multi-blocked (four-fold) cutting-in tackle that was led to the top of the main mast. The cutting-in tackle was shortened as the blubber was stripped off the whale, the men removing the layer of blubber in one continuous piece, as if they were peeling the skin off an orange. A second cutting tackle was hooked into the blubber when the first was closed up, block to block. The first strip of blubber or 'blanket piece' was then cut off, and lowered below the upper deck into the upper hold or 'blubber room'. Here men, on their hands and knees, cut a blanket piece into four-foot by six-foot sections or 'horse pieces': when the ship rolled, these men would slide, the decks greasy with oil and blubber. On deck the men chopped the horse pieces into smaller 'books', or 'Bible pieces', before

the blubber was melted down in enormous kettles set on a brick-sided 'tryworks'. After cooling, the oil was run in canvas hoses to storage barrels in the lower hold. The head of a sperm whale contains, in a special cavity, a white, waxy substance, spermaceti, then much prized as a fuel for lamps or candlemaking. Sometimes whalemen were forced to enter this head cavity and, up to their armpits in congealing spermaceti, bale out the semi-liquid. Spermaceti was also melted down in the tryworks and stored in barrels alongside the whale oil. By day and night the process continued; at night the scene was lit by the fires of the tryworks and crude candles, made from rope yarns twisted together and stuck into small chunks of blubber.

In 1871, 32 whalers from New Bedford were caught in the Arctic ice and all were destroyed. If they had had engines, they might have escaped. It was the beginning of the end of the sailing whaler; soon steam engines were to replace sails, explosive-headed harpoons, fired from guns on the foredeck, were to replace harpooner's iron and the double-ended whaleboat.

Today the *Charles W. Morgan* is preserved at Mystic Seaport, Connecticut, in the USA. The hull is painted black with a white stripe on the main rail,

93 *Steamship whaler,* Southern Cross, *c1900, with whaleboats and a barrel for a look-out position. (National Maritime Museum, Greenwich)*

and its two narrow, raised deckhouses in the stern are distinct features of all sailing American whalers. The *Morgan* is now rigged as a double topsail bark, the working rig from 1867 to 1921, and the favourite rig of whalers. It was an easy rig to work and the main braces were kept aloft, well clear of davits and whaleboats. The *Morgan* is not only the last of the sailing whalers, but also the last example of the hull type seen in the tonnage cheaters of the first half of the nineteenth century.

Faster sailing ships

After 1850, and following the repeal of the British tonnage laws and Navigation Acts, ocean traders gradually became longer, flatter-floored, more streamlined and shallower, and as a result much faster. More and more vessels were given a third mast and sailed as fully-rigged ships or barques, (barks), with greater sail-power and a smaller crew.

But it was the Americans who, since the very beginning of the eighteenth century, had led the way towards faster ships. American privateers, schooners, brigs and the 'Baltimore Clippers', regularly out-sailed the British Navy during the war of 1812. These American ships, often built of softwoods, had high, long bows and a deeper draught aft than forward ('deep drag'). Speedy Baltimore Clippers,

built in Baltimore and around 90 ft long by 24 ft in the beam, were actually able to enter British convoys, cheekily pick off prizes, and out-run any pursuers. Baltimore Clippers, flush-decked, topsail schooners with raked masts, undoubtedly had a strong influence on the development of the later American clipper ships. Fast Baltimore-built ships, between 100–400 tons and rigged as schooners and brigs, were used as slavers in the first part of the nineteenth century and replaced the eighteenth-century British slavers or 'Guineamen', which were usually snows and frigates.

Undoubtedly another source of influence on American clipper development was the packet ship of the first quarter of the nineteenth century. American packets were hard-driven, and man-killing, as they were pushed across the Atlantic by captains, ruthless to meet punishing schedules. Under 400 tons and around 100 ft, full-rigged craft, early packet ships like the *James Monroe* would set out in the most appalling conditions so as to sail on time. From 1818 to 1823 the average passage time for ships of the Black Ball Line, running between New York and Liverpool, was 23 days, travelling eastwards to England, and 40 days westwards, half the passage time of ordinary ocean traders.

By 1825 these transatlantic passage ships, along with American ex-privateers, were often sent to

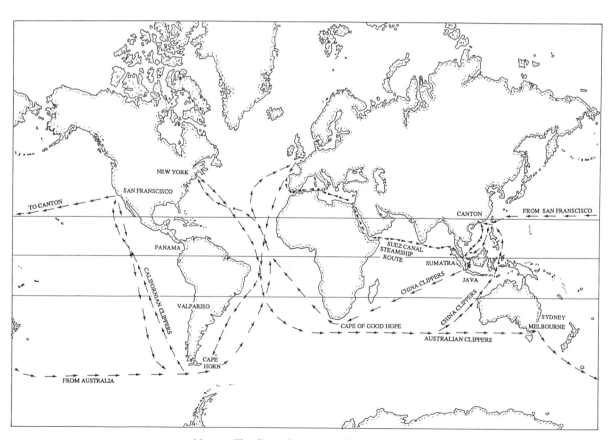

Map 7 *The clipper ship routes. (after Knight, 1973).*

140

finish their working lives on the China trade: Americans had acquired a taste for tea. These ships were soon succeeded by the new clippers, a fore-runner of which was the Baltimore-built 493-ton, *Ann McKim*. Launched in 1833, she was 143 ft long, and the largest ship in the American merchant fleet. Although incorporating many of the features of other Baltimore fast ships, her bows were still barrel-shaped (convex), but the hull was extremely wedge-shaped aft, and had a large afterdrag.

In 1845 the New York shipbuilders, Smith and Dimon, turned the *Ann McKim's* bow 'inside out' when they built the *Rainbow*, with sharp, *concave* bows foreward, and a much reduced afterdrag and deadrise. Although *Rainbow* has often been heralded as the first of the 'true clippers', Smith and Dimon only incorporated, into one ship, a number of features that had already been tried and tested in smaller ships (see C. Cutler, *Greyhounds of the Sea*). Nevertheless, in 1845 the 752-ton *Rainbow* was the largest ship with concave bows then built: 159 ft long, 31 ft 10 in. abeam and 18 ft 4 in. deep (abbreviated in this chapter to 159 × 31.10 × 18.4). The *Rainbow* was built for the China trade, and joined an American fleet of 44 full-rigged ships and two barques.

At the beginning of the century the term 'clipper' was generally used to mean a fast ship, probably making its appearance during the War of 1812 (possibly from the Dutch word 'kleeper' or 'fast horse'). But from 1845, with the launch of the *Rainbow*, 'clipper' took on a definite meaning. Carl Cutler wrote that they were:

Clean, long, smooth as smelt. Sharp arching head. Thin hollow bow; convex sides; light round and graceful stern... Aloft, large built, iron-banded lower masts; taunt tapering smaller masts, long proportioned spars from lower skysail yards.

Another Smith and Dimon clipper followed the *Rainbow*, the 908-ton *Sea Witch*, 170.3 × 33.11 × 19.0, (most dimensions in this chapter follow the format, and are from, the appendices in Cutler's *Greyhounds of the Sea*), also destined for the China tea trade. When launched in New York in 1846, *Sea Witch* was considered to be the most beautiful of all American ships. Fully-rigged, with royals set on all three well-raked masts, the stern was square and the bow even more concave than on *Rainbow*. Captained by Robert 'Bully' Waterman, who drove his frightened crews with pistol, knuckle-duster and belaying pin, *Sea Witch* beame the first ship to break the 100-day passage barrier round Cape Horn from New York to San Francisco. *Sea Witch's* 78-day passage from Canton to New York was never beaten.

North of New York, in Boston, there was a clipper builder who became even more famous than Smith and Dimon: Donald McKay. He built ships for the California, China and Australia clipper-routes, and was responsible for such beautiful creations as the *Sovereign of the Sea, Flying Cloud, Stag Hound,* and the *Great Republic.* For British shipowners he built, amongst others, *Lightning, Champion of the Sea* and the *Donald McKay.* In 1850 McKay built the first of the true clippers, the *Stag Hound*: 1534 tons, 215.0 × 39.8 × 21.0. Clippers were now coming in all shapes and sizes: out-and-out racers were called extreme clippers, others, medium and half clippers. All types were in demand, and they made large profits often recouping building costs on maiden voyages. In 1851 McKay launched the extreme clipper, *Flying Cloud*—1782 tons, 229.0 × 40.8 × 21.6— which became the 'Queen of the Californian Clippers' for over four years. Captain Josiah Cressy drove the ship on her maiden voyage from New York to San Francisco in 89 days 21½ hours.

In 1850 the *Oriental* unloaded tea in London, the first American clipper to enter Britain after the repeal of the Navigation Acts. *Oriental*, built in 1849 of white oak, live oak, locust and cedar, 1050 tons, 185.0 × 36.0 × 21.0, was then the largest American clipper, and like all true American clippers set 'skysails' above the royals. On some clippers 'moonsails' were even set above skysails. *Oriental's* appearance in London caused a sensation, and immediately British tea firms chartered the vessel. By 1855, 24 American-built clipper ships were carrying tea to England from China, securing the cream and much of the trade.

The period from 1845–1860 was the great epoch of the American clippers. In 1852, the golden year of the American clipper, 95 clippers sailed from the east coast of America for San Francisco and 17 made the trip in less than 110 days. In 1853 McKay's *Sovereign of the Sea* sailed 421 miles in 24 hours, an unbeaten clipper ship performance. In the same year McKay launched the huge four-masted sailing ship, the *Great Republic.* She was the largest clipper ever built at 4555 tons, 335.0 × 53.0 × 38.0, and the topsails were so big that MacKay divided them into 'double-topsails', to make them easier to handle.

Despite this dominance by the Americans in the 1850s, by 1860 British ships were back in force on the China runs. The forerunners of British fast ships were the 'opium clippers' that smuggled opium from India into China c1830 to 1850. Opium clippers were not true clippers. They were fast ships, brigs, schooners and a few full-rigged vessels. They were usually small, as bars of silver or balls of opium required little hold space. One of the most famous opium clippers, operated by Jardine, Matheson & Co., was the *Falcon*, of 351 tons. Built in 1824 as a yacht, *Falcon* was 107.2 × 27.4, square-rigged, with

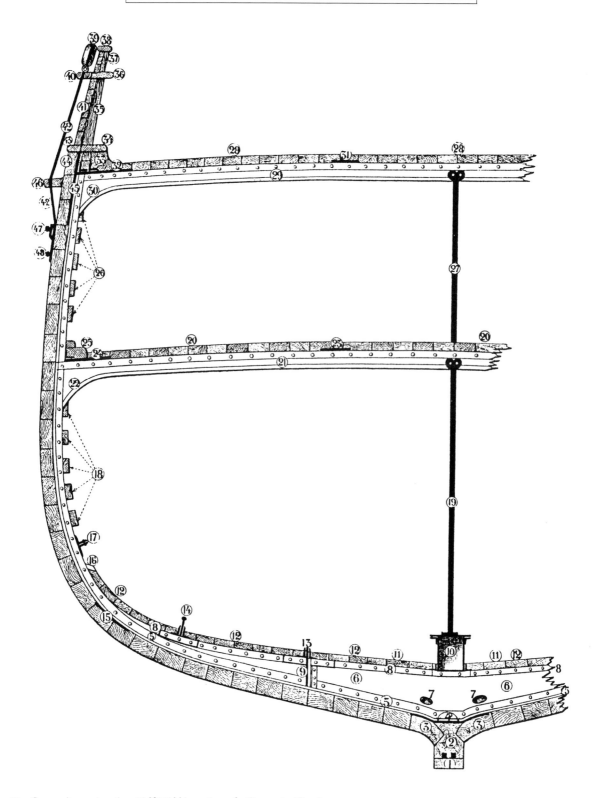

94 *Composite construction. Half-Midship-section of a Composite Vessel:*

1 False-keel; 2 Keel; 3 Garboard-strake; 4 Keel-plate; 5 Frame; 6 Floor; 7 Limbers—Water-course; 8 Reversed-frame; 9 Side-intercostal-keelson; 10 Middle-line (box) keelson; 11 Limber-boards; 12 Ceiling; 13 Side-keelson; 14 Bilge-keelson; 15 Bilge-plate, Iron-bilge-strake, Bilge-strake-plate; 16 Covering-board; 17 Bilge-stringer; 18 Cargo-battens (in hold); 19 Hold-pillar; Hold-stanchion; 20 Lower-deck; 21 Lower-deck-beam; 22 Bracket-end (of lower-deck-beam); 23 Lower-deck-beam-tie-plate; 24 Lower-deck-stringer, Lower-deck-beam-stringer-plate; 25 Lower-deck-waterway; 26 Cargo-battens (betwixt-deck); 27 Upper-deck-pillar, Upper-deck-stanchion; 28 Upper-deck; 29 Upper-deck-beam; 30 Bracket-end (of upper-deck-beam); 31 Upper-deck-beam-tie-plate; 32 Upper-deck-stringer, Upper-deck-beam-stringer-plate; 33 Upper-deck-waterway; 34 Covering-board; 35 Bulwark-stanchion; 36 Main-rail, Roughtree-rail; 37 Topgallant-bulwark-stanchion; 38 Topgallant-rail; 39 Dead-eye; 40 Upper-channel; 41 Bulwark-planking; 42 Chain-plate; 43 Planksheer; 44 Sheerstrake; 45 Iron-sheerstrake; 46 Lower-channel; 47 Chain-bolt; 48 Preventer-bolt. (from Paasch, 1890)

royals on all three masts. Flush-decked with eight gun ports a side, *Falcon* sailed for 15 years in the opium trade before disappearing in 1855.

British shipbuilders took up the challenge as American clippers swept all before them. In Aberdeen, Scotland, Alexander Hall and Sons had for some time being building fast schooners, like the *Scottish Maid*, with extended stems. In 1848 they launched the full-rigged ship *Reindeer*, with this new type of bow—the Aberdeen bow. The foremost part in an Aberdeen bow was greatly extended, so that the 'cutwater', as it was known, was carried forward to create a more streamlined stem. Aberdeen-built ships were smaller, beamier and less heavy than the American clippers, and out-performed them in light to moderate winds. Fast Aberdeen clippers such as *Stornaway* (1850)—595 tons NM, 157.8 × 28.8 × 17.8 —and *Chrysolite* (1851) 149.3 × 29.0 × 17.0— followed *Reindeer*. By the 1860s the British clipper took the lead and held it until sail gave way to steam. Extreme British clippers were of composite construction, often of teak and oak, and although

hard-driven, lasted longer than the softwood American clippers. The latter tended to last only four or five voyages, and when mercilessly driven their hulls soon became twisted, wracked and waterlogged.

Other Scottish, Clyde-side yards built famous extreme British clippers, including *Ariel, Taeping* and *Sir Lancelot*. Throughout the 1860s and 1870s British tea clippers raced home from China to be first to deliver the new season's tea. The races grew out of the commercial advantage of arriving first in port with a new cargo of tea, but the tea races caught everyone's imagination in Britain, and wagering soon became an important part of the race. The 'Great Tea Race', reported in the *Illustrated London News*, took place in 1866. *Ariel* (1865)—853 tons, 197.4 × 33.9 × 21.0—was narrowly beaten by *Taeping* (1863)—767 tons, 184.0 × 31.1 × 19.9.

95 *The Great Tea Race. Note—the* Serica *was not built of iron.* (Illustrated London News, *22/9/1866*)

THE GREAT SHIP-RACE FROM CHINA TO LONDON.

THE great race between nine of the swiftest clipper sailing-ships in the China trade—competing with each other all the way from Foo-Chow-Foo to London for the premium offered by the London tea importers on the arrival of the first cargo of this season's teas—was decided on Wednesday, the 5th inst., when the Taeping got into London Docks at 9.45 p.m., the Ariel, which came next, getting into the East India Dock half an hour later, and the third ship, the Serica, into the West India Dock at half-past eleven that night.

The following are the names of the nine ships, their owners and commanders, their tonnage, the ports where they were built, and the respective departures from Foo-Chow-Foo :—

Names.	Ton-nage.	Captains.	Where Built.	Owners.	Date of Sailing.
Ada	686	Jones	Aberdeen	Wade and Co.	June 6.
Ariel	853	Keay	Greenock	Shaw and Lowther	May 30.
Black Prince	750	Inglis	Aberdeen	Findlay and Co.	June 3.
Chinaman	688	Downie	Greenock	Park Brothers	June 3.
Fiery Cross	689	Robinson	Liverpool	J. Campbell	May 29.
Flying Spur	731	Ryrie	Aberdeen	Robertson and Co.	June 6.
Serica	708	Innes	Greenock	Findlay and Co.	May 30.
Taeping	767	M'Kinnon	Greenock	Roger and Co.	May 31.
Taitsing	815	Nutsfield	Glasgow	Findlay and Co.	May 31.

The struggle, however, was between the Fiery Cross, Ariel, Taeping, and Serica. The Fiery Cross obtained a start of one day over the others. The Serica, Ariel, and Taeping crossed the bar of Foo-Chow-Foo in company together, May 30. The Taitsing started the following day. There was a fair wind (N.E.) blowing, which the Fiery Cross kept to 19·20 N., when they met with a few hours' calm and southerly wind. North-east wind, fresh, again set in, which carried them to the Parcells reef on June 3, though they were not sighted. The Serica, Taeping, and Ariel met with similar weather. The Fiery Cross saw nothing of them until noon of June 7, in lat. 9·87, when she passed a large ship on the opposite tack', believed to have been the Ariel. To the southward of the Parcells they met with strong S.W. winds. As far as we have been enabled to ascertain, the ships passed the lighthouse at Anjer, Strait of Sunda, as follows :—Fiery Cross, at noon of June 18 ; Ariel, on the morning of June 20 ; Taeping, on the afternoon of June 20 ; Serica, at six p.m. of June 22 ; Taitsing, at ten p.m. of June 22 ; Black Prince, on June 29.

At this time the Fiery Cross was evidently holding the lead, while the Taitsing, which left Foo-Chow-Foo on the day after the others, had caught up with the Serica, the Fiery Cross heading both by two days. From Anjer they carried good trade winds to the meridian of Madagascar. The Fiery Cross passed Mauritius on June 30, the Ariel on July 2. The Cape of Good Hope was sighted by the Fiery Cross on July 15, the Ariel rounded the Cape the next day, wind S.E. to E. and N.N.E. The Serica rounded the Cape on the 22nd.

On Aug. 9, in lat. 12·29 N. the Fiery Cross signalled the Taeping, and continued in company till the 17th, with wind variable and light. In lat. 27·58, long. 36·54 W., a fresh breeze sprang up, and took the Taeping out of sight from the Fiery Cross in four or five hours. The Fiery Cross was becalmed, and was not making one knot per hour for twenty-four hours. This circumstance is alleged to have lost her the race. On the 29th she reached lat. 41·5 N., long. 35·51 W., and at ten a.m. of Sept. 6 she sighted the Isle of Wight, it bearing N.N.W., with a wind W.S.W., blowing hard.

At eight o'clock on the morning of Wednesday, the 5th inst., the Ariel and Taeping, which had lost sight of each other for seventy days, found themselves off the Lizard, running neck and neck up the Channel under every stitch of canvas that could be set, with a strong westerly wind. The two ships appear thus in our Illustration, the Taeping in front. During the whole day the two ships kept their position, dashing up the Channel side by side in splendid style, sometimes almost on their beam ends, every sea sweeping their decks. On approaching the pilot station off Dungeness the next morning they each fired blue lights to signalise their position. At daybreak the pilots boarded them at the same moment, and the race was continued in the same exciting manner till they arrived in the Downs, where they both took steam-tugs to tow them to the river. The ships had to shorten sail to enable the tugs to come up and pick up the hawsers to take them in tow. This was about eight o'clock a.m., the tugs starting almost simultaneously, and both ships still neck and neck. The Taeping, however, was fortunate enough to have a superiority in the power of the steam-tug, and reached Gravesend some time before the Ariel. The Serica followed closely upon them. She passed Deal at noon, and got into the river with the same tide which carried the Taeping and Ariel up the river to the docks. when the result of this extraordinary race was declared to be as follows :—

1st. Taeping, docked in London Dock .. .. 9.45 p.m.
2nd. Ariel, docked in East India Dock .. .. 10.15 p.m.
3rd. Serica, docked in West India Dock .. .. 11.30 p.m.

The Taeping, therefore, was the winner of the premium, 10s. per ton extra to be paid to the first sailing-vessel in dock with new teas from Foo-Chow-Foo. The Fiery Cross arrived in the Downs on the 7th, and was compelled to bring up to an anchor on account of a heavy gale blowing, where she remained some time. She, however, managed to get into the London Dock by eight o'clock on Saturday morning, about twenty-eight hours after the Taeping. The fifth ship, Taitsing, arrived in the river some hours after.

The three first ships—the Taeping, Ariel, and Serica—were all built by Messrs. Steele and Co., of Greenock. The Taeping and Ariel were constructed on the composite principle, wood and iron. The Serica is iron built.

The cargoes of the ships were—Taeping, 1,108,709 lb. of tea ; Ariel, 1,230,900 lb.; the Serica, 954,236 lb.; Fiery Cross, 854,236 lb.; and the Taitsing, 1,093,130 lb.

The time occupied on the voyage by the three ships has been ninety-nine days, being seven days shorter than the time occupied by the Fiery Cross and Serica last year. The Taeping, indeed, though not in the race of last year, made the passage in five days less time than they did. Captain Mackinnon, the commander of the Taeping, is a native of the island of Tyree, in Argyleshire, and a Lieutenant in the Royal Naval Reserve.

September 22, 1866.

G: Dutton, del. et lith.

London, Published Nov.

The Great
The Clipper Ships "TAEPIN
ON THEIR HOMEWAR
To Alex Rodger Esq (owner of the Taeping)

'Taeping' started 30ᵗʰ May 1866.
arrived in London Dock 6ᵗʰ Sept 9·45 PM

'Ariel' started 30ᵗʰ May 1866.
arrived in E.I. Dock 6ᵗʰ Sept 10·15 PM

96 Taeping *v.* Ariel *in the Great Tea Race. (Science Museum, London)*

Foster, 17, Billiter Street, E.C.

~hina Race~
& "ARIEL" passing the Lizard Sept. 6th 1866.
FROM FOO-CHOW-FOO.
~ Shaw, Lowther & Maxton (owners of the Ariel,)
Print is most respectfully dedicated by their Obedient Servant, W.m Foster

97 **top** Torrens *alongside The Adelaide Wool Store, Australia. (National Maritime Museum, Greenwich)*

98 **bottom** Torrens *at sea, 1875. (National Maritime Museum, Greenwich)*

In 1868 the extreme Aberdeen clipper *Thermopylae*—947 tons, 212.0 × 36.0 × 20.9—was built by Walter Hood. On *Thermopylae*'s maiden voyage to Melbourne, Australia the outward passage time was a record 60 days. Continuing from Newcastle, Australia to Shanghai a new trans-Pacific record was made when this voyage was completed in 28 days. Loading tea in Foochow, *Thermopylae* took part in the 1869 tea race, coming second to the extreme clipper, *Sir Lancelot. Taeping* was well beaten.

The famous *Cutty Sark*, now preserved at Greenwich, London, was built in 1869, specifically to challenge *Thermopylae* in the tea races. Constructed at Dunbarton in Scotland and designed by Hercules Linton, the ship incorporated the latest techniques of composite construction. Most of the extreme British clippers taking part in the China tea races were of composite construction, a form of building introduced c1840 and consisting of covering iron frames with planking, and used extensively for about a dozen years on both tea and Australian wool and passenger clippers.

The *Torrens* was the last fully-rigged composite passenger-carrying clipper, built by James Laing of Sunderland. Launched in 1875—1276 tons, 221.0 × 38.1 × 21.5—the *Torrens* was 'a ship of brilliant qualities', according to the writer Joseph Conrad, who joined the ship as second mate in 1891. *Torrens* sailed to Adelaide in 64 days and logged 300–350 miles a day, when running in the strong winds of the roaring forties.

The *Cutty Sark*—963 tons gross, 212.5 × 36.0 × 21.0—carried, like all clippers, an enormous spread of canvas: ringtails on the spanker, royal stunsails and watersails under the lower stunsail, staysails on every stay, double topsails on all three masts, and a sky sail above the royal on the main mast. A 'patent truss' was used to attach the lower yards to the mast. The truss kept the yard some distance off the mast, so that when the *Cutty Sark* was close-hauled, and the square sails angled into the wind, the leading edge of the sail could be brought closer in to the wind. The forecourse could be boomed out, and a 'Jamie Green', set along the jib boom under the jib and staysails. The Jamie Green was filled with the down draught coming off the headsails. The best 24-hour run the *Cutty Sark* ever made was 363 miles, the longest run ever made by a British tea clipper, sometimes travelling at over 17 knots.

99 *The* Cutty Sark *viewed from the bow. (M.W. Marshall)*

100 Cutty Sark *viewed from the stern. (M.W. Marshall)*

The *Cutty Sark* was launched the same year that the Suez Canal was opened, when steamers were about to make the tea clippers obsolete. But *Cutty Sark* did make eight trips to China between 1869 and 1877, then, for the following five years, traded between London, Shanghai and Sydney. The Australian wool trade, from 1883 until 1895, was where she ended her days under the British flag.

The California and China tea clippers were only a very small percentage of the total number of sailing ships carrying the world's trade in the nineteenth century, but their cargoes were probably one of the most valuable. In their old age, and because of over-production, some beautiful American clipper ships, like the *Bald Eagle* and the *White Falcon*, ended up transporting bird-lime (guano) from Peru; others worked with cut-down rigs in the grain and lumber trades. The *Sea Witch* ended her days in 1856 on a Cuban reef, whilst carrying a cargo of Chinese labour in the 'coolie trade' from Amoy in China to Cuba.

101 *The three-masted barque* Still Water, *built in Portland, Oregon, USA in 1879. Dimensions in register (The Record): length 177 ft, breadth 37.5 ft, depth 23.4 ft, 1090 tons registered. (National Maritime Museum, San Francisco)*

After the world wide abolition of slavery, the colonizing nations experienced a severe labour shortage on their cocoa, coffee and sugar plantations: the freed slaves had had enough! Labourers were sought in China, and later India, with their large populations of peasant classes. In the 1850s Chinese labourers were transported in the coolie trade from their homeland, in conditions that were little better than the slave trade. Poor Chinese workers, either sold by relatives or lured by false promises, were carried to the Peruvian, Cincha Islands and forced to dig guano. Basil Lubbock, in *Coolie Ships and Oil Sailers*, vividly describes their conditions:

A coolie's day's work digging guano was considered to be 6 to 8 tons. The men, half naked, and working in clouds of guano dust, were kept to it by the whips of the cruel overseers. Under these conditions those Chinese who did not commit suicide by some means or other speedily succumbed to overwork, breathing the guano dust, and a want of sufficient food.

Survival times was often only a few months. Between 1850 and 1860 there were between 50 to 80 ships, many of them ex-tea clippers, waiting to load guano at Peru's Cincha Islands.

Plantations in the British West Indian colonies were probably saved by the importation of Indian labour. From 1853, to Trinidad and Guyana, Demerara, Mauritius and the Cape of Good Hope, a controlled, reasonably humane exportation of Indian labour was over-seen by the British government. The ships were often Blackwall frigates and some travelled as far as Fiji in this 'Indian coolie trade'. Conditions could not have been as bad as for the Chinese labourers, as Indian labourers would sometimes sign on for two or three consecutive work periods.

Down easters and schooners

Before, throughout and after the period of clipper ships, much ocean trade was carried by merchantmen not involved in the glamorous China and Californian clipper-ship runs. Three- and four-masted barques and full-rigged ships carried the bulk cargoes: lumber, wheat grain, wool, jute, rice and iron goods. In the 1870s and 1880s, America developed a large class of all wooden, 1000–2000 ton, full-rigged ships, such as medium clippers, and known as 'down easters'. They were built 'down east' on the New England coast, at places like Bath and Maine, from local woods—white oak and pitch pine—and were often used to carry grain to Britain from San Francisco. They were large, like the *Henry B. Hyde*, which was built in 1884 and was 290 ft long and 2580 tons gross. The *Henry B. Hyde* sailed on her maiden voyage with a cargo of wheat from San Francisco to Liverpool and between 1890 and 1893 made four consecutive voyages from the east to west coast of America, around Cape Horn, averaging 108 days per voyage. The 2526-ton *Ocean King* built in Maine in 1874 was rigged as a four-masted barque.

The Americans were also experimenting with multi-masted schooners. From small two-masted schooners (100 to 130 tons) c1800, they had developed, by the 1880s, four-masted schooners of 700 tons with only a nine-man crew. The *David Dows*, launched in 1881, was the first of over 50 five-masted American schooners that were c2700

102 *The three-masted, full-rigged ship* Abner Coburn. *Built in 1882 in Bath, USA, and rigged with double topsails. Length 223 ft, breadth 43 ft, depth 26.8 ft, 1879 tons registered. (National Maritime Museum, San Francisco)*

19thAND 20th CENTURY

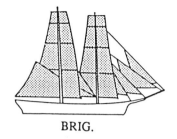

BRIG.

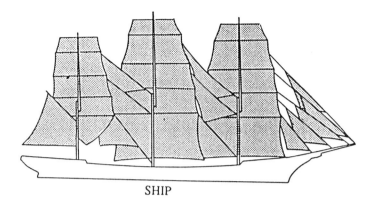

SHIP

BRIGANTINE

FIVE MASTED BARQUE

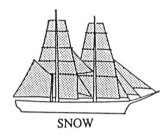

SNOW

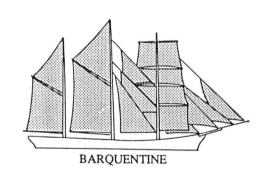

BARQUENTINE

TOPSAIL SCHOONER

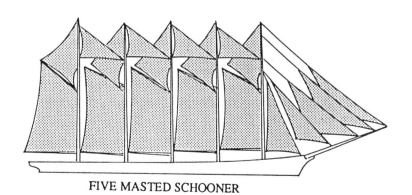

FIVE MASTED SCHOONER

103   *Sail plans. (after Kihlberg, 1986)*

tons. In 1900, the 3402-ton *Eleanor A. Percy* was the first six-masted schooner, followed nine years later by the longest wooden sailing ship ever built, the 3731-ton *Wyoming*. These enormous wooden ships, like McKay's *Great Republic*, were braced with fore and aft iron stiffeners. The only seven-masted schooner, *Thomas W. Lawson* (395.0 ft × 50.0 × 35.0), was launched in 1902. Her hull was made of steel, the twentieth-century ship-building material. The schooner-rig was so efficient that the *Thomas W. Lawson* had a crew of only 16 men. The only five-masted, ship-rigged ocean trader was the *Preussen*, which was launched in the same year as the *Lawson*. (There were a few five-masted barques built.) Although 407 ft long, 54 ft beam and 5081 tons gross, the German-built, steel-hulled *Preussen* needed a crew of 47 to work her 46 sails. However the *Lawson* was a clumsy ship and made only two voyages under sail, while the *Preussen* made numbers of successful voyages (two round voyages a year) on the nitrate trade.

Iron and steel sailing ships

In 1838, one of the first iron-hulled sailing ocean traders was launched—the 270-ton *Ironside*. Built in Liverpool with dimensions 99.0 ft × 23.6 × 13.8, *Ironside* was a full-rigged ship, including skysails, and sailed on the South American trading routes. The ship was a success and soon other iron-hulled vessels followed. The iron-hulled British clipper, *Lord of the Isles*, was built for the China tea run, but never outsailed the composite-built ships. Iron hulls were therefore not used for sailing tea-clippers, as they were said 'to sweat' and cause water damage to the delicate cargo. Iron hulls were also subject to underwater marine growth, since in the early days of metal ship-building satisfactory anti-fouling did not exist. Marine growth can markedly reduce a ship's speed through the water.

Iron and steel sailing ships dominated, for a while, the long-haul bulk routes, until they were ousted by the more flexible, steam-engine, iron-hulled tramps.

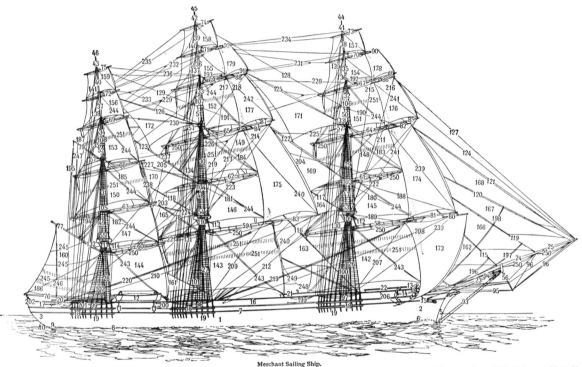

Merchant Sailing Ship.

1, hull; 2, bow; 3, stern; 4, cutwater; 5, stem; 6, entrance; 7, waist; 8, run; 9, counter; 10, rudder; 11, davits; 12, quarter-boat; 13, cathead; 14, anchor; 15, cable; 16, bulwarks; 17, taffrail; 18, channels; 19, chain-plates; 20, cabin-trunk; 21, after deck-house; 22, forward deck-house; 23, bowsprit; 24, jib-boom; 25, flying-jib boom; 26, foremast; 27, mainmast; 28, mizzenmast; 29, foretopmast; 30, maintopmast; 31, mizzentopmast; 32, foretopgallantmast; 33, maintopgallantmast; 34, mizzentopgallantmast; 35, foreroyalmast; 36, mainroyalmast; 37, mizzenroyalmast; 38, foreskysailmast; 39, mainskysailmast; 40, mizzenskysailmast; 41, foreskysail-pole; 42, mainskysail-pole; 43, mizzenskysail-pole; 44, fore-truck; 45, main-truck; 46, mizzen-truck; 47, foremast-head; 48, mainmast-head; 49, mizzenmast-head; 50, foretopmast-head; 51, maintopmast-head; 52, mizzentopmast-head; 53, foretop; 54, maintop; 55, mizzentop; 56, dolphin-striker; 57, outriggers; 58, foreyard; 59, mainyard; 60, crossjack-yard; 61, fore lower topsail-yard; 62, main lower topsail-yard; 63, mizzen lower topsail-yard; 64, fore upper topsail-yard; 65, main upper topsail-yard; 66, mizzen upper topsail-yard; 67, foretopgallant-yard; 68, maintopgallant-yard; 69, mizzentopgallant-yard; 70, foreroyal-yard; 71, mainroyal-yard; 72, mizzenroyal-yard; 73, foreskysail-yard; 74, mainskysail-yard; 75, mizzenskysail-yard; 76, spankerboom; 77, spanker-gaff; 78, maintrysail-gaff; 79, monkey-gaff; 80, lower studdingsail-yard; 81, foretopmast studdingsail-boom; 82, foretopmast studdingsail-yard; 83, maintopmast studdingsail-boom; 84, maintopmast studdingsail-yard; 85, mizzentopmast studdingsail-boom; 86, foretopgallant studdingsail-boom; 87, maintopgallant studdingsail-boom; 88, maintopgallant studdingsail-yard; 89, foreroyal studdingsail-boom; 90, foreroyal studdingsail-yard; 91, mainroyal studdingsail-boom; 92, mainroyal studdingsail-yard; 93, bobstays; 94, bowsprit-shrouds; 95, martingale-guys; 96, martingale-stays; 97, forechains; 98, main-chains; 99, mizzen-chains; 100, fore-shrouds; 101, main-shrouds; 102, mizzen-shrouds; 103, foretopmast-shrouds; 104, maintopmast-shrouds; 105, mizzentopmast-shrouds; 106, foretopgallant-shrouds; 107, maintopgallant-shrouds; 108, mizzentopgallant-shrouds; 109, futtock-shrouds; 110, futtock-shrouds; 111, futtock-shrouds; 112, forestay; 113, mainstay; 114, mizzenstay; 115, foretopmast-stay; 116, maintopmast-stay; 117, spring-stay; 118, mizzentopmast-stay; 119, jib-stay; 120, flying-jib stay; 121, foretopgallant-stay; 122, maintopgallant-stay; 123, mizzentopgallant-stay; 124, foreroyal-stay; 125, mainroyal-stay; 126, mizzenroyal-stay; 127, foreskysail-stay; 128, mainskysail-stay; 129, mizzenskysail-stay; 130, foretopmast-backstays; 131, maintopmast-backstays; 132, mizzentopmast-backstays; 133, foretopgallant-backstays; 134, maintopgallant-backstays; 135, mizzentopgallant-backstays; 136, foreroyal-backstays; 137, mainroyal-backstays; 138, mizzenroyal-backstays; 139, foreskysail-backstays; 140, mainskysail-backstays; 141, mizzenskysail-backstays; 142, foresail or forecourse; 143, mainsail or maincourse; 144, cross-jack; 145, fore lower topsail; 146, main lower topsail; 147, mizzen lower topsail; 148, fore upper topsail; 149, main upper topsail; 150, mizzen upper topsail; 151, foretopgallant-sail; 152, maintopgallant-sail; 153, mizzentopgallant-sail; 154, foreroyal; 155, mainroyal; 156, mizzenroyal; 157, foreskysail; 158, mainskysail; 159, mizzenskysail; 160, spanker; 161, mizzenstaysail; 162, foretopmast-staysail; 163, maintopmast lower staysail; 164, maintopmast upper staysail; 165, mizzentopmast-staysail; 166, jib; 167, flying jib; 168, jib-topsail; 169, mainroyal-staysail; 170, mizzentopgallant-staysail; 171, mainroyal-staysail; 172, mizzenroyal-staysail; 173, lower studdingsail; 174, foretopmast-studdingsail; 175, maintopmast-studdingsail; 176, foretopgallant-studdingsail; 177, maintopgallant-studdingsail; 178, foreroyal-studdingsail; 179, mainroyal-studdingsail; 180, forelift; 181, mainlift; 182, mizzen-lift; 183, fore lower topsail-lift; 184, main lower topsail-lift; 185, mizzen lower topsail-lift; 186, spanker-boom topping-lift; 187, monkey-gaff lift; 188, lower studdingsail-halyards; 189, lower studdingsail inner halyards; 190, foretopmast studdingsail-halyards; 191, maintopmast studdingsail-halyards; 192, foretopgallant studdingsail-halyards; 193, maintopgallant studdingsail-halyards; 194, spanker peak-halyards; 195, signal-halyards; 196, weather jib-sheet; 197, weather flying-jib sheet; 198, weather jib topsail-sheet; 199, weather fore-sheet; 200, weather main-sheet; 201, weather crossjack-sheet; 202, spanker-sheet; 203, mizzentopgallant staysail-sheet; 204, mainroyal staysail-sheet; 205, mizzenroyal staysail-sheet; 206, lower studdingsail-sheet; 207, foretopmast studdingsail-sheet; 208, foretopmast studdingsail-tack; 209, maintopmast studdingsail-sheet; 210, maintopmast studdingsail-sheet; 211, foretopgallant studdingsail-sheet; 212, foretopgallant studdingsail-tack; 213, maintopgallant studdingsail-sheet; 214, maintopgallant studdingsail-tack; 215, foreroyal studdingsail-sheet; 216, foreroyal studdingsail-tack; 217, mainroyal studdingsail-tack; 218, mainroyal studdingsail-sheet; 219, forebrace; 220, mainbrace; 221, crossjack-brace; 222, fore lower topsail-brace; 223, main lower topsail-brace; 224, mizzen lower topsail-brace; 225, fore upper topsail-brace; 226, main upper topsail-brace; 227, mizzen upper topsail-brace; 228, foretopgallant-brace; 229, maintopgallant-brace; 230, mizzentopgallant-brace; 231, foreroyal-brace; 232, mainroyal-brace; 233, mizzenroyal-brace; 234, foreskysail-brace; 235, mainskysail-brace; 236, mizzenskysail-brace; 237, upper maintopsail-downhaul; 238, upper mizzentopsail-downhaul; 239, foretopmast studdingsail-downhaul; 240, maintopmast studdingsail-downhaul; 241, foretopgallant studdingsail-downhaul; 242, maintopgallant studdingsail-downhaul; 243, clue-garnets; 244, clue-lines; 245, spanker-brails; 246, spanker-gaff vangs; 247, monkey-gaff vangs; 248, main bowline; 249, bowline-bridle; 250, foot-ropes; 251, reef-points.

104 *Full rigged ship c1890. (Science Museum, London)*

105　Ships, barks and coal at Sandridge railway pier, Melbourne, Australia in 1890. (National Maritime Museum, Greenwich)

106　Building the schooner Sotoyome in Albion, California, USA, a fine example of skeleton construction. Launched in 1905.
Dimensions in register: length 165 ft, breadth 36.8 ft, depth 10.3 ft, 398 tons registered. (National Maritime Museum, San Francisco)

Grain, case-oil and cotton from America; wool, and later grain, from Australia; coal and manufactured goods from Britain; lumber from North America; phosphates, nitrates and guano from South America; jute and rice from the East, were the cargoes carried on the long-haul routes by the last of the square-rigged ocean traders.

As iron, and then steel, were increasingly used in British ship-building, the yards moved to the north of England, and to Scotland, close to the iron deposits and coal fields. By 1866 the techniques of making steel were perfected and when launched the British medium clipper *Formby*, was the first sailing ocean trader built in steel. Square-rigged, *Formby* was 1271 tons and measured 209.1 ft × 36.0 × 23.4. By the end of the 1880s, steel had replaced iron as the first choice for hulls: steel hulls were some 15% lighter.

With iron and steel there is almost no limit to the size of ship that can be built: sailing ships got longer, up to 400 ft and 5000 tons, masts taller and sails larger. By 1870 it was common practice to rig 'double topgallants' for ease of sail handling and for owners to economize on crews! Another mast was added and ocean traders were often rigged as four-masted barques. A 'stump or spike bowsprit' replaced the long jib boom and flying jib boom and, in order to accommodate the headsails, the foremast was stepped further aft. Masts and yards were made at first of iron and then, by 1880, of tubular steel. The lower masts and topmasts were built as one continuous steel tube. The steel 'rigging screw', attached to the in-board side of bulwarks, replaced channels, deadeyes and lanyards. The rigging screw,

used to replace tarred hemp rope, was far more effective at tightening up iron and steel standing rigging.

By 1865 nearly all large British sailing ocean traders were square-rigged and iron-hulled. By the mid-1870s large, iron-hulled ocean traders were mainly sailed as four-masted, full-rigged ships, but by the 1880s, four-masted barques were the most common ocean traders. In the late 1890s some giant, five-masted barques, such as the British-built *France* and the second, even larger, French-built *France*, and the German-built *Potosi*, were launched, to carry up to 7000 tons of nitrate back to Europe from South America. During the 1870s and 1880s, sailing ships continued to score economically over tramp steamships, on routes where water (for boilers) and coaling ports were in short supply and time not a factor. Later, in the early twentieth century, about a dozen four-masted barques (e.g. the *Magdalene Vinnen*) were designed with auxiliary engines, but they were never really successful, the engine and its fuel wasting cargo space incurring high initial and maintenance costs.

Around 1850, in America, and about 1870 in Britain, the 'barquentine' (or barkantine or three-masted brigantine) rig was developed, that is, a ship that is square-rigged on the foremast, and fore- and

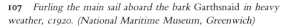

107 *Furling the main sail aboard the bark* Garthsnaid *in heavy weather, c1920. (National Maritime Museum, Greenwich)*

aft-rigged on the other masts. In 1885 the first all-steel barquentine, the *Hedwick*, was built. Like four-masted barques, (and multi-masted schooners), a barquentine rig helped to split sail area by distributing sails over four (or more) masts: thus requiring smaller crews to operate them. The *City of Sydney*, for example, was launched in 1875 as an iron-hulled steamship, but was re-rigged as a six-masted barquentine in 1916. Over 300 ft in length she was a large, ugly vessel, but the barquentine rig extended her working life, making her economically competitive in the twentieth century.

By 1880, in Britain, only small sailing ships, under 500 tons or so, were being constructed in wood: brigs, barquentines and schooners. Large, metal-hulled barques and full-rigged ships were still being built, even though steam tramps were beginning to make serious inroads into the long-haul trading routes. In 1885 the English company R.W. Leyland launched a two-deck, full-rigged ship, the *Southgate*, later named the *Wavertree*, 2170 tons gross, 279.0 ft × 40.2 × 24.4. The hull was of iron, and five square sails, set on each of the three masts, powered the ship as it tramped its way around the world on the long-haul routes searching for cargoes. Speed was never important on the long-haul routes. The *Wavertree* set no skysails or stunsails, and there were no double topgallants. Single topgallants were difficult sails to handle on any large square-rigger,

but especially when rounding Cape Horn, from east to west, in a gale. In *The Wavertree* Alan Villiers wrote:

The big full-rigged ship, too, could be brutish to tack, for the main and mizzen yards must all swing at the right moment, or else. Some of these big ships were apt to be hard-mouthed, sluggish big bullocks to swing across the wind, man-killers for their small crew; and their long, open decks were awash as they rolled down there off the Horn...

On 7 December 1910, the *Wavertree* arrived in Port Stanley, the Falkland Islands, towed in after the mainmast had been snapped off when trying to beat to windward in a gale some 200 miles south of Cape Horn. The cargo had shifted, the holds were awash, and three men had had their legs broken by seas that had crashed aboard. The carpenter later went mad.

Today the *Wavertree*, partially restored, can be seen at South Street Seaport Museum, New York, USA. One of the last iron-hulled, sailing ocean traders. Alongside her is the steel-hulled *Peking*. Built in 1911 for the famous German 'Flying P Line' (all their ships had names beginning with 'P'), F.C. Laeisz and Co. of Hamburg. Laeisz was the last ocean trading company to build sailing merchantmen. *Peking* is one of three, steel-hulled, four-masted barques: the other two, the *Passat* and the *Padua*, are also still afloat. Another former 'P'-Line ship still afloat is the steel, four-masted, stump-topgallant barque the *Pommern*, built for Laeisz in 1904. The *Peking* spent her working life carrying coal or manufactured goods out from Europe to Valparaiso

108 *The* Wavertree, *New York, 1988. (M.W. Marshall)*

in Chile, via Cape Horn; then a short passage north, in ballast, to load bags of nitrate from Chilean desert ports such as Antafagasta or Iquique; then the return passage to Europe, again via Cape Horn. In 1932 *Peking* was laid up when nitrate demand decreased with the increase use of synthetic fertilizers. Today *Peking* and *Wavertree*, side by side in New York harbour, are to many the embodiment of all sailing merchantmen: but they represent only the last of a long line that stretches back over 5000 years.

109 *The four-masted barque or bark* Peking, *New York, 1988.* Peking *carried 32 sails and was square-rigged on the fore, main and mizzen masts, and fore- and aft-rigged on the one aftermost mast—the jigger. On the jiggermast, she set a lower spanker, an upper spanker and a spanker topsail. There were royals on the fore, main and mizzen masts, and topsails and topgallants were doubled to make sail handling easier. On the bowsprit, from forward to aft, there was a flying jib, an outer jib, an inner jib, and a fore topmast staysail. (M.W. Marshall)*

CHAPTER SEVEN

Compound Engine and Container Ship

Two dramatic changes took place in this century and the last. Both commenced in the 60s, and both radically altered the nature of ocean trade. The first was when steam tramps replaced sailing ocean traders; the second was when conventional cargo vessels were replaced by container ships. Containerization expanded into ocean trade so fast that few men at sea in the 1960s would have believed that within almost a decade conventional cargo ships would be practically obsolete.

Steam, war, oil and container (1830–1990)

In the early nineteenth century shipowners realized that fast ships, sailing on regular schedules across the Atlantic and carrying passengers and mail, were extremely profitable. But steamships could make faster, more reliable passages than even the hardest-driven sailing packets, and wooden-hulled paddle steamers soon challenged their monopoly. In the latter part of the nineteenth century more efficient, iron-hulled, screw-driven steamships replaced the paddle steamers (see C.E. Fayle's *A Short History of the World's Shipping Industry*, R.A. Fletcher's *Steam-ships and Their Story*, and E. Corlett's *The Ship*, Vol. 10.)

The middle to late nineteenth century saw the birth of many famous shipping companies on the trans-Atlantic route, and throughout the world. Lucrative Post Office mail contracts were a major incentive for the formation of some of the earliest, and most successful, British shipping companies. In 1839 the British and North American Royal Mail Packet Steam Company was created, which later became the Cunard company. In the early 1830s, because of the patronage of the royal houses of Spain and Portugal, the Peninsular & Oriental Steam Navigation Company—P&O—began operating a regular steamer service to the Iberian peninsular. In

1837 P&O was contracted by the British Post Office to carry mail to Gibraltar, and eight years later the company had the mail contracts from Britain to Egypt, and then to India, via the 'overland route': ships would dock in Alexandria; the passengers, mail and some valuable freight would then travel by canal boats to the Nile, where they would be transferred to a river steamer for the passage up the Nile to Cairo. Then the 84 hot, dusty, desert miles of the overland route, from Cairo to the Red Sea, were in horse-drawn coaches. At Suez, passengers, mail and cargo joined another ship and steamed down the Red Sea and across the Indian Ocean to Calcutta. In the same year, 1845, P&O extended its mail run to Singapore and Hong Kong, and by 1859 the company was operating screw-driven steamships on regular mail runs to Singapore, Australia and Japan. In 1869 the Suez Canal was completed and brought an end to the P&O's overland route.

The opening of the Suez canal was a dramatic event for the ocean trader. The initial drive for the canal came from Ferdinand de Lesseps (1805–1894), a French diplomat in Egypt between 1831 and 1838, while the British, at first strongly opposed to the canal, were one of its main benefactors. In 1854 Lesseps obtained a concession from Egypt to build the canal and digging started in 1859, ten years later the canal was opened. The canal cut the route to India, one of Britain's richest colonies, by over one-third and dramatically shortened longer voyages to the Far East. This aided and increased the development of the iron-hulled steamship by reducing the number of coal bunkering stations, and stimulating the bulk cargo trades, like rice and coal, between East and West. In 1888 Britain obtained the right to 'guarantee the neutrality of the canal' and became the major user of the canal.

In 1852 the loss of a wooden-hulled, paddle-

110 *Port Said, c1865, 15 years after the opening of the Suez Canal: Three island steamships, rigged as ships and barques. (National Maritime Museum, Greenwich)*

wheeled mail ship caused the British Post Office to decide that in future mail ships were to have iron hulls and be driven by propellers—the iron-hulled steamship finally had official approval. At first, fast steamships or 'liners' carried mail, passengers (often emigrants or immigrants), but little cargo on the scheduled runs. 'Intermediate liners' were soon developed, ships which carried fewer passengers but more cargo; and these were followed by 'cargo liners', general cargo ships which kept a regular schedule and carried only a dozen or so passengers. To meet published schedules all three liner classes sometimes put to sea with accommodation, or cargo holds, not completely filled. To safeguard profits several British shipping companies operating liners, in 1875, called the first of a number of 'liner conferences' where shipowners agreed to regulate sailings on different trade routes and, more importantly, set fixed freight rates. Thus shipping companies cushioned themselves against the effects of the ruthless, free-market competition then in operation. Shipping cartels were also used by the owners when shipping companies amalgamated to form large conglomerates which, although supposedly operating independently, had only one financial policy and directive.

Despite attempts at protectionism, the ships of the liner companies were, by the end of the nineteenth century, less numerous than the tramp steamers. Tramp ships went where the freights were; they sailed when holds were full or when they could make

a profit; they acted as cross-carriers for the liner companies and, as steam engines became more efficient, they began to challenge the sailing ships as bulk carriers on the long-haul ocean routes. Many a sea captain spent his retirement playing the freight markets by having shares in, or owning, a second-hand tramp steamer. In 1914, two thirds of all ocean-going steamships were owned by Great Britain: 60% of this tonnage was in tramp ships.

Just before World War I, although other countries were beginning to challenge this maritime supremacy, Great Britain was still firmly in control. Fayle, in this *World's Shipping Industry*, shows that the relative percentages of the world's gross steam tonnage owned by the maritime nations in 1914 was: British Empire 47.7%, Germany 12%, Norway, France, USA (excluding its Great Lakes ships), Japan, Holland and Italy each between 4.5% and 3.4%, while Spain had only 2.1%. Of Portugal there was no mention: the old Iberian Empires had long since lost control of the ocean trading routes as well as many of their colonies.

After winning the Spanish-American war, America, aware of its ever increasing international power, annexed Cuba, Puerto Rico and the Philippines, and in 1898, Hawaii: colonies were still important symbols of national prestige. The USA acted rather like its old colonial master when it decided to build the Panama Canal. In 1903 the Americans aided some Colombian revolutionaries to set up the independent state of Panama, and in return, the new Republic of Panama granted the USA a 'canal zone', five miles on each side of any future canal, which the Americans could fortify in order to maintain the 'neutrality of the canal'. The advantages of a Panama Canal had been evident to the USA since the early days of the California Gold Rush, when a canal-passage would have avoided the long, dangerous passage around Cape Horn. But is was the extraordinary Frenchman, Ferdinand de Lesseps, who, in 1881, not satisfied with building the Suez Canal, set out to construct the Panama Canal. However ten years later, tropical diseases and lack of money finally forced him to abandon the project. In 1907 the USA bought out the defunct French canal company and continued to dig. After the loss of hundreds of lives, and a capital outlay that was four times that of the Suez Canal, a lock-gate canal was finally built to link the Caribbean Sea with the Pacific Ocean. The Cape Horn trade route, which had claimed the lives of countless sailors, ended in 1914 as the first steamships worked their way through the canal's many lock gates. By 1924, the Panama Canal was being used by some 5000 ships a year, as many as the Suez Canal.

Another developing world power in the early twentieth century was Germany. United after the Franco-Prussian war (1870–1871), which politically divided France, Germany had sufficient reserves of iron and coal to be independent of Britain. The Imperial German navy was rapidly expanded, and ten German liner companies, representing some 60% of all German tonnage, amalgamated to form a united, competitive front against British liners. Germany as was customary in any expanding nation, began collecting colonies but, inevitably, clashed with Britain, the greatest colonizer since the Romans. The Boer Wars (1880–1 and 1899–1902) had fuelled the rivalry between the two nations, and when the German army marched into Belgium in 1914 the British Empire went to war. In the opening stages of the war Britain, regardless of the effects of neutral nations, mined the North Sea. Germany retaliated by declaring the seas around Britain and Ireland a 'war zone'. It was 'total war', when warships and submarines sunk defenceless merchantmen and commandeered neutral shipping. After the confrontation between giant British and German battleships at the Battle of Jutland, which in less than an hour ended in a draw (the two battlefleets sunk a total of 25 ships and killed some 10,000 seamen), the German surface fleet returned to port, blockaded for the rest of the war by the British war-fleet.

Germany quickly realized the value of submarines. They were cheaper than the huge battleships of the surface fleets, more deadly, and the British were unprepared to fight them. During the war Germany's small submarine fleet sank some seven million tons of commercial shipping, and Britain had only six weeks supplies of food left when America entered the war in 1917. Once in the war, the USA used its huge resources of men and materials to rebuild her depleted merchant fleet; partly to restore her old maritime power; and partly to relieve the submarine blockade of Britain. The industrial power of the USA was such that production of ocean traders by the end of the war had increased by four-fold, more than sufficient to relieve the submarine blockade. After the war, in 1919, Great Britain still had the world's largest merchant fleet, about 16 million gross tons, but the USA, with nearly 10 million tons, had risen to second place.

There was a short post-war shipping boom, but this only lasted until 1920. The economic disruption caused by the war and governments' subsidies for building merchant fleets (often as part of national maritime policies) caused freights to drop as world tonnage increased. Between 1914 and 1933 British ship production did not fall, and this was one of the major causes of the massive over-production of world tonnage of the 1920s and 1930s. By 1925, Germany was exporting more ships than Britain. Japan had started on a mercurial rise which was to make her one of the world's major shipbuilders and shipowners. Despite the slump in ocean trade, world gross tonnage continued to rise, from 50 million tons in 1924 to 68 million tons in 1933 (the blackest part of the economic depression) to 65.5 million tons in 1939, just before World War II. One result of the excess of steamship tonnage was that sailing traders became uneconomical: in 1924 Gustav Erikson was the only shipowner left operating sailing ocean traders. A significant fraction of the new tonnage was composed of tankers, as throughout much of the developed world, oil was beginning to replace coal as the new energy source.

In 1850 oil was a little-understood substance used for medicinal purposes and for caulking wooden ships. But by the 1860s it was realized that a distillate of oil, kerosene, made a very effective fuel for wick-lamps. In America, oil was fairly easily obtained by drilling, but the liquid was difficult to transport, especially overseas. At first stowed in sailing ship's holds in barrels, and then in five gallon tins packed in wooden boxes, the distillate became known as 'case oil'. By the 1890s case oil was being carried all over the world from the USA in metal-hulled, three- and four-masted ships and barques; and in 1900, a number of 3000-ton plus, steel-hulled 'oil sailers' were built specially for the trade. Oil sailers were soon replaced by specially built steam-powered tankers, for in 1886, the first ocean-trading, tank steamer *Gluckauf* had already been launched in the northeast of England.

Oil not only became an important lighting and

**Gross tons
(Millions)**

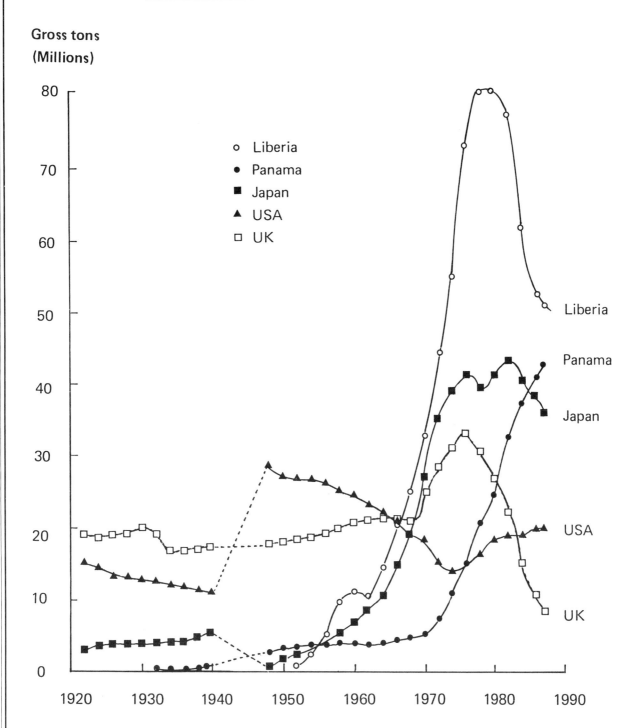

Liberia
Panama
Japan
USA
UK

III   *Gross tonnage changes since World War I. (source: Lloyds Register of Shipping, statistical tables)*

energy source on land; at sea it began to replace coal as the fuel of making steam. In 1902 only 1% of the world's ocean traders used oil to make steam, by 1918 this had increased to 15%. The fast, trans-Atlantic passenger liners were some of the first ships converted to burning oil, rather than coal, to make steam. Oil fired boilers were more efficient, they did not require a large labour force for bunkering (the oil could be pumped aboard) and, most important for

shipowners, they required less labour to operate them (trained crews are expensive). Fuel oil also took up to one third less hull space than coal, especially when stored in 'double bottom tanks' that had the added advantage to shipowners of being exempt from tonnage dues.

Britain, whose coal and iron resources were one of the corner-stones of her nineteenth-century maritime supremacy, was a country without oil, and slower than most industrialized nations to change over to the new fuel, despite its many advantages. Oil became increasingly important as the developed world entered the 'petroleum age', such that by 1970 the world was consuming oil at the rate of two billion tons annually, half of it carried by tankers.

The 90-year monopoly of the reciprocating steam engine was eventually challenged by an oil-fired marine engine when, in 1903, a German engineer, Rudolf Diesel (1858–1913), developed a new form of internal-combustion engine. Submarines were driven by diesel engines during the World War I, and diesels were used as auxiliary engines by one of the last of the sailing ocean traders. The *Vulcanus* in 1910 and the Danish trader *Selandia* two years later became the first cargo ships to use marine diesel engines. *Selandia* was twin-screwed, 7400 tons deadweight, and built for the East Asiatic Company of Copenhagen; her oil consumption was so low that she went from Denmark to the Far East and back without re-fuelling.

In 1906 the northeast England shipbuilding firm of William Doxford also began to consider diesel engines as a means of ship propulsion. In 1921, after years of research, the yard, successfully installed their first motor vessel, the *Yngaren*, a 3000-horsepower (hp) Doxford diesel. Soon oil-powered motor vessels were operating on all the ocean routes, and just before World War II about a quarter of all ocean traders were powered by diesel engines. By the late 1940s, Doxford diesels were world famous and from the 1950s onwards diesel engines were used in many ocean traders. The reciprocating compound steam engines were now obsolete but steam turbines, which had been invented in 1884 by Charles Parsons, were still to be found in some ships. Turbine steam engines were especially developed for warships and were used by the Atlantic passenger and cargo liners that needed to make fast passages.

In 1961 the atomic-powered merchant ship *Savannah* was launched, but atomic energy has not yet replaced oil as the fuel for ocean traders. Since the oil crisis of the 1970s, the emphasis nowadays is on fuel-efficient engines, and ocean traders are still fitted either with diesels or steam turbines. Today most diesel engines are operated at slow or medium speeds, the propeller shafts rotating at between 100 to 450 revolutions per minute. Steam turbines although smaller, lighter, and cheaper to build and maintain than diesel engines, are less manoeuvrable and consume more fuel oil (see W. Packard's *Sea-trading* Vol. 1). There are even a few experimental ships with steam turbines that have travelled a full cycle and have been fitted with coal-fired boilers!

In the early part of the twentieth century a very important advance was made in shipbuilding when, in 1919, the first all welded ship, the *Fullagar*, was launched. Later, welded ships were to play an important role in winning World War II for the Allies. The origins of the World War II were many and complex, but suffice it to say that Germany, Italy and Japan built up their merchant fleets as part of the expansionist policies of totalitarian regimes: it was well known that sea trade was an important element in any expansionist philosophy. Once again German submarine action against commercial shipping brought Britain to the brink of defeat. Once again the USA entered the war at a crucial moment and helped bring about victory with a massive shipbuilding programme. America, with its enormous industrial capacity, applied well-tried mass-production techniques to shipbuilding. The result was the 'Liberty' ship and the 'British Empire' ship. The first Liberty ship was launched in the USA in 1941; by 1945 100 new American shipyards had gone into operation and well over 2500 ships had been built. It was said they could construct a Liberty ship in a week.

By 1950 the USA had increased its total merchant fleet from a pre-war figure of 11.4 million tons gross to nearly 27.5 million tons. Britain had gained about a million gross tons to 18.2 million, despite the British Empire having lost almost 60% of its merchant fleet during the war. In the post-war period, trade made a quick recovery, and the shipping boom continued well into the 1950s. But de-colonization programmes in the 1960s brought many new nations into world trade, all eager to own merchant fleets. Government subsidies to the shipyards of Scandinavian, European and Far East countries once again brought about an over-production of world tonnage, aided by developing nations insisting on carrying their own cargoes, American protectionism of its coastal ships, and the USSR continuing to produce a large state-owned merchant fleet. Tanker over-production was especially bad, further aggravated by the fall in ocean trade as world oil prices were increased dramatically in the 1970s. Shipping went into another recession, which still continues.

A feature of post-World War II shipping was the rapid rise of 'flags of convenience' tonnage, where ships were registered in different countries to the nationality of the owners. The great advantages to shipowners was that they paid less tax on the high earnings obtained during the boom years of the 1950s. Convenience ships were freed from stringent shipping legislation, and also allowed owners to employ cheaper labour, as labour and safety legislation was often less demanding in countries like Panama and Liberia. Surprisingly the safety record of convenience ships is only a little worse than that of the more established maritime nations. From almost zero tonnage in 1939, today Liberia and Panama have most of the world's registered tonnage of ocean traders. Undoubtedly many of the rich western nations have many million of tons registered with flags of convenience countries.

In 1945 the passenger line *Queen Elizabeth* made her maiden voyage. By 1958, for the first time, the number of passengers carried by air across the Atlantic exceeded those who went by sea. By the 1960s cheap air travel had killed off the magnificent trans-Atlantic passenger liners, such as the *France*, the *Queen Mary* and *Queen Elizabeth*, and the *United States*.

In 1965 Sealand introduced containerization on the North Atlantic run: the end of the conventional cargo ship was in sight. From the 1960s to the late 1980s, world shipping underwent its second revolution in a hundred years. New types of ship, new practices, new ports and new shipbuilders in the Far East, finally broke the hold of the traditional maritime nations.

Britain suffered the most, losing thousands of seafarers, hundreds of ships and tens of companies and yards. Nowadays, perhaps, British shipping industry's main hope is to capture the more sophisticated end of the ocean trader market.

The first revolution

Before steamships were economically viable as ocean traders, and able to replace the sailing merchantmen, there were four advances in shipbuilding technology that had to take place (Fayle *A Short History of the World's Shipping Industry*). The first was that ships had to be built strong enough to withstand the vibrations imposed on them by both the early reciprocating steam engines, and the rotation of long, iron propeller shafts. The second was that before steamships could compete on the long-haul ocean trading routes they had to solve the problem of reducing the bunker, engine room and boiler spaces relative to the ship's cargo carrying capacity. Primitive reciprocating steam engines, especially, needed large amounts of coal. Wooden hulls could not be built much longer than 350 ft, nor could they withstand the vibrational stresses. Iron hulls solved both of these problems. Nineteenth-century iron steamers owed much to an eighteenth-century British industrialist, Heny Cort (1740–1800), who invented the 'puddling process' as well as a technique of producing iron bars using grooved rollers. After iron ore is smelted to give pig iron, Cort 'puddled' the

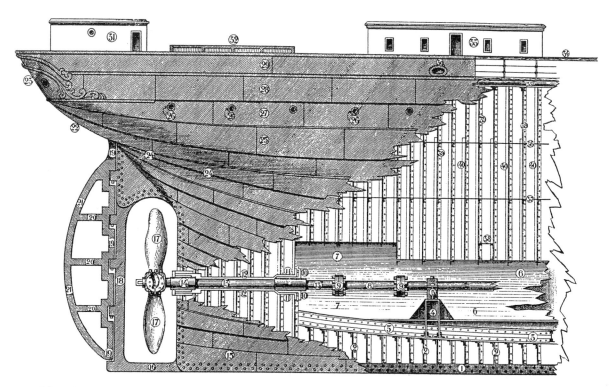

112 *Afterend of a screw-steamer (showing part of tunnel, etc.):*

1 Keel; 2 Floors; 3 Keelson; 4 Pedestal; 5 Plummer-block; 6 Tunnel, Shaft-tunnel; 7 Tunnel-recess; 8 Adjusting-shaft; 9 Couplings, Shaft-couplings; 10 Stuffing-box-gland; 11 Stuffing-box; 12 Stern-tube; 13 Propeller-shaft, Tail-shaft, Tail-end-shaft, Screw-shaft, Stern-shaft; 14 Stern-bush; 15 Garboard-strake; 16 Sole-piece (of Stern-frame); 17 Propeller-blades; 18 Stern-post; 19 Main-piece (of Rudder); 20 Rudder-stays; 21 Rudder-frame, Bow of rudder; 22 Counter, Lower-stern; 23 Stern, Upper-stern; 24 Buttock; 25 Main-sheerstrake, Main-deck-sheerstrake; 26 Side-lights, Side scuttles; 27 Topside-strake; 28 Upper-sheerstrake, Upper-deck-sheerstrake; 29 Bulwark-plating; 30 Mooring-pipe; 31 Wheel-house; 32 Cabin skylight; 33 Cabin-companion; 34 Main-rail, Roughtree-rail; 35 Upper-deck; 36 Main-deck; 37 Lower-deck; 38 Semi-box-Orlop-beam; 39 Frames; 40 Reversed-frames. (after Paasch, 1890)

pig iron using wooden poles to burn out excessive amounts of carbon. This purified the pig iron to such an extent that, although still like a paste, it could be rolled into bars and plates which could be riveted together to make iron hulls.

The third requirement for an economically viable steamship was that they had to be driven by screw propellers. The paddle wheels of paddle steamers were vulnerable to breaking seas, they dipped in and out of the water when ships rolled in heavy weather and they were inconvenient when docking. An American, John Stevens, had in 1804 driven a 24-ft boat around New York Harbour with twin screw propellers. But it was Francis 'Screw' Smith (1808–1874) and John Ericsson (1803–1879) who, in 1836, independently developed, and both took out a patent for, the first screw-propelled ships. In Britain, Smith formed the Ship Propeller Company in 1839, which built the *Archimedes*, the first screw-driven ship to go to sea. A year later, in 1840, the problem of a watertight bearing for the propeller shaft as it went through the circular hole in the stern of the ship was solved. A very hard, oily wood, *lignum vitae*, was used on the bearing surface of the 'stern gland', to help overcome wear of the iron propeller shaft and create the seal. Also, by 1840, the sterns of steamships were sufficiently well designed to allow screw-propellers to operate in clear streams of water, for maximum drive, and correctly shaped to prevent the propeller blades from fouling the rudder. This

progress probably made Isambard Kingdom Brunel (1806–1859) convert, in 1840, from paddle wheels to screw propellers after work on his famous ship, the *Great Britain*, had already started.

Brunel's *Great Britain* was almost the first shipping revolution in one ship: made of iron, large (then the biggest ship afloat), and screw-driven. Brunel was only without an efficient marine engine: the compound steam engine had yet to go to sea. Before embarking on the *Great Britain* project, he had already experienced building a large, pioneering ship. He had designed for the Great Western Steamship Company the first custom built steamship for the trans-Atlantic passenger and mail trade. A wooden-hulled paddle steamer, the *Great Western* (236 ft long, 35 ft 4 in. beam and 1340 tons, BOM), which, when launched, was the largest steamship in the world. Built like a wooden battleship, with iron diagonals, *Great Western* was driven by steam powered reciprocating cylinders that were $73\frac{1}{2}$ in. in diameter, had a stroke of 7 ft and developed between 400 and 750 hp. The *Great Western* left Bristol on her first trans-Atlantic voyage on 7 April 1838 and arrived in New York on 23 April. But despite this very fast crossing, it was Samuel Cunard's shipping company that obtained the important North American mail contract.

113 *The* Great Britain *in the Thames off Gravesend, just before having her engines removed, 14 August 1875. (National Maritime Museum, Greenwich)*

Undaunted, the Great Western Steamship Company decided, in 1839, to lay down the keel of another large ship, the *Great Britain*. Brunel first designed the *Great Britain* as a wooden-hulled paddle steamer, but finally, after five major design changes, arrived at a screw-propelled iron ship with an overall length of 322 ft, beam 50 ft 6 in. and 3443 tons, BOM, or 1016 tons under the new measurements. The screw propeller was driven by four direct-acting, steam-driven cylinders; each cylinder was 88 in. in diameter and had a stroke of 6 ft. Boilers, heated by 24 furnaces, operated at steam pressures of 5 psi. Like all early steamships, *Great Britain* carried a set of sails to reduce coal consumption and for emergency use in case of engine failure. Brunel rigged the *Great Britain* as a six-masted schooner—the world's first. *Great Britain* consumed about 40 tons of coal a day and was expensive to run. In 1881 she finally became, when her engines and passenger accommodation were removed, a long-haul sailing trader working the Cape Horn route. After failing to round Cape Horn in a gale, and loaded with coal, she ran aground off the Falkland Islands, to lie at anchor there, first as a floating warehouse, later as a hulk, from 1866 to 1936, before being sunk and abandoned in the shallow waters of Sparrow Cove.

114 *The* Great Britain, *Bristol dry dock, 15 July 1987. (M.W. Marshall)*

In 1970 the *Great Britain* was salvaged, and returned to the dry-dock in Bristol where she was built. Today, restored, she is a national monument to the engineering skill of Isambard Brunel. (see E. Corlett's, *The Iron Ship*, for the story of this.)

In the 1850s the failure of the Irish potato crop in Europe and the discovery of gold in America and Australia created a huge demand for passenger ships—steam and sail-driven. In 1852. Brunel designed two, iron-hulled, screw-driven ships for the Australian run, but they were not successful as they had to make expensive coal-bunkering stops on the outward journey. In order for a ship to make a non-stop run to Australia, Brunel designed the *Great Eastern* with a bunkering capacity of some 10,000 tons! To hold this enormous amount of coal the *Great Eastern* was six times larger than any ship afloat—680 ft long, 83 ft beam and 18,914 gross tons. She had a designed speed of around 14.5 knots, and was powered by both paddle wheels and screw propellers. Brunel, no doubt exhausted by the complexity of the project and the numerous delays before launching, died a week after the *Great Eastern* left on her maiden voyage, and never knew that his last ship was a commercial failure. The *Great Eastern* became a cable ship, before finally being scrapped in 1888: a ship, and a man, ahead of their time.

The fourth requirement for the development of an economically viable steamship, was the introduction

115 **top** *The* Great Eastern, *12 August 1855, showing cellular construction below the waterline, with longitudinal framing, in and out plating and transverse, watertight bulkheads. (National Maritime Museum, Greenwich)*

116 **bottom** *The* Great Eastern, *2 November 1857, nearing completion with paddle wheels partially constructed. (National Maritime Museum, Greenwich)*

of an efficient steam engine into the iron-hull of a screw-driven ship. This was partially achieved in 1854, when John Elder (1824–1869) built, on the banks of the River Clyde near Glasgow, the 764-tons gross *Brandon* and fitted her with a compound steam engine, a more efficient power unit than the multiple, single cylinders used up to then to turn a propeller shaft. A compound steam engine has two cylinders working in tandem, steam is introduced into the first, or high-pressure, cylinder and after forcing down a piston, is allowed to exhaust into a second, lower-pressure cylinder where it can continue to do work, before finally being passed on to a condenser. Compound steam engines had long been used ashore. Patented in 1781, they were much used for pumping water out of coal mines and they worked at higher steam pressures than simple, less efficient, one cylinder steam engines. But, especially aboard ships, high-pressure steam requires safe, reliable boilers and condensers, and these were not really available until good-quality, mild steel could be produced. Henry

Bessemer (1813–1898) in 1853, and later William Siemens (1823–1883) in 1861, developed mild steel manufacturing technology to such an extent that, by the 1880s mild steel had almost taken over from iron in shipbuilding. Mild steel has the great advantage that it can be melted, cast and easily rolled into plates and, further, ships constructed of steel are about 15% lighter than those of iron.

The rise of steam pressure in ships' boilers throughout the nineteenth century can be used to follow the advances made in boiler technology (see E. Smith's *A Short History of Naval and Marine Engineering*). For example, in 1838, the *Great Western* worked her single cylinders with steam pressures of 5 psi. The iron-hulled, screw-driven P&O passenger liner, the *Bengal*, when launched in 1853 was the largest steamer afloat (296 ft long, 38 ft beam, 25 ft draught, and 2185 tons gross). Her two, single cylinders each had a diameter of 80 in. and a 5 ft stroke; and were operated at steam pressures of around 12 psi when sailing at 9 knots. By the 1860s boilers could produce steam pressures of up to 30 psi, which had increased to 60 psi by c1865. By 1866, Elder and his partner Randolph had built 48 compound engines into ships, mostly for use in the Pacific Ocean where bunkering stations were few, and coal expensive. P&O were the second steamship company (after the Pacific Steam Navigation Company) to fit compound steam engines, as they

117 *The* Bengal, *a single-screw steamship, at anchor. The diameters of the cylinders of the main engine were 80 in. and 60 in., with a 5 ft stroke. Steam pressure was 12 p.s.i.* Bengal *consumed 45 tons of coal a day. (National Maritime Museum, Greenwich)*

too operated ships on distant ocean routes away from bunkering stations.

A Liverpool engineer turned shipowner, Alfred Holt, developed his own version of the compound engine. In 1866 he built three iron-hulled steam ships—*Agamemnon, Ajax* and *Archilles*—for the Far East run via the Cape of Good Hope for his Ocean Steamship Company, the famous Blue Funnel line. *Agamemnon* could carry 3500 tons of cargo, and sailed 8500 miles from England to Mauritius without a bunkering stop: the steam-driven ocean trader had finally arrived.

In 1880 John Elder's Company fitted the first triple expansion (compound) steam engine into the 16-year old steamer the *Propontis*. Steam was allowed to expand and do work through high, intermediate and low pressure cylinders before it was finally condensed. But the boilers on *Propontis* were not really good enough to take the high steam pressures required for a triple expansion engine. In 1881, when the 3616-tons gross *Aberdeen* was launched, her steel boilers were capable of creating steam pressures of 125 psi and her triple expansion steam engine was a complete success. By the end of the nineteenth century steam pressures of 200 psi were not uncommon. Quadruple expansion engines had, by then, been developed and twin screw ships had been in operation for nearly 20 years.

118 *The* Bengal *ashore at Bishops College, Calcutta after a typhoon. A channel had to be dug to refloat the ship. (National Maritime Museum, Greenwich)*

119 Agamemnon, *one of the first steamship ocean traders. (National Maritime Museum, Greenwich)*

Over 100 years ago in 1888, in Govan Park, opposite the bustling, modern Govan shipyard, a statue was erected to John Elder. On the plinth is written:

By his many inventions, particularly in connection with the compound engine, he effected a revolution in engineering second only to that accomplished by James Watt, and in great measure originated the developments in steam propulsion which have created modern commerce.

By 1900 forced draught in the furnaces enabled cheaper, poorer quality coal to be burnt, to give a further improvement in engine economic efficiency. Triple-expansion steam engines were then so efficient that they used, for every ton of ship and knot of speed, only a half an ounce of coal. The energy equivalent of burning a couple of sheets of good quality Victorian notepaper! (T.H. Beare, quoted by R. Craig in *The Ship*, Vol. 5).

Steamships evoke nostalgia: the smoking funnel of a steam tramp, the steady rhythm of propeller and engine, the smell of oil, the hiss of steam and the silky slide of polished metal through the water. But the steam engine requires many coal-burning furnaces which, in the tropics, made a stokehold a living hell. In an article in the magazine *Sea Breezes*, A.D. Blue wrote of 'the record-breaking passages of yesteryear ... only made possible by the backbreaking labour of the men in the stokehold'. He recalled life aboard a twin-engined, refrigerated ship in the mid to late 1920s, and what follows is based upon his article.

A World War I built, twin-engined, fast cargo liner, of around 10,000 tons, would carry some 3000 tons of bunker coal. Five boilers could be heated by a total of 20 furnaces which might consume some 90 tons of coal a day. In the stokehold, the ten-man watch would consist of a junior engineer, five firemen and four trimmers. The men worked four hours on, eight hours off, round the clock, until the ship was in port and the engines closed down.

Firemen would wield steel shovels and slice bars. Slice bars were heavy rods, nine feet long, flattened at one end, and used to break up clinker and prise open smouldering coal lumps. Foremen raked, 'pitched'—that is threw in large quantities of coal—and 'patched'—sprayed a light covering—with the skill of long practice. Trimmers supplied the firemen

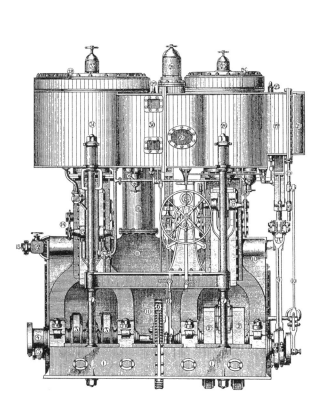

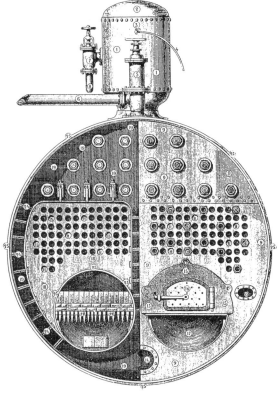

120 *The Triple Expansion Steam Engine: 12 Condenser; 25 High-pressure-piston-rod; 28 Intermediate-piston-rod-crosshead; 29 Low-pressure-piston-rod; 33 High-pressure-cylinder; 35 Intermediate-cylinder; 37 Low-pressure-cylinder. (from Paasch, 1890)*

121 *Front tube plate of a boiler with furnace door etc., on the right hand. Inside-view of Back-end-plate; Back-tube-plate etc., on the left hand: 7 Auxiliary-steam-valve; 11 Boiler tubes; 15 Furnace-front; 16 Furnace-door, Fire-door; 17 Ash-pit; 21-Fire-bridge, Furnace-bridge; 24 Fire-box-stays, Combustion-chamber-stays. (from Paasch, 1890)*

122   *The Columbo, built 1853; length 286 ft 6 in., breadth 36 ft, depth 26 ft 8 in.; Wrecked on Minicoy Island, 1862. (National Maritime Museum, Greenwich)*

with coal, bringing it from bunkers to the furnace doors in wheelbarrows. As the voyage progressed, and coal was used, trimmers had to make long trips with their wheelbarrows to reach the back of the coal bunker. Coal-burning always makes a clinker and ash, lots of it is of poor quality, and it was the trimmers who shovelled it into a hoist for dumping overboard.

As hard-driven steamships travelled the Red Sea with a following wind, temperatures in the stokehold would soar. Firemen and trimmers often collapsed with stomach cramps through drinking too much iced-water, and from heat exhaustion. Unable to climb the ladder out of the hold, some were hoisted out by derricks and revived with buckets of sea water. They worked to the roar of the furnaces, a blinding, searing coal-heat, and the steady clank of rake, slice bar and shovel. The bad ventilation caused sweat to run in rivulets down half-naked bodies, blackened with shiny coal-dust and gritted with ash. As the wind increased and the ship began to roll, the men had difficulty in keeping their footing, but firemen continued to pitch and patch, and trimmers

to push their coal-laden wheelbarrows. On each four-hour watch tons of coal were shifted and burnt. The high steam pressures of the triple expansion engines needed to be maintained, even as the weather worsened. The life of everyone aboard depended on keeping the engine running and the propeller turning. When diesel oil replaced coal, a breed of very hard men died.

Structure and form: 1830 to 1960

In the nineteenth century, steamship yards developed in northern Britain, not far from coal and iron ore deposits, and near good harbours and deep rivers. Shipyards tended to specialise. In Scotland, on Clydeside, passenger liners, cargo liners and naval ships were built, while in Northern Ireland, Belfast built some of the large, early tankers. The northeast of England specialized in cargo tramps, colliers, some liners and naval ships.

The internal structures of these first iron steamships were like wooden sailing traders; wooden ribs and hull planks were replaced by iron, angle-bar frames and plates. Angle bars were bent to give the shape of the hull, and iron plates riveted to the frames to give the outside shell. Ship's bulwarks and decks were made of wood, and deck planks were laid longitudinally, supported on transverse, iron deck beams. Deck beams were supported by vertical pillars, attached to a fore and aft running centre girder positioned over the iron keel. 'Stringers', fore and aft iron angle bars, gave increased resistance to longitudinal bending, and bulkheads, made of iron plates, stiffened the ship transversely. Early iron ships like the *Great Britain* were clinker-built, the iron hull plates overlapping one-another as did the hull planks of a Viking longship. It is relatively simple to cut wooden frames to fit wooden planks, but more difficult with iron frames and plates. On *Great*

Britain, tapered 'liners' were used to fill the space left between the frames and clinker-laid hull plates.

Scott Russell (1808–1882), a Glasgow-born engineer, developed an 'in and out' system of hull- or 'shell'-plating an iron ship. Alternate 'in' plates are first riveted to the frames, and then 'out' plates are laid on top. The advantage of Russell's system was that uniform, and not tapered, liners were required under each hull plate, to fill the space left between frame and 'out' plate. Rivets were spaced along the edges of the 'out' plates where they overlapped the 'ins'. This 'alternate' or 'in and out' system, was a popular method of shell-plating until machines were developed that were powerful enough to 'joggle' (indent) either the plates at their overlapping seams,

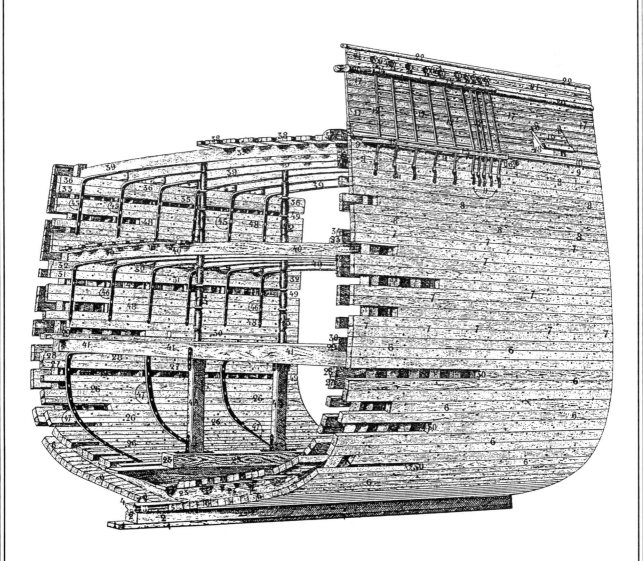

123 *Outside, and part inside view of the middle portion of a wooden sailing ship: 1 False-keel; 2 Keel; 5 Garboard-strake; 7 Wales, Bends; 9 Sheerstrake; 12 Chain-plates; 13 Lower-channel; 14 Upper-channel; 15 Dead-eyes; 23 Floor; 24 Keelson; 25 Rider-keelson; 26 Hold-ceiling. (from Paasch, 1890)*

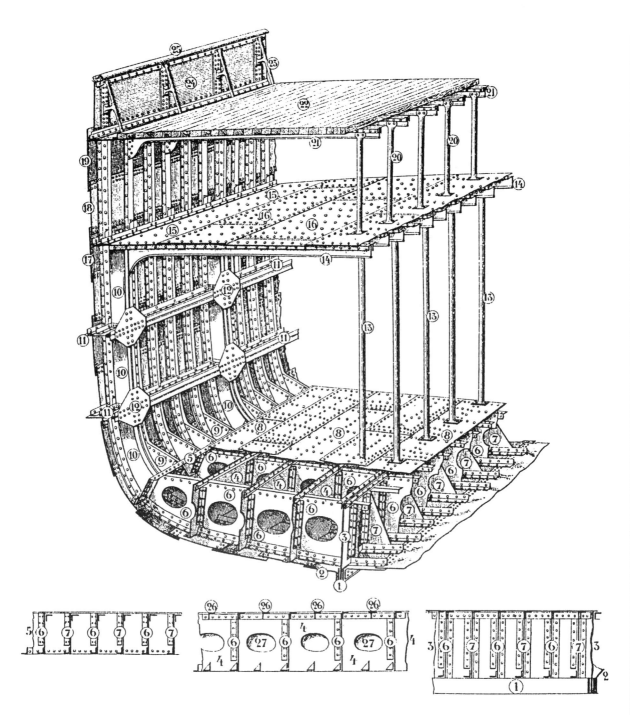

124 *Part of a web-frame steamer, having a cellular-double-bottom, with continuous girders: 1 Keel, Side-bar-keel; 2 Garboard-strake; 6 Floors, Intercostal-floors; 8 Inner-bottom, Top of Double-bottom, Top of Tank; 10 Web-frames; 13 Hold-pillars; 14 Main-deck-beams; 18 Topside-strake; 19 Upper-sheerstrake, Upper-deck-sheerstrake. (from Paasch, 1890)*

or the frames themselves. With joggling, liners were no longer necessary.

Russell worked with Brunel on the *Great Eastern* and they used 'in and out plating', and a unique, longitudinal, system of girders to support the hull plates, as well as conventional transverse frames and bulkheads. Below the waterline, *Great Eastern* had a cellular construction of longitudinal and transverse frames that supported the outside hull and an inner,

also watertight, hull. Once, when the ship ran aground, the inner hull remained watertight despite a long gash in the outer hull. *Great Eastern*'s double hull was one of the forerunners of the 'double bottom tank' that are still common in general cargo ships. *Great Eastern* and *Great Britain* were incredible ships and, although outside the mainstream development of the iron-hulled ocean trader, were pioneers of shipbuilding in iron.

172

A less grand forerunner of the double bottom tank was a little Geordie collier, the *John Bowes*, built of iron in the northeast of England at Palmer's yard, Newcastle upon Tyne, in 1852. For centuries, colliers had travelled from Newcastle to London loaded with coal, and returned with gravel or sand in ballast. The 485-gross tons, 150-ft long 25-ft 7 in. beam, *John Bowes* was fitted with iron tanks which, when filled with sea water, were used as ballast tanks for the return trip to Newcastle. Ballast tanks were an immediate success, and were quickly made a structural part of colliers' hulls. Around 1860, a new design gave the first true 'double bottom' ballast system. In this 'McIntyre system', a number of fore- and aft-running girders, riveted to the bottom of the ship, supported a watertight 'inner bottom' whose edge was supported on a fore and aft 'margin plate', itself riveted to the turn of the bilge. By the 1880s watertight double bottoms were being built with additional transverse framing to give a cellular form of double bottom tank. Full-length, cellular, watertight, double bottom tanks were gradually incorporated into ocean traders, to avoid carrying ballast, and also to store fresh water and fuel oil. They became the rule in ocean traders as soon as the enclosed space between inner and outer bottom became exempt from tonnage measurements.

By the 1880s mild steel was well on the way to replacing iron in British shipbuilding. Shipowners continually complained that the hulls of iron ships contained too many decks, transverse beams and vertical pillars: they preferred larger, unobstructed spaces for working and stowing cargo. With the more versatile building material of steel, ships could be built with fewer transverse beams, decks and pillars, and with deeper holds. To maintain transverse strength, special, extra-wide 'web frames' were added at every sixth frame, and stringers were made stronger, and wider, to align with the edges of the web frames. Later all transverse frames were increased in width, to give the hull structure of the cargo ships of the 1930s, 40s and 50s.

The *Great Eastern*'s longitudinal framing system was similar to the fore and aft system that was developed, c1908, by Joseph Isherwood. Heavy longitudinal frames were supported at widely spaced intervals by strong, transverse frames, and ships built with the Isherwood system are stronger and lighter than transversely framed vessels. Although Isherwood proposed his system for all types of ships, at the time it was unpopular with general cargo shipowners: longitudinal frames reduced cargo space more than transverse frames. But for tankers the system was ideal, as they are especially susceptible to fore and aft bending stresses and, after World War I, the system was increasingly used in tanker construction, as demand and size for this type of ship rapidly

increased. Around 1918, a composite framing system was developed for general cargo ships using longitudinal stringers and frames along the ship's bottom and deck, in conjunction with heavy transverse framing, with girders and struts, that ran across the ship. This composite system was also used in ships of the 1930s and 1940s.

As large wooden traders had been for centuries, the lines of early steamships were designed as plans or models. Also as they had done for wooden ships, loftsmen chalked out in the 'mould loft' (a spacious area with a large, wooden, often black-painted, floor) from the ship's plans, every transverse frame, full-sized, on the loft floor. The frames would be transferred, or 'scrived' (scrieved), onto wooden templates or 'scrive boards' which were taken to the bending slabs: large, flat, cast-iron plates drilled with numerous holes. The outside shape of a frame was taken off the scrive board with a 'set iron'—a thin, flat metal bar secured to the bending slab. Angle bars were heated in a furnace, and then hammered and forced into the shape of the set iron by the men of the plating squad. A wooden scale model of the ship was also prepared to give a three dimensional aspect to the lofting process. From the model the overlapping joins of the hull and deck plates were established, as were the approximate shapes of the plates. Hull plates were curved using heat, hammers, rollers, and later hydraulic presses, from templates made of wooden battens obtained from the mould loft.

During the nineteenth century workers in a shipyard were organized into squads or gangs, that specialized in operations like plating, riveting, deck-laying and framing. Shipbuilding was very labour intensive and the men worked mostly outside: skill, muscle and sweat built the ships. At the building berth, open to all the elements, there were no cranes and, hand operated derricks hoisted and lowered plates, frames and beams. Extensive wooden staging was built around the ships and long ladders gave the men access to work areas. Prior to the 1930s ships were riveted throughout, the rivet holes, at first all hand-drilled, were later punched by machines.

The noise made by the hammers of the riveters could be unbearable. One old shipyard worker likened entering a shipyard to walking directly into a 'wall of dirt and noise'. Before long, most men in a riveting squad, one or two riveters, a holder-up, a catcher lad and a heater lad, would be suffering from partial deafness; cotton wool stuffed in to their ears was their only form of protection. The heater lad, a young boy, an old man or, during war-time, a woman, heated up the iron rivets in a portable, gas-fired furnace. When red hot, they would be thrown to the catcher lad, also sometimes a woman, to be passed to the holder-up. Working on the inside of

'prefabrication', where large sections were made away from the ship, later to be hoisted aboard and welded in place. One great advantage of welding over riveting, is that there is no need to overlap joining plates. During the 1930s, instead of hammers, compressed air was increasingly used to close many rivets, and pneumatic and hydraulic riveting were used on structures that could be brought to the presses. By the 1950s riveting was gradually being phased out, and steel plates were being cut with gas torches. Labour was still organized in gangs but there were now more machines, bending rollers, shearers and planers, punches, drills and counter sinks, and mobile cranes, capable of handling up to 40 tons. In many yards in the 1940s and 1950s building was still largely piecemeal: keel plate, then double bottoms; next frames and deck beams; and finally shell and deck plates from the bottom upwards. Staging around the hull was primitive, but now boilers and funnels were usually added before launching.

Prefabrication techniques were continually being developed after World War II and became increasingly sophisticated. By the early 1960s an advanced shipyard could build a standardized general cargo tramp ship from some 300 pre-fabricated units, each of around 12 tons. The ship would be about 90% welded, and radical changes would have taken place in the mould loft with the introduction of optical lofting. Scaled down onto photographic film, lofting drawings were used to give instructions to automatic machine tools for plate cutting and profiling.

The *form* of the 1960s ocean-going cargo ships was not greatly different from the screw-driven ocean traders of the late nineteenth century—there was a forecastle, a bridge and a poop deck. But by 1890 steamships were very different from the first iron steamship. In both structure and form the earliest iron steamships resembled the flush-decked, wooden sailing traders. The steamers were even rigged with masts and sails and classified as brigs, barques, ships etc.

Seas breaking aboard a flush-decker would sweep it from stem to stern, and funnels and engine room openings located midships were extremely vulnerable. Steamships soon had raised, protective deck and bridge erections. A high forecastle gives good protection to head seas and, by housing the crew in a forecastle situated above the upper deck, shipowners gave themselves more hold space forward. In the aft part of the ship a protective covering for the steering gear became the poop deck which, when raised above the upper deck, gave more hold space aft. These three erections on a flush-decked ship resulted in the appearence of c1870, the classical 'three island' cargo ship (see Fig. 130). There were many variations. For example, to balance cargo hold space

125 *The building of the* Queen Mary, *1934, showing rivet holes in joggled hull plates, framing and extensive scaffolding. (Science Museum, London)*

the hull, he inserted the hot rivet and held it up with a large hammer, before two riveters on the outside flattened over the rivet end with hammers. Holders-up and riveters needed strong arms and powerful wrists to deliver, hour after hour, the strong hammer blows and to withstand the incessant, jarring crash of metal on metal.

The first job at a building berth in the 1800s and early 1900s was the setting up of the wooden blocks by the shipwrights to receive the horizontal keel plate. Then the fore and aft centre girder was erected, before the cellular double bottom tanks were constructed for the whole length of the ship. The shipwrights secured the vertical hull frames by bolting them to the transverse floor frames, and checked the hull shape before tying the hull frames together with the transverse deck beams. Nuts and bolts held the whole structure together before riveting began. The ship was decked and 'shelled' at each level, from the bottom upwards, and rudders and stern frames were strong castings that were riveted into the ship. The propeller and the propeller-shaft were added before the launch, while steam engines, boilers and funnels were fitted after the launch.

During World War II, electric arc welding was used extensively on American Liberty ships and, similarly-constructed, British 'Empire' ships, as was

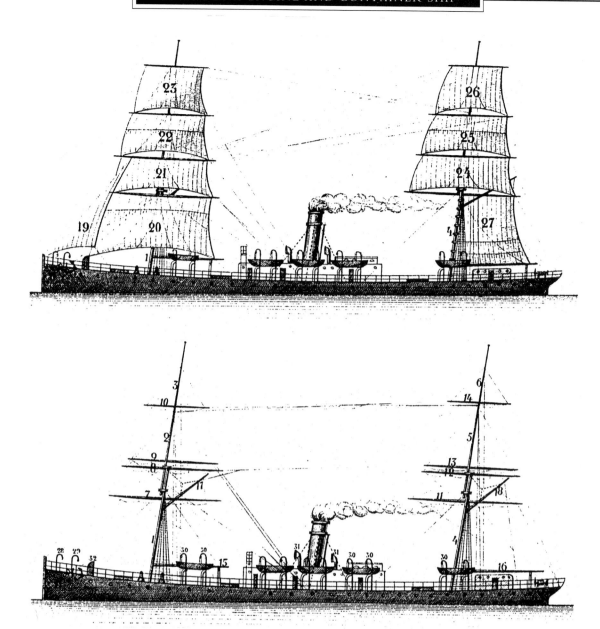

126   Steamer (Brig): 1 Fore-mast; 2 Fore-topmast; 3 Fore-topgallant-mast; 4 Main-mast; 5 Main-topmast; 6 Main-topgallant-mast; 7
Fore-yard; 8 Lower-fore-topsail-yard; 9 Upper-fore-topsail yard; 10 Fore-topgallant-yard; 11 Main-yard; 12 Lower-main-topsail-yard; 13
Upper-main-topsail-yard; 14 Main-topgallant-yard; 15 Fore boom, Fore-trysail-boom; 16 Main-boom, Main-trysail-boom; 17 Fore-gaff,
Fore-trysail-gaff; 18 Main-gaff, Main-trysail-gaff; 19 Fore-topmast-staysail; 20 Fore-sail; 21 Lower-fore-topsail; 22 Upper-fore-topsail; 23
Fore-topgallant-sail; 24 Lower-main-topsail; 25 Upper-main-topsail; 26 Main-topgallant-sail; 27 Main-trysail; 28 Cat-davit; 29 Fish-davit;
30 Boat-davits; 31 Ventilators; 32 Crew-space-companion. (from Paasch, 1890)

fore and aft (in the aft hold, space was lost to the
engine machinery and to a 'tunnel' for the propeller
shaft) the whole of the aft, upper deck was raised, to
give a 'raised quarter deck' ship. Forecastle, bridge,
and poop deck were sometimes connected to give a
'spar-' or 'awning-decked' vessel. A temporary or
'shelter deck', was first used to protect cattle carried
on deck across the Atlantic. The space enclosed
within this deck was exempt from tonnage dues,
provided it was open at both ends, and so became a
semi-permanent fixture. When at sea these openings
were sealed with hatch boards, and the shelter deck

was often used to carry light cargo. A typical 1870,
three-island steamer was c1000 tons gross. Each year
ships increased in size and by the 1880s, for example,
ocean traders were up to around 3000 tons gross.

In 1893 the first of the 'turret' ships, the *Turret*,
was launched by William Doxford of Sunderland in
the northeast of England. The topsides were strongly
curved to form a central turret. In cross-section, the
ships looked like squat bottles, and had one great
advantage, they paid lower tonnage dues than normal
freighters. Turret ships were strongly built, and well-
established British shipping companies like P&O,

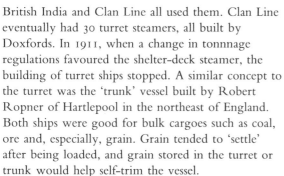

127 **top left** Clan Farquhar, *turret deck, steel steamship with two decks, built in 1899 by W. Doxford: length 439 ft, breadth 51.6 ft, depth 28.9 ft. Triple expansion steam engine, 27½ in. × 45½ in. × 75 in. cylinder diameters with a 5 ft stroke; 5858 gross tons. (Scottish Maritime Museum)*

128 **bottom left** *Cargo liner* Patonga: *length 152.3 m, breadth 19.72 m, depth 12.81 m; broken up 1977. (P & O Group)*

129 **above** British Queen, *built 1849 for the Cunard line, (National Maritime Museum, Greenwich)*

British India and Clan Line all used them. Clan Line eventually had 30 turret steamers, all built by Doxfords. In 1911, when a change in tonnnage regulations favoured the shelter-deck steamer, the building of turret ships stopped. A similar concept to the turret was the 'trunk' vessel built by Robert Ropner of Hartlepool in the northeast of England. Both ships were good for bulk cargoes such as coal, ore and, especially, grain. Grain tended to 'settle' after being loaded, and grain stored in the turret or trunk would help self-trim the vessel.

By 1900 some oil tankers were built like today's tankers with their engine room and stokehold aft, although the bridge and accommodation were still in the middle of the ship. Transverse bulkheads were split by longitudinally-running bulkheads to give tanks with separate compartments. The engine-room was separated from the tanks by a small space, the 'cofferdam', enclosed between two oil-tight, transverse bulkheads. Pump rooms were located in the cofferdams and the first tankers used steam-driven reciprocating pumps to discharge their oil. Later, rapid-flow, steam-turbine driven centrifugal pumps were developed to discharge the oil, and these were used in conjunction with small 'stripping pumps' which finally sucked out the last remnants of oil from a tank. In World War II a tanker, the 'T2'

tanker, was produced in large numbers in America, using a 'direct-line system' where each pipe-line had its own centrifugal pump. In the direct-line system, three pipelines, for example, driven by three turbine rotary pumps, might work 30 oil compartments.

Coal-fired, three-island tramp steamers were at their peak during World War I. In World War II, American 'Liberty' ships and British 'Empire' ships were produced in large numbers. They were not greatly dissimilar in form to World War I British steam tramps. R. Craig, in Vol 5 of the *The Ship*, describes the standard Liberty ship as being 7176 tons registered gross, 4380 tons net, and carrying about 10,400 tons of deadweight cargo. When steaming at 11 knots the ship consumed 30 tons of coal a day. The Liberty design was based on the *Dorington Court*, and ocean trader launched in 1939, by Joseph Thompsons, a shipyard at Sunderland in the northeast of England.

In 1963, I sailed to Australia in the P&O cargo liner *Patonga*, a steam-turbine powered 'dry' cargo ship launched ten years before. The general lines of the *Patonga* were not much different from the *Dorington Court*, or the tramp motor vessel, *Akri Hill*, built in 1924, or even the steamship, *British Queen*, built in 1849. From the 1850s, the hulls of general cargo ships become larger, squatter and more stream-lined. Cargo handling became more sophisticated, with the introduction of heavy-lift derricks and improved facilities ashore. All four ships were, however, built on the three-island principle; there was a single funnel amidships and passengers and some crew were accommodated in this region. Cargo handling was by derricks working off fore and mizzen masts.

In contrast the container ship, *Al Mariyah*, built in 1983, is very different. Capable of transporting the same cargoes as the other four ships, it does so much more efficiently. *Al Mariyah*'s funnel and accommodation are both aft, there are no masts or derricks, and the deck is full of containers, each container one lorry load. By 1983 the second dramatic change to ocean trade had taken place: the container had well and truly arrived.

130 Akri Hill, *built 1924 by W. Doxford, a motor tramp ship with three cylinder Doxford diesels: length 375 ft, beam 52.6 ft, depth 25.7 ft; 4359 gross tons. (National Maritime Museum, Greenwich)*

131 *The Al Mariyah, built in 1983 for the United Arab shipping company: length 211.46 m, maximum breadth 32.26 m, maximum draught 11.27 m; 32,534 tons gross and capable of loading 1846 TEUs. (Air photo)*

132 *Govan shipyard. The first of the double bottom units has been lifted into place to start building the first of the two China Ocean container ships. (M. W. Marshall)*

Structure and form: 1960–1990

As a direct result of World War II, shipbuilding underwent dramatic changes. Specialized fighting ships evolved into new forms of merchant vessels: the tank landing craft taking part in the Allied invasion of France were the forerunners of today's 'roll-on/ roll-off' ferries and container ships (see E. Corlett *The Ship*, Vol. 10). The unit, block and modular building approach, now so successful in building ocean traders, had its origins in the arc-welded, pre-fabricated units of World War II 'Liberty' ships. Once these production engineering techniques were fully applied to shipbuilding there were huge reductions (often 60%) in the labour force.

'Design for production' is the key phrase of 1980s shipbuilders. Digital computers play a major role in ship design, work allocation, and in the manufacturing process. A modern British yard, such as Govan Shipbuilders on the Clyde, makes extensive use of mainframe and micro computers to run large, iterative software packages like CADAM: Computer Aided Design and Manufacture. In the late 1980s Govan Shipbuilders is the only yard building large general cargo ships in Britain. The two container ships being built for the China Ocean Shipping Company of Shanghai, are each 236 m long, 32.2 m in breadth 18.6 m in depth and 46,100 tonnes deadweight—DWT (a tonne is a metric ton = 1000 kg). (The first was launched in March 1989. The second will be completed soon.)

Govan Shipbuilders build their units and modules using production-line techniques. Ships are 100%

welded and made from prefabricated units that can weigh up to 80 tons. After arriving at the yard, the steel plates and sections enter the 'plate preparation shop' on rollers, where they are shot blasted and painted. Steel plates are then cut using multi-headed burning machines that burn within tolerances of $\pm$ 2 mm, and cutting machines that cut to within $\pm$ 2/1000 th of an inch. Hull and deck plates are shaped using heavy presses and rollers, or locally applied heat (heat line bending). Frames are bent using special machines. In the 'fabrication shop' men weld together the frames and plates of the 70 to 80 ton units on a 'work-station principle', an important aspect of modern shipbuilding. There are a number of special 'module-building shops', where free-standing, macro and small-equipment modules are constructed, as well as complete cabin modules, fitted with showers and telephones. There are computer-controlled 'pipe-bending shops' and special 'paint cells' where all the welds are shot-blasted before the complete modules and units are painted. A the building berth mobile cranes, capable of lifting 120 tons when working in tandem, lower the painted units into place.

Nowadays ship construction does not start with the laying of a keel plate on wooden blocks. Instead, two prefabricated, double-bottom units are craned onto the building berth and welded together by automatic welding machines. Construction begins amidships and continues in both directions, fore and aft, as more and more units are welded in. Module and unit construction continues in the fabrication shops in parallel with unit assembly at the building

133   *The general cargo ship,* Coromandel, *built in 1949 and powered by Doxford diesels; 7065 tons gross. (P & O Group)*

berth. Before decking-over, engines, auxiliary machinery and cabin modules are added to the ship. At launch time the funnels are welded in, and the engine room and most electrical and pipe work is at an advanced stage of completion.

To many seamen modern cargo ships lack the romance of the older tramps and cargo liners. But their beauty is their sheer bulk and power: to be at sea in a small yacht and look up at a giant ocean trader under way creates a form of paralysis; their very size is mesmerizing. People at sea in small boats fear the story of a large tanker arriving at the end of an Atlantic voyage with a yacht's mast and rigging entangled in the anchor, the mast only noticed while the anchor was being made ready to let go.

The *form* of most modern cargo ships is based around a long rectangular box, ideal for containers, oil and ores, with engines and accommodation aft. Nearly all have bulbous bows to aid propulsion and in some ships, to increase their manoeuvrability, there are bow and stern thrusters—athwartships propellers located on each side of the ship in transverse tunnels. As well as double-bottom ballast and bunker tanks, there are floodable holds and large wing tanks to help ballast the ship when sailing without cargo. Many modern ships use slow-revving, fuel-efficient diesel engines that burn cheap, poor-quality bunker oil. The bridge contains sophisticated satellite navigation equipment, and there is a move towards unmanned engine rooms, with engineers operating computer

controlled mimic diagrams, switches, alarms and monitors from remote, control rooms.

The three-island type cargo ships, like my first ship the P&O general cargo liner, the *Coromandel* (launched in 1949; 147.7 m long, 19.2 m beam, 7065 tons gross/10,049 DWT; and powered by Doxford diesels) have all but disappeared. Their departure was hurried by containerization and the rapid increase in oil prices of the 1970s that made their oil-hungry diesel engines uneconomical. A class of ships like the British 'SD 14' are intermediaries between these more traditional general cargo ships and the container and multipurpose cargo ships of today. The SD 14s have their engines and accommodation aft, but still forward of a fifth hold in the stern. They are 141 m long, 20.5 m beam, 9000 tons gross/15,2000 DWT, and their main engines are low-speed diesels, specially designed for economical fuel consumption. Double-bottom ballast tanks are augmented with the capability of flooding the third cargo hold. These ships are today's tramp ships, they can carry crated, bagged and bulk cargoes as well as containers.

Modern, multipurpose, general cargo ocean traders, like the Japanese 'Freedom' ships, have their engines and accommodation right aft. The Freedom ships are 164 m long, 23 m beam and 13,600 tons gross. They have one 'tweendeck', box-shaped holds for containers and palletized goods, and carry cranes capable of working their own cargoes.

Today containers exist in a number of internationally-accepted standard sizes. The two most

179

commonly used are the TEU containers (Twenty foot Equivalent Units, 20 ft long, 8 ft high) and the FEUs (40 ft × 8 ft). The Govan container ships for the China Ocean Shipping Company can, for example, carry 2700 TEUs. A 'fully cellular' container ship is one that has holds fitted with special framing, or 'cell guides', into which the more common TEUs are slotted. The Govan ships have fixed cell guides for TEUs in the first two holds, and in the other five holds, there are guides for FEUs, with additional special sockets and stacking cones for TEUs. In 1987 there were over 21 million gross tons of fully cellular container ships in the world. Many container ships are without derrick or cranes, relying on the ports' cranes to load and discharge them. Containers revolutionized ports as well as ships: many new ports were built, others were radically altered to deal with the logistics of fast inflow, outflow, and loading or discharging of containers. Many traditional ports, unable to adapt to the new methods, died.

Some specialized container ships carry refrigerated containers that work off the ships' generators while at sea (the Govan container ships can carry 90 refrigerated TEUs). Other specialized ships treat floating barges or lighters as if they were containers. LASHs (Lighter Aboard Ships) transport barges that are craned aboard after being floated into the stern of the mother ship or, in another system, barges are lifted aboard on submersible lifts. Some roll-on/roll-off, RO-RO, container ships load and discharge 'horizontally'. Horizontal loading of containers is by trucks, or specialized vehicles, driving up straight, slewed or angled ramps that are led through special openings in the ship's stem, stern or sides.

Nowadays the largest percentage of world shipping, and the world's largest ocean traders, are oil tankers (some 120 million tons out of a 1987 world total of 403 million gross tons). In 1900 there were only about 100 tankers in the world of more than 2000 tons. This had increased in 1919 to some 450, and by 1939, to c1500. Around the 1950s, oil refineries were being built away from the oil-producing countries and larger ships could be utilized to bring crude oil to Europe and North America for refining, to give 'oil products' such as petroleum and many basic chemicals for the plastics industry. The Suez Canal was temporarily closed in 1956 and voyages around the Cape of Good Hope once more became a reality.

Larger ships are of course cheaper to operate, and by 1959 the first 100,000 DWT-tonnage tanker had been launched, although most tankers at that time were only a quarter that tonnage. The 37,000-DWT P&O tanker Garonne, built in 1959, (which I sailed in for about a year) was then an example of a fairly large tanker. Powered, like most tankers, with steam

turbines, Garonne was 210.5 m long, 27.5 m beam and 11 m draught. Tankers continued to become longer, and by the late 1960s super tankers had arrived. Today some crude oil carriers are so large, over half a million tons deadweight, that they can only sail on a few ocean routes. The world's largest tankers are known as Ultra Large Crude Carriers (ULCCs), 300–550,000 DWT and, often loading and discharging at special off-shore terminals, they carry oil from the Arabian Gulf to America, Europe and the Far East. A second class of tankers is the Very Large Crude Carriers (VLCCs), between 200–299,000 DWT, they can pass only in ballast through the Suez Canal. A third class is the Medium Size Crude Carriers, (MSCC), 70–130,000 DWT, which can pass through the Suez Canal partially, or even fully, loaded with oil.

Some recent oil traders, known as 'combination carriers', mix liquid and dry cargoes. Those that carry oil and bulk cargoes are known as Ore-Oil, OO, carriers, there are Ore-Bulk-Oil, OBO, carriers or even more sophisticated, Products (refined crude oils)-Ore-Bulk-Oil, PROBO, carriers. Combination ships are more flexible than straight ore, bulk, or oil carriers, and were designed to change from dry to liquid cargoes depending on availability, but they have problems. Tank cleaning is often difficult, and international regulations prevent the simultaneous carriage of ore and oil.

Bulk cargo carriers, transporting ores and bulk cargoes, make up the second largest class of modern ocean traders (110 million gross tons). They may be large as 150,000 DWT and carry, for example, grain, ore, coal, fertilizers, lumber and even containers. They may be general bulk carriers, or specialized 'bulkers' for cargo like cement, ores, lumber and cars. Most modern bulkers are simply constructed with engines and accommodated aft, box-shaped holds and no cranes or derricks, relying on the ports to discharge and load them. Sloping wing tanks in the upper corners of holds act as self trimmers, like the turret in the turret ships (p 175), and wing tanks can be used for ballast or the carriage of additional free-running cargoes like grain. Lower wing tanks are sometimes fitted for extra ballast and to prevent cargo shifts, always a problem in the carriage of bulk cargoes. Some bulkers are specially built for trade through the Panama Canal, their dimensions limited by the length and width of the locks (about 275 m by 32.3 m). Govans build the 66,500 DWT 'Panamax'

134 top *The Garonne: bridge and officers' accommodation midships, engine room aft; length 690 ft 3 in., breadth 90 ft 5 in., maximum draught 36 ft 7 in.; 24,513 tons gross. (P & O Group)*

135 bottom *The Globtik, London, VLCC tanker built in 1973: length 378.8 m, breadth 62 m, and maximum draught 28.2 m; 238,000 tons gross. (Air photo)*

type bulk carriers (225.5 m long, 32.2 m beam) specifically to travel through the Panama Canal as well as the 35,000 DWT 'Lakers' (222.5 m long, 23.1 m beam) to trade in the Great Lakes of North America. To obtain some idea of the relative size of today's ships, Ronald Hope, in *The Merchant Navy*, made an interesting comparison when he wrote that, given their increased speed and diminished turn-round time, 'one fair size bulk carrier could carry as much as the entire merchant fleet of Queen Elizabeth I'.

Rapid advances in technology since the 1960s have also resulted in the development of some extremely specialized ocean traders. For example, there are over 9 million gross tons of liquid gas containers in the world. These sophisticated ships, like LPG (Liquid Petroleum Gases), transport liquified butane and propane gas in insulated, cylindrical, aluminium cargo tanks at temperatures of $-20°C$. Other gas-carrying ships, the LNGs (Liquid Natural Gases), carry ethane and methane at temperatures as low as $-176°C$, the spherial aluminium tanks often appearing above deck level.

Some of the most spectacular new generation, custom-built ocean traders are the heavy lift ships. The single heavy lift derrick, working off the foremast of a 1960s general cargo ship has been gradually superseded by 'Stulcken'-type heavy lift derricks, often rigged on a specially-constructed heavy lift ship, with extra-strong decks, wide hatches, and sometimes with RO-RO facilities. A semi-submersible class of heavy lift ship has also been developed, and often used alongside the off-shore oil industry. One of the world's largest semi-submersibles is *Ferncarrier*. These vessels are submerged by flooding their holds with sea water, and floated under their gigantic loads, which are lifted as the sea water is pumped back out.

Perhaps a voyage carried out by *Ferncarrier* exemplifies the ocean traders of today. This remarkable semi-submersible carried on her deck a huge off-shore oil rig over 11,000 miles from South Korea to Scotland. The rig weighed over 15,000 tons, extended 20 m either side of *Ferncarrier*'s deck and was over 100 m high. *Ferncarrier* averaged an incredible 13 knots for the whole voyage.

136 top *The Khannur, liquid natural gas carrier, built in 1977; length 293 m, breadth 41.6 m, and maximum draught 11.7 m; 84,000 tons gross. (Air photo)*

137 bottom Fern Carrier, *semi-submersible. (Foto Flite)*

Conclusion

At sea in the 1960s, I was very much aware of the long periods spent in port, but which, when in some exotic country, were often to my liking. Crew on a tramp ship, or a general cargo liner like my first ship, the *Coromandel*, would have plenty of shore leave. We were often in harbour for weeks, sometimes months, at a time, unable to load because of rain, waiting for freight, or strike-bound. Loading and unloading were labour intensive and inefficient, especially if working cargoes in small ports with the ship's derricks. Cargo packaging was often smashed, sometimes deliberately; pilfering was always a problem. Only certain cargoes could be loaded alongside one another for fear of contamination, and making and keeping to a stowage plan was always very difficult. Opening and closing hatches was extremely time-consuming. Holds were covered by wooden hatch boards laid on steel beams which had to be pulled and then locked into place. Hatches were made watertight by covering them with canvas tarpaulins that had to be dragged across and secured with steel bars and wooden wedges driven into cleats.

Nowadays container ships and bulk carriers turn round in days, perhaps hours, almost independently of the weather. New functional and efficient harbours have been designed to take the new ships and load and discharge them in close cooperation with land transport. Ship and port revolutionized both ocean trade and trader, and few of us, at sea in the 1960s, would have predicted it. In Britain, traditional 'break-bulk' cargo ports like London and Liverpool have almost died as new container ports, like Southampton and Felixstowe, have developed and flourished.

Shipping companies have also changed. A modern British shipping company, like the P&O Group, have diversified into all aspects of shipping and shipping-related businesses. Although some passenger cruise ships were recently built, the group's main shipping

interests since 1960 is the new generation ocean traders: giant tankers, bulk carriers, roll-on/roll-off ferries, ocean-going tugs, liquid gas carriers and, above all, container ships. Ocean shipping is increasingly part of transnational trading corporations, often working within an integrated transport system involving land, sea and air. Ships are often registered under a flag of convenience.

One of the difficulties with this form of registration is that it is often difficult to trace the shipowners. For example when the tanker, the *Torrey Canyon*, ran aground at the entrance to the English Channel in 1967 it was manned by an Italian crew. The ship was operating under a Liberian flag, on charter to an American corporation, which had leased the ship from a subsidary of British Petroleum. Cleaning costs ran into millions of pounds, as 120,000 tons of crude oil ran into the sea, but the true owners of the ship were never found. The *Torrey Canyon* incident highlighted some of the complexities of modern shipping, the old system that allowed the retired ship's captain to own a second-hand tramp steamer and play the freight markets is long since gone.

One way of measuring technological progress, and perhaps ocean trader efficiency, is to divide a ship's tonnage by the number of crew required to operate the ship, to give ship tons per crew member. Ronald Hope, in *The Merchant Ship*, quotes approximate values for the change in ocean trader ton per crew member, over a 400 years period. In the 1600s it was c7 tons per man; by the 1750s, some 15 tons; around 1850, c35 tons; while by 1980 it had risen to an incredible 330 tons per crew member.

Throughout the centuries, from *fluyt* to bulker, there are many examples of rigging and hull changes that directly resulted in a reduction of crew numbers—shipowners were always aware that one of the most expensive recurrent costs in operating a ship was crew wages. Ship safety and design were often adversely affected by the profit motive. Coffin ships caused the death of many a seaman, and slow, unweatherly ships were built to obtain maximum advantage to the owners under existing tonnage laws. But tonnage laws did not always adversely affect ship design, and technological advances not only occurred because shipowners wished to increase profits; new technology was also liked and used by the seamen if it meant less manual labour and safer ships. Although there had been a massive increase in the ships tons per crew member in the latter part of the twentieth century and undoubtedly the shipping industry has become more efficient, seamens' jobs were at stake. In Britain the astonishing advances made since the 1960s in ship size, design and structure, aided by a world slump in trade, dramatically reduced the number of men working at sea. The National Union of Seamen was down from a membership of 62,500 in 1960 to around 20,000 in 1988.

As ships became larger the number of shipyards became smaller. In the 1950s the British shipbuilding industry was the largest in the world. In 1977 British shipyards were nationalized. In 1978, British Shipbuilders had 28 yards and nearly 87,000 employees, but in a decade this was down to four yards and some 6000 employees. One of them was the Govan yard that was sold in 1988 to Norway's Kvaerner group. The dramatic decline was partly caused by a huge, world over-production of (government subsidized) tonnage, and also by British shipowners having their ships built elsewhere. In the decade before nationalization two-thirds of British registered tonnage was built abroad, while in contrast, Japan had not placed a domestic ship order outside her yards since 1948. The maritime nations turned, and continue to turn, to South Korea, Taiwan, and Japan for ocean traders, where shipyards, aided by government subsidies, high productivity, and low labour costs produce most of the non-communist world's shipping. Korean yards were at one time quoting the price for a new ship that was sometimes below the price of the materials for the same ship built in a British yard. In 1987 no ocean traders were being built in the USA, and only two in Britain, both at the Govan yard.

However, there are signs that the world slump is over. The amount of laid-up tonnage is decreasing, the present world tonnage is ageing and scrapping programmes are on the increase. Japan and South Korea, the largest producers, have rising labour costs and have also agreed to try to limit supply to meet real world demand. Many of their yards are now working at near-full capacity. Ocean trade and traders are on the move again, but Britain, once the world's largest owner and producer of ships, will be playing a minor role.

Select Bibliography

Abell, W. 1948. *The Shipwright's Trade.* Conway
Maritime Press, London.

Anderson, R.C. 1927. *The Rigging of Ships in the
Days of the Spritsail Topmast, 1600–1720.*
Conway Maritime Press, London.

Anderson, R. and R.C. 1963. *The Sailing Ship.*
W.W. Norton, U.S.A.

Anonymous. c1625. *A Treatise on Rigging.* Society
for Nautical Research, London. (also Anderson,
R.C. 1921.)

Arnold, D. 1983. *The Age of Discovery.* Methuen,
London.

Blue, A.D. 1988. *The Reality of Steam.* in *Sea
Breezes*, Vol. 62, pp 339–342. Liverpool.

Bowman, F.L. and Roper E.J. 1924. *Traders in East
and West.* Sheldon Press, London.

Burwash, D. 1969. *English Merchant Shipping 1460–
1540.* David & Charles Reprints, Newton Abbott.

Corlett, E. 1975. *The Iron Ship.* Moonraker Press,
Wiltshire.

Cotter, C. 1968. *A History of Nautical Astronomy.*
Hollis & Carter, London.

Culver, H. 1924. *Book of Old Ships.* Doubleday,
Doran & Co., New York.

Cutler, C.C. 1930. *Greyhounds of the Sea.* Halcyon
House, New York.

Davis, R. 1962. *The Rise of the English Shipping
Industry.* David & Charles, Newton Abbott.

Divine, D. 1973. *The Opening of the World.*
Collins, London.

Falconer, W. 1769. *Universal Dictionary of the
Marine.* London.

Fayle, E. 1933. *A Short History of the World's
Shipping Industry.* George Allen & Unwin,
London.

Fletcher, R.A. 1910. *Steam-ships and Their Story.*
Sidgwick & Jackson, London.

Foreman, S. 1986. *Shoes and Ships and Sealing Wax.*
HMSO, London.

Freitas, W. 1963. *Camoes and His Epic.* Institute of
Hispanic, American and Luso-Brazilian Studies,
Stanford, U.S.A.

Greenhill, B. (gen. ed. last vol.) 1981. *The Ship.* 10
volumes. HMSO, London.

Greenhill, B. and Allington, P. 1985. *The Great
Britain. Maritime Wales*, No. 9, pp 3–28.
Gwynedd.

Hart, H. 1951. *Searoad to the Indies.* William Hodge
& Co., London.

Haws, D. 1985. *Ships and the Sea.* Chancellor Press,
London.

Hedderwick, P. 1794. *Treatise on Marine
Architecture.* London.

Hewson, J. 1951. *A History of the Practice of
Navigation.* Brown, Son, & Ferguson, Glasgow.

Hope, R. 1980. *Merchant Navy.* Stanford Maritime,
London.

Johnstone, P. 1980. *The Seacraft of Pre-history.*
Routledge, London.

Jones, V. 1978. *Sail to the Indian Sea.* Gordon &
Cremonesi, London & New York.

Kihlberg, B. (ed.) 1986. *The Lore of Ships.* Crescent
Books, New York.

Knight, F. 1973. *The Clipper Ship.* Collins, London

Laird Clowes, G. S. 1932. *Sailing Ships. Their history
and development as illustrated by the collection of
ship-models at the Science Museum.* The Science
Museum, London.

Leavitt, J. 1973. *The Charles W. Morgan.* Mystic
Seaport, USA.

Lever. D. 1808. *Young Officer's Sheet Anchor.*
London.

Lubbock, B. 1914. *The China Clippers.* Brown, Son,
& Ferguson, Glasgow.

Lubbock, B. 1924. *The Blackwall Frigates.* Brown,
Son, & Ferguson, Glasgow.

Lubbock, B. 1955. *The Coolie Ships and Oil Sailers.*
Brown, Son & Ferguson, Glasgow.

Martinez-Hildago, J. 1966. *Columbus' Ships*. Barre, Mass.

MacGregor, David. 1984 (last vol.). *Merchant Sailing Ships*. 3 volumes: 1775–1815, 1815–1850, 1850–1875. Conway Maritime Press, London.

McGrail, S. 1987. *Ancient Boats in North-west Europe*. Longman, London.

Moore, A. 1925. *Last Days of Mast & Sail*. Oxford University Press, Oxford.

Morison, S.E. 1971. *The European Discovery of America*. 2 volumes. Oxford University Press, Oxford.

Morton Nance, R. 1955. *The Ship of the Renaissance*. Mariner's Mirror, Vol. 41, Pt. I, pp 180–192. & Pt. II, pp 281–298. London.

Moyse-Bartlett, H. 1937. *A History of the Merchant Navy*. G. Harrap & Co., London.

Paasch, H. 1890. *Illustrated Marine Encyclopedia*. Author's Edition.

Packard, W. 1984. *Sea-Trading*: Vol. I, *The Ships*, Vol. II, *Cargoes*, Vol. III, *Trading*. Fairplay, London.

Paris, E. 1882–1908. *Souvenirs de Marin*. 6 volumes. Le Musee de Marins du Louvre, Paris.

Smith, E. 1937. *A Short History of Naval and Marine Engineering*. Cambridge University Press, for Babcock & Wilcox, London.

Smith, J.W. and Holden, T.S. 1946. *Where Ships are Born*. Thomas Reed & Co., Sunderland.

Smith, R. 1985. *Vanguard of Empire*. Terrae Incognitae, Vol. 17, pp 15–27.

Steel, D. 1794. *Elements and Practice of Rigging and Seamanship*. 2 volumes. London.

Steel, D. 1804. *Elements and Practice of Naval Architecture*. 2 volumes. London.

Sutton, J. 1981. *Lords of the East*. Conway Maritime Press, London.

Taylor, E.G.R. 1956. *The Haven Finding Art*. Hollis & Carter, London.

Torr, C. 1894. *Ancient Ships*. Cambridge University Press, Cambridge.

Vaudrey Heathcote, N.H. 1936. *Early Nautical Charts*. Annals of Science, Vol. 1, pp 13–28.

Villiers, A. 1953. *The Way of a Ship*. Charles Scribner's Son, New York.

Villiers, A. 1969. *In 'The Wavertree'*. South Street Seaport, New York.

Waters, D.W. 1958. *The Art of Navigation in England in Elizabethan and Early Stuart Times*. Hollis & Carter, London.

Williamson, J.A. 1946. *Cook and the Opening of the Pacific*. Hodder & Stoughton, London.

Index